SECOND EDITION

Interdisciplinary Elementary Physical Education

Theresa Purcell Cone, PhD
ROWAN UNIVERSITY

Peter H. Werner, PED
UNIVERSITY OF SOUTH CAROLINA

Stephen L. Cone, PhD
ROWAN UNIVERSITY

Human Kinetics

Library of Congress Cataloging-in-Publication Data

Cone, Theresa Purcell, 1950-
  Interdisciplinary elementary physical education / Theresa Purcell Cone, Peter H. Werner, Stephen L. Cone. --
2nd ed.
      p. cm.
  Rev. ed. of: Interdisciplinary teaching through physical education / Theresa Purcell Cone ... [et al.]. c1998.
  Includes bibliographical references and index.
  ISBN-13: 978-0-7360-7215-1 (soft cover)
  ISBN-10: 0-7360-7215-2 (soft cover)
  1. Education, Elementary--Curricula. 2. Interdisciplinary approach in education. 3. Physical education and
training--Study and teaching. I. Werner, Peter H. II. Cone, Stephen Leonard. III. Interdisciplinary teaching
through physical education. IV. Title.
  LB1570.I5669 2009
  372.19--dc22

                          2008033362

ISBN-10: 0-7360-7215-2
ISBN-13: 978-0-7360-7215-1

The Web addresses cited in this text were current as of July 2008, unless otherwise noted.

Acquisitions Editor: Scott Wikgren; **Developmental Editor:** Jacqueline Eaton Blakley; **Assistant Editors:** Lauren B. Morenz and Anne Rumery; **Copyeditor:** Joyce Sexton; **Proofreader:** Kathy Bennett; **Indexer:** Bobbi Swanson; **Permission Manager:** Dalene Reeder; **Graphic Designer:** Bob Reuther; **Graphic Artist:** Denise Lowry; **Cover Designer:** Keith Blomberg; **Photographer (cover):** Tom Roberts; **Photo Office Assistant:** Jason Allen; **Art Manager:** Kelly Hendren; **Associate Art Manager:** Alan L. Wilborn; **Illustrator:** Jennifer Gibas; **Printer:** Sheridan Books

Printed in the United States of America   10 9 8 7 6 5 4 3 2 1

Human Kinetics
Web site: www.HumanKinetics.com

United States: Human Kinetics, P.O. Box 5076, Champaign, IL 61825-5076
800-747-4457
e-mail: humank@hkusa.com

Canada: Human Kinetics, 475 Devonshire Road Unit 100, Windsor, ON N8Y 2L5
800-465-7301 (in Canada only)
e-mail: info@hkcanada.com

Europe: Human Kinetics, 107 Bradford Road, Stanningley, Leeds LS28 6AT, United Kingdom
+44 (0) 113 255 5665
e-mail: hk@hkeurope.com

Australia: Human Kinetics, 57A Price Avenue, Lower Mitcham, South Australia 5062
08 8372 0999
e-mail: info@hkaustralia.com

New Zealand: Human Kinetics, Division of Sports Distributors NZ Ltd., P.O. Box 300 226 Albany, North Shore City, Auckland
0064 9 448 1207
e-mail: info@humankinetics.co.nz

Contents

Preface

It has been 10 years since we collaborated on the first edition of this book. Ten years ago, the concept of integrating movement with other subject areas was considered cutting edge. Now, interdisciplinary teaching is readily accepted as a conventional teaching strategy that mirrors how knowledge and skills are applied in everyday life. As authors, we have seen an increase in materials, articles, and texts that address interdisciplinary teaching and, more important, the acceptance by physical education teachers that interdisciplinary education offers a challenging and renewing way to teach.

This second edition revisits the premise that interdisciplinary teaching in physical education is a valued and effective teaching strategy. Research has been updated to reflect current theory, and new practical ideas for classroom use have been added. The revision process has caused us to reflect on our original goal for writing the book and to assess our changes in perspective and knowledge as a result of research and experience. We have critically looked at our own work in interdisciplinary teaching to ascertain whether the models, strategies, and ideas we initially presented still stand as strong examples of practical application.

The book presents a strong argument for continuing our journey to discover the infinite possibilities of interdisciplinary teaching. We believe, now more than ever, that interdisciplinary teaching speaks to the complex skills and knowledge needed to approach the challenges of everyday life. We know that learning and applying knowledge and skills are more varied and multifaceted than the way content is taught and classified in separate subject areas. The elementary curriculum is an ideal place to link concepts from two or more subject areas. Classroom teachers are primarily responsible for delivering content in multiple subjects and can dissolve the barriers established by traditional subject groupings.

Physical education teachers understand the value of teamwork and have experience in adapting content for different environments, schedules, and student abilities. Together, the classroom teacher, other curricular area specialists, and the physical education teacher can help students see how the different content areas are complementary and provide multiple ways to make meaning of the world around us.

In planning for this edition, we considered other terms such as "cross-disciplinary," "pluridisciplinary," "transdisciplinary," and "multidisciplinary"; yet while we recognize that these terms are applicable, we felt that staying with the term "interdisciplinary" clearly defined our intent for combining subject areas. We continue to advocate for recognizing the integrity of each discipline and its inherent concepts and skills and for recognizing that learning in a specific subject area provides a foundation for future interdisciplinary learning. What finally determines whether subject areas should be integrated is directly linked to identifying what students will gain as a result of this experience. Teaching and learning are effective and motivating when personally meaningful to the teacher and the student.

The purpose of this book is to introduce the reader to experiences that use active learning to help teach concepts and skills addressed throughout the elementary curriculum. The intended audiences are elementary physical education teachers, elementary and early childhood teachers, and faculty and students in professional preparation programs who are interested in promoting a broader understanding of the connectedness we share among our disciplines.

The book is divided into two parts. Part I presents the theoretical need for and benefits of interdisciplinary education and identifies the various models for planning and implementing interdisciplinary learning experiences. Included in the discussion of implementing an interdisciplinary experience are ideas for getting started, building a support network, and assessing learning. Part II includes five chapters that describe detailed sample learning experiences in each of the academic disciplines of language arts, mathematics, science, social studies, and the arts; these chapters also include additional ideas for developing more learning experiences. Within each of the disciplinary chapters are a suggested scope and sequence of concepts for each grade level and a description of the concepts and skills appropriate for primary- and intermediate-grade students.

We hope you will join us in exploring interdisciplinary teaching as a way to develop new activities, help students transfer knowledge and skills from one subject to another, and discover new strategies for presenting content to your students. As teachers, our responsibility is to prepare students for the future as effective thinkers, problem solvers, and creators of new ways of living. It is through interdisciplinary education that students will gain the multiple perspectives to be successful in our ever-changing world.

Acknowledgments

We want to thank all our family, friends, colleagues, and students who are always there to support, encourage, and offer confirmation that our work is meaningful and makes a difference.

How to Use This Book

You are invited to join us as we explore the possibilities of interdisciplinary education. This book was written for novice as well as veteran teachers willing to take risks and enjoy the benefit of professional and personal growth. We offer this book as a means to help you understand the richness and complexity of this approach to teaching and learning. Our goal is to provide you with background information, strategies for developing and implementing interdisciplinary learning experiences, and concrete examples that you will find useful and interesting.

We suggest that you begin by reading the background information presented in chapters 1 and 2. This information will give you a sense of how we view interdisciplinary education when physical education is integrated with other subjects. Ensure that you are well acquainted with the national standards. They will provide you with the basic curricular framework on which you will be able to ground your ideas for developing your own interdisciplinary learning experiences. The three selected interdisciplinary teaching models developed by the authors are unique to this book. As you review each model, keep in mind that the models are guides to how to organize your content, how to collaborate with others, and how to create meaningful activities that affect student learning. You can use the ideas and models in the book to initiate a conversation and build support with another teacher, your administrator, your students, or parents.

Use the tables and figures as a quick reference. They give you a good overview of the "what and how" of interdisciplinary education. You can see that table 2.1, "Strategies for Developing an Interdisciplinary Learning Experience," gives you seven strategies to help you develop an effective interdisciplinary experience. We have included examples of three assessment instruments for you to try as is, to adapt, or to use as a starting point to create your own. Remember to tie the assessment directly to the objective.

The second part of this book includes five chapters that describe how physical education is integrated with language arts; mathematics; science; social studies; and music, theater arts, and visual arts. Each chapter uses a common format, with a brief introduction followed by the K through 6 scope and sequence of each subject. Next, complete learning experiences illustrate the application of the interdisciplinary teaching models in a practical setting. A quick look at the focus and delivery of each learning experience is offered. Teachers should feel free to use these lessons as described or to modify them to meet the needs of their situation.

Each complete learning experience includes a ready-to-use lesson containing all the components needed to get started. The description of each learning experience has the following format:

- **Name** of the learning experience.
- **Suggested Grade Level.**
- **Interdisciplinary Teaching Model.** One of the three interdisciplinary teaching models presented in chapter 1 (connected, shared, or partnership) is identified. Specific skills and concepts used as the focus of the experience are listed with their respective curricular area.
- **Objectives.** The specific skill and concept outcomes resulting from participation in the learning experience.
- **Equipment** needed to complete the learning experience.
- **Organization** within which students will be working: individual, partner, small group, or large group.
- **Description** of the total learning experience, explained as if a teacher were actually

presenting the learning experience to children.

- **Assessment suggestion(s).** Examples of different assessment instruments that can be practically applied during or following the learning experience.

- **Look For.** Key points for you to keep in mind when informally observing students' progress in the learning experience.

- **How Can I Change This?** Ways you can vary the organization of the students, introduce new skills or concepts, or change the level of difficulty, thus allowing all students to be challenged at their ability levels.

- **Teachable Moment(s).** Opportunities either during or after a lesson to emphasize a specific skill or concept related to what has occurred in the learning experience.

The final sections of chapters 3 through 7 contain additional ideas for developing learning experiences and ongoing strategies for the physical education classroom. These brief descriptions offer ways in which you can use movement to integrate the skills and concepts being taught. The sample learning experiences are intended to give you a starting point for developing your own complete learning experiences. Because teachers and schools differ in background, levels of expertise, equipment, and facilities, this section provides a broad range of ideas.

Now it's your turn. Take the ideas and run. Good luck!

Introduction to Interdisciplinary Education

IN THE END, OUR WORK LIVES ITS ULTIMATE LIFE
IN THE LIVES THAT IT ENABLES OTHERS TO LEAD.

Elliot Eisner

Teaching is about seeing and celebrating moments of meaningful learning. These moments cannot always be predicted, but the teacher and student know when they happen. We share the following moment as an illustration of an interdisciplinary moment of learning. A physical education teacher was collaborating with the second grade teacher to integrate movement with a social studies project, which focused on ecological conservation through study of the work of Dr. Jane Goodall. One goal of this interdisciplinary collaboration was to gain an understanding of gorilla family communities, their movements, and their social behaviors. The students, in response to their reading and viewing video about the gorillas, created movements that demonstrated their understanding of how gorillas eat, groom, play, sleep, and care for their young. The teachers' roles were to facilitate the students' exploration, and not to organize or impose their ideas.

Two students wanted to re-create the moment when one of the gorillas that Dr. Goodall was observing made contact with her for the first time. The students started by sitting on the floor and, without discussion about what they were going to do, began to improvise their dance. One of them, dancing the part of Dr. Goodall, sat motionlessly observing the other as she portrayed a gorilla that was eating. The two students slowly lifted their heads, making eye contact, and moved toward each other while maintaining their roles. When they were about a foot apart, both still sitting on the floor, each slowly and deliberately lifted her right index finger, reaching to make a gentle touch by connecting with the other's fingertip. The teachers were in tears as they watched this moment and realized that these students had embodied their experiences and knowledge and used this unrehearsed moment to express their understanding and empathy. The moment could not be choreographed. There was no way of predicting that these two children would create a moment that clearly illustrated the power of expressing their understanding through movement.

Education can be seen as a process of change that continues throughout a lifetime. How we integrate all that is learned and transfer knowledge and skills from one experience to another depends on the types of learning experiences we had while in school and what types of learning experiences we continue to explore. The foundation of interdisciplinary education is our innate need to make meaning from discrete pieces of understanding. It is on this premise that this book's content reveals background information and strategies for making interdisciplinary education meaningful.

Part I comprises two chapters that offer the rationale and theoretical perspectives underpinning the use of movement as a way of teaching and learning subject area skills, topics, and concepts. Interdisciplinary experiences may be used to supplement, support, or enhance the teaching of basic skills and concepts in an elementary school's physical education curriculum. They can also be an essential way of learning for children in any subject area.

Chapter 1, "Foundational Beginnings," discusses the theoretical aspects of interdisciplinary education and explores the advantages and challenges related to planning and implementation. Standards-based curriculum is addressed through recognition of the national standards for physical education, dance, teacher preparation, and other subjects. An overview of interdisciplinary teacher models precedes the presentation of a continuum of three models developed by the authors: connected, shared, and partnership.

Chapter 2, "Successful Planning and Implementation," addresses the more practical aspects of interdisciplinary teaching. The chapter describes the process for reviewing curricular content, selecting a teaching model, developing a learning experience, and addressing the logistics of implementation. A section on assessment strategies and examples is included, along with a vital section on developing a support network of administrators, colleagues, students, and parents.

chapter

1

Foundational Beginnings

This chapter provides an introduction to interdisciplinary education and outlines a framework and theoretical background for integrating subject areas in an elementary school's curriculum. The purpose is not only to give you information on interdisciplinary education but also to motivate you to try this exciting approach. The chapter covers the benefits and challenges of interdisciplinary education, provides a historical perspective of interdisciplinary efforts in physical education, and outlines how interdisciplinary education addresses national standards. We have also included three selected interdisciplinary teaching models that range from simple to complex and describe several approaches for integrating the skills or knowledge of two or more subject areas.

What Is Interdisciplinary Education?

Interdisciplinary education is a process in which two or more subject areas are integrated with the goal of fostering enhanced learning in each subject area. The disciplines may be related through a central theme, issue, problem, process, topic, or experience (Jacobs, 1989). Implementing an interdisciplinary program brings teachers together to create exciting learning experiences for students and to discover new ways of delivering the curriculum. The concept of interdisciplinary education acknowledges the integrity and uniqueness of each subject area, yet recognizes the interrelationships among subjects.

Interdisciplinary education is not new. Numerous examples illustrate teachers' efforts to integrate a variety of subjects such as the language arts with mathematics, the visual arts with social studies, mathematics with science, or music with physical education. A vivid example of teaching across subject areas appears in Whitin and Wilde's (1992) *Read Any Good Math Lately?* The book highlights children's books that focus on selected mathematical concepts in an integrated way. Chard and Flockhart (2002) described a project approach used to study a local park that focused on integrating reading, writing, science, social studies, and math. Heidi Hayes Jacobs, author of *Interdisciplinary Curriculum: Design and Implementation*

(1989), states that "there is no longer as much discussion among educators about whether to blend the subject areas, as about when, to what degree, and how best to do it" (Association for Supervision and Curriculum Development, 1994, pp. 1-2). Integration of the curriculum emerged from what educators knew about learning, child development, and the ways in which school prepares a child to be a productive member of the community. Children's interest in their environment is not subject specific; it crosses many disciplines. This idea is reflected in the interdisciplinary integration approach proposed by Drake and Burns (2004). Teachers organize the curriculum around common themes, concepts, and skills across disciplines to facilitate learning. This approach, in contrast to a discipline-based approach to learning, seeks to connect the disciplines through points of attachment. It proposes to unify understanding by organizing skills and knowledge along lines of connection and convergence rather than along lines of divergence and differentiation.

Interdisciplinary learning is nourished by the content offered in multiple subject areas. The specific content of each subject is composed of skills and knowledge that constitute what is integrated. Skills are the abilities or techniques a student learns and uses to perform a movement or demonstrate a concept or idea, such as throwing, measuring, or drawing. And knowledge is defined as concepts, principles, theories, beliefs, or topics inherent to each subject area. There is no one model that describes all the ways interdisciplinary learning can be delivered. Eisner (1998) states, "What we ought to be developing in our schools is not simply a narrow array of literacy skills limited to a restrictive range of meaning systems, but a spectrum of literacies that will enable students to participate in, enjoy, and find meaning in the major forms through which meaning has been constituted" (p. 12). The act of linking or finding connections among various knowledge domains provides a deeper conceptual understanding of the features, dimensions, and characteristics common within those domains. Through interdisciplinary education, both teachers and students can experience a wide spectrum of possible relationships between diverse subject areas. As educators, the kinds of experiences we offer students influence the kinds of skills and knowledge they develop.

Making those learning experiences relevant, meaningful, and transferable to future learning is the goal of interdisciplinary teaching.

Benefits

Interdisciplinary learning experiences enhance and enrich what students learn (see table 1.1). Proponents of interdisciplinary programming believe that children learn best with use of this approach. In *Children Moving: A Reflective Approach to Teaching Physical Education* (7th ed.), Graham, Holt/Hale, and Parker (2007) emphasize that integration enhances learning by reinforcing curricular content in a variety of educational settings. Wasley (1994), a senior researcher with the Coalition of Essential Schools and author of *Stirring the Chalk Dust: Tales of Teachers Changing Classroom Practice,* makes a strong argument for interdisciplinary programming by addressing the issue of relevance. She observes that by breaking through disciplinary boundaries, teachers can make the curriculum more relevant because they can embed knowledge and skills in real-life contexts. An interdisciplinary approach mirrors daily life, in which we are constantly called on to cross disciplines. As a result, this approach to learning is more readily embraced by students, and they are excited about learning.

One of the most often cited works is Gardner's (1983) *Frames of Mind: The Theory of Multiple Intelligences.* Gardner provides convincing evidence that humans possess multiple intelligences: linguistic, musical, logical-mathematical, spatial, tactile-kinesthetic, intrapersonal, and interpersonal intelligence. He contends that children deserve to have all seven intelligences nourished so they may function at their full potential. He also notes that each person has different strengths in each of the intelligences and that those strengths affect the person's learning mode. When the multiple intelligences are used to teach a skill or concept, the experience naturally becomes an interdisciplinary learning experience.

According to Piaget (1969), young children are in a preoperational stage of learning operations and gradually move into a concrete stage. This means that children profit from concrete, practical, active learning experiences that bridge the gap between abstract concepts and the hands-on real world. Through exploration and play, children learn about their world. Further, Tarnowski (quoted in Wilcox, 1994) tells us that the "interdisciplinary nature" of children's own play should become our model for planning and teaching.

Interdisciplinary learning speaks to children with different learning styles and often combines the modalities of seeing (visual), hearing (auditory), and doing (tactile-kinesthetic), allowing

Table 1.1

Benefits of Interdisciplinary Education

▪ Provides new ways to present and use concepts and skills.
▪ Encourages critical thinking skills such as analysis, synthesis, and evaluation.
▪ Builds in students a collaborative approach to learning. Students can use this strength to contribute to addressing the learning task or problem.
▪ Motivates students because learning is fun and meaningful.
▪ Encourages teachers to collaborate, gain an understanding of other content areas, and develop collegial relationships.
▪ Increases the ability to recognize and accept multiple perspectives.
▪ Nurtures divergent and creative thinking.
▪ Teaches students to use multiple sources to approach an issue.
▪ Demonstrates transfer of knowledge from one learning context to another.

children the opportunity to use their strengths to learn what they are taught. Children make sense of the world through expressing their thinking in a variety of ways. "For the young child, movement is the first and foremost vehicle through which she is able to communicate her feelings about herself and her world to others" (Fraser, 1991, p. 2). Movement as a language is a natural and powerful way to express ideas and demonstrate understanding. A child's ability to be proficient at using movement as a means of communication and learning is directly related to the range of movement experiences he or she encounters. It is through the physical education program, as part of an interdisciplinary approach to learning, that students gain the essential kinesthetic learning experiences that will enhance their ability to learn both movement and other subject areas through movement.

Additional support (Gilbert, 1992; Connor-Kuntz and Dummer, 1996; Gallahue and Cleland, 2003; Gilbert, 2004; Grube and Beaudet, 2005; Overby, Post, and Newman, 2005) for interdisciplinary programs emphasizing a movement orientation includes the following:

1. Using movement promotes active involvement in learning (vs. passive learning) that leads to increased understanding.

2. For young children, movement is a natural medium for learning. As children learn fundamental concepts such as height, distance, time, weight, size, position, and shape, movement gives meaning to an abstract system of language symbols.

3. Movement stimulates development of the motor and neurological systems.

4. Movement can be experienced as a means of expression and communication.

5. Movement activities motivate children and capture their interest.

Teachers, like students, benefit from interdisciplinary learning because it builds understanding of other subject areas and fosters appreciation of the knowledge and expertise of other staff members. It facilitates teamwork and planning as teachers work together to weave a theme across several subject areas. In addition, students benefit when they see teachers working in different subject areas, teaching in different classroom spaces, and making similar points across subject

areas. Their learning is reinforced in a powerful and meaningful way. As a result of participating in and observing a variety of interdisciplinary activities in the school, students begin to realize how the skills and knowledge in one subject area can transfer into another and ultimately be applied to life experiences.

Challenges

Despite all the interest in interdisciplinary programming, some educators and parents raise concerns or cautions. The concern most often voiced is that moving from a discipline-based curriculum to one using interdisciplinary learning will cause important content to fall by the wayside. Teachers, especially at the upper grade levels, fear that the "purity" of their subject areas and the logical scope and sequence will be lost in integrated units. They may be reluctant to change content priorities and unwilling to adapt content to be taught in a new way. The concern over losing important content in one's own subject area is very real. Jacobs (1989) emphasizes that teachers should integrate disciplines only when doing so allows them to teach important content more effectively. By providing a context in which students can see relationships among information and skills learned across subject areas, interdisciplinary teaching can improve students' retention.

Another common concern is that one subject area will be allowed to greatly overshadow another in the pursuit of integrated work. Trade-offs are inevitable and inherent in any interdisciplinary learning endeavor. Along with difficult decisions about what to integrate, teachers' concerns include planning time for their own interdisciplinary efforts and arranging a common planning time with other teachers. Collaboration involves dealing with interpersonal issues that require blending different teaching styles, agreeing on a theme topic or activity, dividing the work to prepare materials, and committing resources of time and energy. Flexibility and compromise are essential for successful implementation, which means that trust and teamwork need to be developed or must already exist.

Teachers may be concerned that they do not possess adequate knowledge in another subject area and will not be able to find ways to interrelate concepts and skills. There are few assessment technique models for teachers to follow that specifically address interdisciplinary learning.

In addition, school districts may not offer opportunities for professional development in interdisciplinary education and can present barriers that limit attendance at conferences and workshops outside the school district. Inadequate professional development will result in poor preparation, unclear objectives, and superficial activities that students may find confusing. The students' enthusiasm and motivation drop off, teachers become frustrated, and administrators withdraw support of future efforts. Even after thorough planning of an exciting interdisciplinary lesson or unit, a teacher can encounter logistical barriers involving restructuring schedules; finding an adequate space for conducting activities; organizing materials; and securing the use of audio and visual equipment, computers, and other technical support.

The time and effort needed to create a quality learning experience for children requires a commitment and a willingness to take a risk. Not all experiences will yield immediate success; however, this should not be a reason for abandoning the attempt at integrating the curriculum. Take the time to reflect on your efforts and make the necessary changes to increase the opportunity for a successful learning experience. You may also find that implementing an interdisciplinary learning experience requires rearranging the order of your teaching to coincide with a concept being taught in another subject area. The opportunities are endless, and interdisciplinary learning serves as a continual source of energy feeding the educational process.

Historical Perspectives on Interdisciplinary Programming in Physical Education

In 1929, Horrigan wrote that teachers of physical education were facing a new problem in the elementary schools. Units of work that were developed in the classroom used all subjects as far as possible to broaden the child's learning experiences. If physical education were to maintain a significant place in the total education pattern, it too would have to make a definite contribution to teaching units.

Since that initial call for teachers to integrate subject matter across subject areas, there have been several cycles in which this type of work has received attention in physical education. In the mid- to late 1960s, Humphrey's *Child Learning* (1965) and Miller and Whitcomb's *Physical Education in the Elementary School Curriculum* (1969) focused on an integrated approach to a total school curriculum by illustrating applications of physical education in language arts, mathematics, science, social studies, art, and music. In the early 1970s, Cratty's *Intelligence in Action* (1973) and *Active Learning* (1971) focused on a more generic approach to interdisciplinary learning by including games and physical education activities to enhance academic abilities. By the late 1970s, Gilbert's *Teaching the Three Rs Through Movement Experiences* (1977) and Werner and Burton's *Learning Through Movement* (1979) encouraged teachers to pursue a more conceptual approach to interdisciplinary learning by providing examples of movement experiences based on problem solving and guided discovery.

The 1980s were a decade of back-to-basics and discipline-based education with the focus on defining the specific content to be learned in a particular discipline, not on integrating subject areas. Led by the Getty Foundation, work in the visual arts emphasized four areas from which the content of discipline-based art education is drawn (Eisner, 1988). These four content areas are art making, art criticism, art history, and aesthetics. In physical education the content is learning about how the body moves using locomotor, nonlocomotor, and manipulative skills in combination with movement concepts related to space, effort, and relationships. Another way to view the content of physical education is by categorizing it under the broad areas of games, dance, gymnastics, and health-related fitness. In essence, the 1980s served to identify the content of what physical educators teach and reaffirmed physical education's place in the curriculum as a disciplinary subject based on an identified body of knowledge.

The last 20 years have been characterized by a resurgence of interest in interdisciplinary teaching. Robin Fogarty, author of *The Mindful School*

(1991a), calls interdisciplinary teaching "a wave that is gaining momentum in the United States, Canada and Australia" (Association for Supervision and Curriculum Development, 1994, pp. 1-2). She goes on to say that this is a trend, not a fad. Leading educational organizations such as the Association for Supervision and Curriculum Development (ASCD), the National Dance Association (NDA), the National Association for the Education of Young Children (NAEYC), and the National Association for Sport and Physical Education (NASPE) support the idea of interdisciplinary teaching. As an example, the NAEYC (Bredekamp and Copple, 1997) and NASPE (2000a, 2000b) documents on appropriate practices support interdisciplinary learning, with specialists working with classroom teachers, to deliver an integrated curriculum. In addition, NASPE's (2003) *National Standards for Beginning Physical Education Teachers* and NDA's (1994) *National Standards for Dance Education: What Every Young American Should Know and Be Able to Do in Dance* require teachers to have content knowledge that allows them to incorporate concepts and strategies into other subject areas.

The popularity of interdisciplinary programming in physical education has been evidenced in leading journal articles for physical education teachers, through Web sites like www. pecentral.com or www.pelinks4u.org, and on national convention programs. For example, the topic of an integrated curriculum was a special feature of the December 1994 issue of *Teaching Elementary Physical Education*. In that issue, in addition to providing several examples of interdisciplinary activities, Stevens (1994) called for the collaboration of physical education and classroom teachers. She further suggested that if "two disciplines can find a way to work together both areas can be reinforced by helping students learn academic concepts from a movement perspective" (p. 7). Werner (1994) wrote about the concepts of whole physical education in the preschool feature of the *Journal of Physical Education, Recreation and Dance*. In 2003, *Teaching Elementary Physical Education* dedicated the July issue to interdisciplinary learning. In addition, several articles on dance education (Gilbert, 1992; Rovegno, 2003; Minton, 2003; Gabbei and Clemmens, 2005) show how an interdisciplinary approach to dance can enrich the experiences of children. A national news-

letter for preschool teachers called *Kids on the Move* (Pica, 1995) often illustrates movement concepts with other subject areas. Clements and Osteen (1995) also emphasize interdisciplinary work with preschool children through the use of movement narratives that draw heavily on integrated themes. Interdisciplinary sessions frequently appear within professional conference programs; and national journals such as *Journal of Physical Education, Recreation and Dance* (Behrman, 2004; Hatch and Smith, 2004; Ballinger and Deeney, 2006), *Strategies: Journal for Physical and Sport Educators* (Griffin and Morgan, 1998; Altman and Lehr, 2003; Elliott, 2003; DeFrancesco and Casas, 2004), and *Teaching Elementary Physical Education* (Cone and Cone, 1999; Carpenter and Stevens-Smith, 2003; Kalyn, 2005; Moulton, 2006) continue to reflect an emphasis on interdisciplinary learning as we move forward in the 21st century.

The No Child Left Behind Act of 2001 offers challenges to all educators. The physical education curriculum can contribute to meeting this federal mandate by promoting interdisciplinary learning experiences (Bennett and Hanneken, 2003). The discipline's unique ability to integrate kinesthetically, cognitively, and affectively with content from other subject areas effectively addresses the needs of the whole child.

Standards-Based Curriculum

As we begin the 21st century, parents, educators, business leaders, and politicians continue to examine the educational system in America. They have asked questions such as "Will our children be ready to meet the demands of the 21st century?" and "What do our children need to know and be able to do to prepare for the future?" As a result, educational reform has received support from the highest levels of government. The nation's president and governors met at an education summit and established goals for the nation. From this effort has emerged a movement to establish nationwide education standards.

The development of national standards does not establish a national curriculum or a predetermined course of study, nor does it dictate specific teaching methodologies. Rather, the standards offer a road map for competence and educational effectiveness that focuses on student learning results. The expectation is that students in every school should be able to reach these standards with adequate support and sustained effort. With the passage of the Goals 2000: Educate America Act in March 1994, educational standards were written into law.

Using the Goals 2000: Educate America Act as an impetus, national and state associations in each of the subject areas have established standards with accompanying benchmarks that indicate what children should know and be able to do at selected grade levels. Key concepts in each of these curriculum frameworks include support for interdisciplinary learning with teachers working together to deliver an integrated curriculum. For example, *National Standards for Arts Education* (Consortium of National Arts Education Associations, 1994) contains specific content standards that focus on making connections between the arts and other disciplines. According to *National Standards for the English Language Arts* (National Council of Teachers of English and International Reading Association, 1996), the language arts are interdisciplinary and provide students with the means to access and process information and understanding from all other disciplines.

Just as standards and curriculum frameworks have been developed at national, state, and local levels for language arts, mathematics, science, the arts, and social studies, so too have they been developed for physical education and dance.

NATIONAL PHYSICAL EDUCATION STANDARDS

The National Association for Sport and Physical Education (1992) published *The Physically Educated Person,* containing the section "Outcomes of Quality Physical Education Programs," in response to needs expressed by NASPE members, other educators, and concerned citizens for a national platform on which to base judgments of quality about physical education programs. Outcomes with appropriate benchmarks at grades K, 2, 4, 6, 8, 10, and 12 indicate the ways in which school programs should transform students by providing guidance for *what* students are able to learn as well as *when* it is reasonable to expect that they have learned it.

Following the publication of the physical education outcomes document, a Standards and Assessment Task Force was appointed by NASPE to develop national content standards and assessment material. The original *National Standards for Physical Education* has since been revised, and *Moving into the Future: National Standards for Physical Education* (NASPE, 2004) established six content standards (outlined in table 1.2) with accompanying sample benchmarks for each standard at the grade levels previously noted. Assessment guidelines were also designed to expand and complement, not

Table 1.2

NASPE Content Standards in Physical Education

A physically educated person
1. demonstrates competency in motor skills and movement patterns needed to provide a variety of physical activities.
2. demonstrates understanding of movement concepts, principles, strategies, and tactics as they apply to the learning and performance of physical activities.
3. participates regularly in physical activity.
4. achieves and maintains a health-enhancing level of physical fitness.
5. exhibits responsible personal and social behavior that respects self and others in physical activity settings.
6. values physical activity for health, enjoyment, challenge, self-expression, and/or social interaction.

From National Association for Sport and Physical Education, 2003, *National standards for beginning physical education teachers*, 2nd ed. (Reston, VA: NASPE).

simply replace, the original physical education outcomes document.

While none of the national physical education standards directly address the concept of interdisciplinary programming, the document recommends that quality physical education programs reinforce knowledge learned across the curriculum and suggests that they can serve as a laboratory for application of content in other subject areas. For example, the application of movement concepts and principles to the learning and development of motor skills supports the many scientific principles that have application in physical education. Learning to understand and respect differences among people provides support for learning across gender, racial, cultural, and other differences such as religion (table 1.3).

NATIONAL DANCE STANDARDS

Dance education is an integral part of a comprehensive physical education curriculum, yet it also appears in education as a component of an arts education curriculum. It can exist in both places (Cone and Cone, 2007). However, dance should always be taught primarily as a means of expression and communication, with students creating dances, learning to perform dances, and responding to their own dancing or the dancing of others. In this book, dance education is included as a content area in the physical education curriculum. All students should have the opportunity to participate in learning experiences that focus solely on the skills and concepts intrinsic to dance education, as well as in interdisciplinary learning experiences linking dance education to another subject area. Many dance education skills and concepts naturally correlate with music, visual arts, theater arts, and language arts and can easily be tied to mathematics, science, and social studies.

In 1994 the National Dance Association, in conjunction with the American Alliance for Theater and Education, the Music Educators National Conference, and National Art Education, published a set of national standards for arts education (Consortium of National Arts Education Associations, 1994) describing what students should know and be able to do in the arts. Specifically, the dance education standards (table 1.4) are a guide for developing meaningful learning experiences in dance education and for suggesting levels of achievement for grades 4, 8, and 12. The dance education standards address the movement concepts and skills that are universal to teaching all types of dance forms, such as creative dance, cultural dance, and social dance. They also describe the basic choreographic principles, processes, and struc-

Table 1.3

Interdisciplinary Applications of Physical Education Standards

Standard 1	When connecting measuring in math with correct jumping technique, the students practice a two-foot takeoff and landing while measuring the jump distance using standard and nonstandard measuring tools.
Standard 2	During a striking lesson using badminton rackets, the science concept of angles is introduced to support the correct arm position for overhead and underhand strokes.
Standard 3	Students maintain a written or tape-recorded journal of their physical activity participation while in and out of school. The journal can be illustrated with photographs, collages, drawings, or audio files.
Standard 4	Students use math skills to calculate their target heart rate zone during a fitness unit. Music, at different tempos, is integrated during the aerobic activities to reach and maintain a target heart rate zone.
Standard 5	Students collaborate to write a list of behavior rules for effective learning in physical education. They use acting skills to demonstrate appropriate and inappropriate behaviors.
Standard 6	During a games unit, students play games from different cultures and then challenge themselves to create a new game. The games are recorded, illustrated, and taught to peers. This activity integrates social studies, language arts, and visual arts.

Table 1.4

Content Standards in Dance Education

1. Identifying and demonstrating movement elements and skills in performing dance
2. Understanding choreographic principles, processes, and structures
3. Understanding dance as a way to create and communicate meaning
4. Applying and demonstrating critical and creative skills in dance
5. Demonstrating and understanding dance in various cultures and historical periods
6. Making connections between dance and healthful living
7. Making connections between dance and other disciplines

From The National Dance Standards from Consortium of National Arts Education Associations, 1994.

tures appropriate for elementary students and emphasize using critical and creative thinking skills when learning to perform and respond to dances.

A strong interdisciplinary focus that speaks to performing and understanding dance as a part of history and culture, maintaining a healthy lifestyle, and making direct connections between dance and other disciplines is evident in several of the standards. We suggest that using the dance education standards will help you develop specific objectives, activities, and assessments not only for learning experiences in dance education but also for interdisciplinary efforts with other colleagues.

NATIONAL STANDARDS FOR BEGINNING PHYSICAL EDUCATION TEACHERS

As national standards have been developed for our nation's schools, organizations such as the National Council for the Accreditation of Teacher Education (NCATE) have been developing new standards for the preparation of teachers. In cooperation with NCATE, NASPE created the beginning physical education teacher standards (NASPE, 2003). Among the 10 stan-

dards, which outline a comprehensive teacher education model, are principles that focus on content knowledge, pedagogical knowledge, teaching and learning styles, and collaboration. Within the principles of content knowledge is a requirement that teachers understand how to relate physical education content with other subject areas. Instruction for diverse populations of learners will require teachers who are well versed in strategies that include direct instruction, problem solving, discovery learning, cooperative learning, independent study, and interdisciplinary instruction. Collaboration fosters teachers' relationships with colleagues, parents, and community agencies to support learner growth and well-being, and calls for teachers who value finding out about all aspects of a learner's experience, including other subject matter areas. From this document it is clear that the teacher of the future will have to be well versed in interdisciplinary programming.

Interdisciplinary Teaching Models

Over the last two decades, experts in curriculum design have identified a variety of models that follow an integrative approach. A model provides a guide or a framework. Teachers can organize their ideas in accordance with a particular model to give them an idea about how involved a particular lesson or unit might become with respect to interdisciplinary work. Nielsen (1989) provided a hierarchical concept continuum that flows from simple or more concrete concepts such as climate and animals to highly abstract concepts such as change, patterns, and variation. The author held that a conceptually based approach to curriculum development and implementation would better help young students to integrate information and develop a set of clearly defined links between themes, topics, and subject areas. Fogarty (1991b) provided an even more complex model with 10 variations along a continuum. Variations begin with an exploration within individual subject areas (fragmented, connected, and nested models) and continue with models that integrate several subject areas (sequenced, shared, webbed, threaded, and integrated models). The continuum ends with models that operate within learners themselves (immersed model) and across networks of learners (networked model). Fogarty's hope for these models was to provide teachers with a solid foundation for designing curricula that help their students make valuable connections while learning.

In all likelihood, you will discover, adapt, or create various models during your interdisciplinary journey. You may already be familiar with the intradisciplinary or the internal interdisciplinary (Nilges, 2003) concept of merging content within one subject area. In this approach, you make links within a subject area, tying one skill to a related skill or linking one concept to another (see table 1.5). Fogarty (1991a) states that the effort is to deliberately relate curricula within the subject area rather than assuming that students will understand the connections automatically. "Connecting ideas within a subject area permits the learner to review, reconceptualize, edit and assimilate ideas gradually and may facilitate transfer" (p. 15). Fogarty also notes that the intradisciplinary approach is useful as a beginning step toward an integrated curriculum. Teachers feel confident looking for connections within their own subject area; as they become adept at relating ideas within the subject area, it becomes easier to scout for connections across subject areas.

Drake and Burns (2004) offer a broader perspective and describe the academic approaches as multidisciplinary, interdisciplinary, and transdisciplinary. Although these models are similar, the central difference is in the perceived degree of separation between content areas. Where one approach would have disciplines remain somewhat distinct, the continuum would evolve to integrating or overlapping concepts to respecting real-world context and, ultimately, to an understanding that we are accountable to standards and assessment.

Models for Physical Education

Although each of Fogarty's models is helpful, the multiplicity of choices is somewhat overwhelming. We have experimented with a variety of approaches to interdisciplinary teaching and have developed three models that function on a continuum from simple to complex (figure 1.1).

The three interdisciplinary teaching models—connected, shared, and partnership—provide approaches for integrating the skills and concepts of two or more subject areas. These models will help you clarify your intent and objectives for using interdisciplinary teaching. They are not meant to be finite models that serve every type of interdisciplinary teaching experience, but rather guides to integration with meaning and purpose. You may develop interdisciplinary learning experiences that do not fit neatly into one of the three models, and you may need to overlap or adapt the models to meet your particular situation.

The *connected* model uses a simple approach in which content from one subject area is used to augment or supplement the learning experience in another subject area. For example, you are teaching Mexican folk dances in a physical education lesson, and you use a map to show where the country is located as a means of connecting the topic with social studies. The *shared* model emphasizes the linkage of similar topics, concepts, or skills from two or more subject areas taught collaboratively with another teacher. In the folk dance example using a

Table 1.5

Interdisciplinary Links

Subject area	Skill or concept	Link
Physical education	Ready position	Volleyball, dance, tennis, basketball
Science	Life cycles	Plants, animals, humans
Language arts	Story structure	Reading or writing, fiction or nonfiction

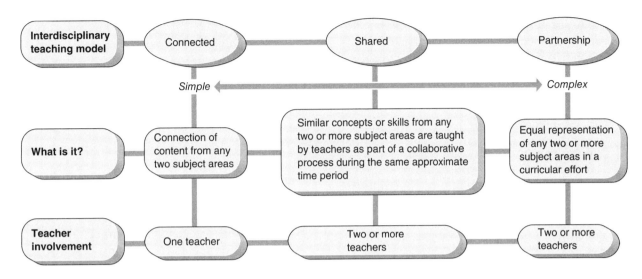

Figure 1.1   A comparison of the connected, shared, and partnership interdisciplinary teaching models.

shared model, the concept of Mexican cultural traditions would be taught concurrently in the physical education and social studies lessons. The folk dances emphasize the cultural traditions, and the social studies lesson focuses on how traditions are part of holidays. The even more ambitious *partnership* model provides a strategy for complex unification of content from two or more subject areas. In relation to this example, the teachers plan and team-teach a unit on Mexico including lessons on the folk dances, cultural traditions, history, games, music, visual arts, and foods.

Another way of viewing interdisciplinary teaching—and one that vividly conveys the continuum of these models—is through imagery. The connected model is like fruit cocktail in which each fruit retains its individual identity. However, the degree of integration is limited. In the shared model, you experience an integration more characteristic of fruitcake than of fruit cocktail. The disciplines persist in recognizable chunks that make sense, but they are embedded in a pervasive and unifying batter in which raw materials are transformed. And finally, the partnership model is similar to a fruit smoothie in which the contents are blended together. Each of the models is designed to give the teacher the structure needed to link one subject area to another. In your planning process, select one or more models that offer the most appropriate means to achieve the goals you identify for the learning experience.

THE CONNECTED MODEL

In the connected model (figure 1.2), the skills, topics, and concepts of the physical education curriculum are the primary focus of the learning experience, and the content from another subject area is used to enhance, extend, or complement the learning experience. This model, commonly used by teachers because they are comfortable with it, allows them to independently plan, schedule, and choose the subject area content for the connection. They can schedule the lesson at a time when it fits into the learning sequence

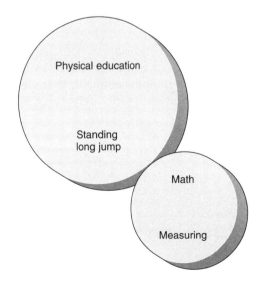

Figure 1.2   Example of a connected interdisciplinary teaching model.

they have planned for the year; choose the subject area and specific skills, topics, and concepts they want to use; and do the planning on their own time. However, they may want to consult with a colleague about resources and accuracy of information.

This model can be used in these ways:

- When you introduce a new skill, topic, or concept, you can use the content from one subject to further explain or illustrate the skill, topic, or concept you are teaching. For example, when introducing the proper technique for a jump, you can use the scientific principle of how a spring works to illustrate the jumping action. You use imagery when you use the notion of a moving spring to make a point about jumping. You cross the bridge from imagery to interdisciplinary teaching when you present the scientific principle of how a spring works as covered in the science curriculum.

- You can use the connected model to stimulate interest in a lesson and demonstrate how the content you are teaching is relevant to the student. For example, at the beginning of a rope-jumping unit, the class reads a poem that expresses the frustrations and joys experienced when one is learning to jump rope. The teacher makes a connection between the language

arts and physical education subject areas through use of the poem.

- You can use the connected model to enhance a lesson by applying a skill from another subject area. For example, students may have just learned the techniques involved in a standing long jump. They can then use the math skill of measuring to see how far they jump.

- The content of a physical education lesson can be used to supplement or reinforce skills, topics, and concepts that come up in other subject areas. A gymnastics lesson can be connected to a writing lesson when students write sentences using words emphasized in the gymnastics lesson, such as tripod, cartwheel, or straddle.

THE SHARED MODEL

A shared model is one in which two subjects are integrated through a similar skill, topic, or concept that is part of the content for both subject areas (figure 1.3). The model requires agreement between the teachers on the theme, skill, topic, or concept and on the time line for teaching. The time line can result in simultaneous presentations in the respective classrooms, or one teacher might explore a common theme, skill, topic, or concept a short time before the other teacher. The shared model may require the teachers to

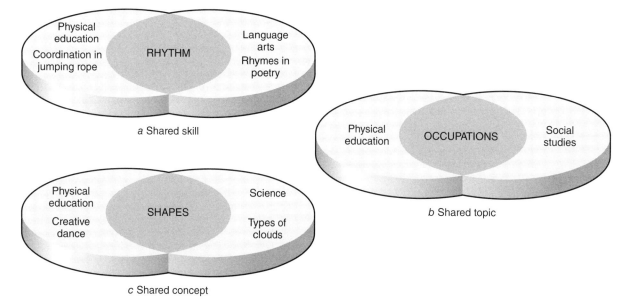

a Shared skill

b Shared topic

c Shared concept

Figure 1.3 Three examples of the shared interdisciplinary teaching model, using *(a)* a shared skill, *(b)* a shared topic, and *(c)* a shared concept.

adjust their sequence of teaching to include the new "shared" content. The integration helps students understand how themes, skills, topics, or concepts can cut across subject areas. The students' learning is reinforced in a meaningful way as they view teachers presenting similar ideas in different classrooms in parallel.

This model can be used in these ways:

- To help teachers take the first step in collaborating with another teacher. The teachers discuss the content they plan to teach during the year and identify common skills, topics, or concepts. Once the content has been identified, they align the sequence of teaching to deliver the common lesson or unit at a similar time. For example, in a social studies unit, students are learning about how communities work together, and the students develop a homework hot line to help other students in the school. At the same time in the physical education class, students are learning about teamwork and participate in team-building activities. The subjects share the concept of how people work together to help one another complete a task.

- To reinforce a selected theme. Several teachers may choose a broad theme for a grade level or as a schoolwide project. Teachers in all subject areas find a way to teach different aspects of the theme (figure 1.4). However, a theme may not be equally important across all subject areas. As an example, you might use the theme of change. In science, students study the changing seasons; the visual arts lessons focus on how changing your perspective while you view a sculpture changes what you see; the language arts emphasize the process of changing a piece of writing to fit different audiences; and in physical education, change is addressed as students study how the sport of basketball has changed over the last 100 years.

- To select a skill, topic, or concept from one subject area to share in both subject areas. For example, in figure 1.3b, the shared topic is *occupations,* which is taught in the social studies curriculum but is not typically part of the physical education curriculum. This use of a shared interdisciplinary teaching model extends the physical education curriculum by adding a new area of content.

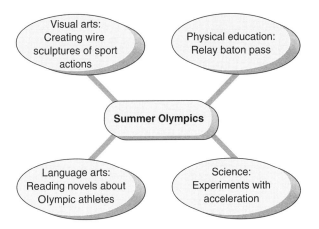

Figure 1.4 Shared interdisciplinary teaching model using a theme.

THE PARTNERSHIP MODEL

A partnership model is defined by the equal representation of two or more subject areas in a curricular effort. The skills, topics, and concepts of two or more subject areas are blended together so that learning takes place simultaneously in all subject areas. Teaching is collaborative and is often accomplished through a team-teaching model. The teachers teach together at the same time in the same classroom, collaborating to deliver an agreed-on content within the curricular areas. This model takes considerable planning, a willingness to seek common areas, the identification of a time block for teaching in this manner, and a significant effort to identify links between specific curricular areas. It often leads to uncharted territory, challenging teachers to view their curriculum from a new and different perspective. The result is a curriculum in which students gain a better understanding of the interconnectedness of all subject areas (figure 1.5).

This model can be used in these ways:

- To demonstrate the value of understanding the relationship between two or more subject areas that would have otherwise been taught as discrete subject areas. Students have an opportunity to apply their knowledge in a different context, thus demonstrating their complete understanding of what they have learned. The application of the mathematical concept of fractions infused with the teaching of the correct mechanics for badminton strokes is one example. A teacher could describe the backswing of

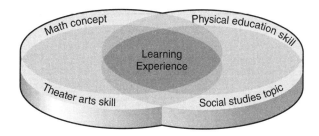

Figure 1.5 Example of a partnership interdisciplinary teaching model.

the stroke as a fraction of a circle or determine the number of successful serves using fractions. Before the learning experience, the two teachers share their content with each other and together create a new way to teach the targeted content.

■ To give teachers the opportunity to restructure or refocus curriculum to provide students with the chance to learn through a new lens. For example, when teaching patterns, the physical education and music teachers create a joint learning experience to enhance the children's understanding of patterns. The teachers select the ABA structure or ternary form as the focus of the experience. The students create movement sequences, such as twist, stretch, twist, and compose music in the ABA form to accompany their movement sequence.

■ To facilitate an integrated event. This type of event usually involves total immersion by all faculty, students, and staff of the school. For example, the school decides to celebrate a particular event and focuses all activities around a theme. The entire school community participates through activities, food, costumes, and customs associated with the event and coordinates learning experiences representing various subject areas. Faculty and staff work with many different students in a variety of activities.

Summary

Interdisciplinary education is a process in which two or more subject areas are integrated with the goal of fostering enhanced learning in each subject area. It adds new meaning and perspectives to the content and reflects how knowledge and skills are used in daily life. Interdisciplinary learning experiences enhance and enrich what students learn and provide an opportunity to reach children with different learning styles. Studies have shown that interdisciplinary programs emphasizing movement bridge the gap between abstract concepts and the hands-on, real world. The primary concern about interdisciplinary learning is the fear that as you move away from a discipline-based curriculum, you will lose important content. The time commitment needed to complete the collaborative process can be discouraging, and issues such as teaching style or restructuring schedules must be addressed.

Interdisciplinary efforts in physical education have evolved as the discipline has defined and redefined its content and its place in the educational enterprise. As we begin the 21st century, the concept of interdisciplinary learning has increasingly taken a place in the redesign and reform of curriculum at the state and national levels. National standards documents in physical education, dance, and teacher preparation describe what students and teachers should know and be able to do in a comprehensive physical education program. These documents serve as the future framework for curricular design and assessment.

A variety of models that follow an integrative approach have been proposed over time; no one model describes all the ways in which interdisciplinary learning can be delivered. These models begin with a relatively simple intradisciplinary approach, include multidisciplinary styles, and move to progressively more complex models of interdisciplinary teaching. We presented three selected interdisciplinary teaching models—connected, shared, and partnership—and introduced, defined, and illustrated these models with examples of practical applications. The selection and application of a model should be based on the desired goals for the learning experience and the level of commitment agreed on by the teachers involved. Chapter 2 introduces several strategies for implementing an interdisciplinary learning experience.

Successful Planning and Implementation

Successful interdisciplinary teaching requires careful thought and planning for the skills and knowledge students will learn in a lesson or unit of lessons. This approach to teaching offers an opportunity for teachers to look at the curriculum from a new perspective. As teachers develop an integrated curriculum, they must identify how integration will increase teaching effectiveness and contribute to expanding student learning.

This chapter was written to answer many of the questions you may have about beginning to teach using an interdisciplinary approach. It provides guidance on how to get started, develop ideas, and locate information. We offer strategies for selecting an interdisciplinary teaching model and outline a process that will help you take your first steps toward implementation. You will also find a section on assessment of interdisciplinary learning with practical examples using the three selected interdisciplinary models. The chapter concludes with suggestions on how to develop a successful support network to help you achieve your initial attempts and to provide the support for ongoing efforts.

Accepting the challenge of integrating content from your curriculum with another subject area is worthwhile. You will find new and interesting ways to teach, become personally invigorated as a learner, and experience the excitement of collaborating with colleagues. Not all lessons need to be integrated with other subjects; however, you should always recognize the association between what is being taught, how it fits into the broader curricular picture, and how it applies to life experiences.

Getting Started

Interdisciplinary education occurs neither automatically nor accidentally. It must be thoughtfully constructed. You will have many questions as you begin your new initiative. Some questions will have fairly easy answers, while others will be answered as you become more engaged in the planning process. Ultimately, these answers will give you the information needed to develop a meaningful lesson or unit. Begin by asking yourself these questions:

- What subjects do I want to integrate?
- Where do I find information to use?

- Whom will I work with?
- What will students learn in each of the subject areas?
- What is the best way to create a learning experience?
- How can the learning be assessed?
- How does integrating subjects meet the national standards for each subject area?

You can create an interdisciplinary learning experience on your own, using the connected model, or through a collaborative effort as in the shared and partnership models. Table 2.1 describes a set of strategies you can use as a guide for developing an interdisciplinary learning experience.

Table 2.1

Strategies for Developing an Interdisciplinary Learning Experience

Review curricular guides and scope and sequences
Select content (themes, topics, issues)
Gather content information
Decide on the interdisciplinary teaching model(s)
Create lesson plans, including specific activities
Determine scheduling, materials, equipment, organization, facilities
Decide how to assess student learning

REVIEW CURRICULUM GUIDES

A good source of information is the curriculum guides adopted by your school district or the yearlong plans designed by other teachers. These curriculum guides describe the content of various subjects, the scope, the recommended grade level, and the sequence in which the content should be taught. Table 2.2 presents a sample scope and sequence of physical education movement concepts and skills taught in elementary schools. Chapters 3 through 7 present scope and sequence summaries for language arts, mathematics, science, social studies, music, theater arts, and visual arts. Reviewing curricular guides lets you see what will be taught during

Table 2.2

Scope and Sequence of Physical Education Concepts and Skills Taught in Elementary Schools

MOVEMENT CONCEPTS	GRADE						
Body awareness	K	1	2	3	4	5	6
Body-part identification	✘	✘	✘				
Shapes	✘	✘	✘	✘			
Action of the whole body and its parts	✘	✘	✘	✘			
Space awareness							
Personal space	✘	✘	✘				
General space	✘	✘	✘				
Levels	✘	✘	✘	✘			
Directions	✘	✘	✘	✘			
Pathways	✘	✘	✘	✘	✘	✘	
Extensions	✘	✘	✘	✘	✘	✘	✘
Effort							
Time	✘	✘	✘	✘	✘		
Force			✘	✘	✘	✘	✘
Flow					✘	✘	✘
Relationships							
Body parts	✘	✘	✘	✘	✘	✘	✘
With other people			✘	✘	✘	✘	✘
MOVEMENT SKILLS	GRADE						
Locomotor	K	1	2	3	4	5	6
Walking	✘	✘					
Running	✘	✘	✘	✘			
Jumping	✘	✘	✘	✘			
Hopping	✘	✘	✘	✘			
Galloping	✘	✘	✘	✘			
Skipping		✘	✘	✘			
Leaping			✘	✘	✘		
Sliding		✘	✘	✘			
Rolling	✘	✘	✘	✘	✘		

(continued)

Table 2.2 *(continued)*

MOVEMENT SKILLS	GRADE						
Nonlocomotor	K	1	2	3	4	5	6
Turning	✕	✕	✕	✕			
Twisting	✕	✕	✕	✕			
Swinging	✕	✕	✕	✕			
Stretching and bending	✕	✕	✕	✕			
Pushing and pulling	✕	✕	✕	✕	✕		
Falling and rising					✕	✕	✕
Starting and stopping	✕	✕	✕	✕			
Balancing	✕	✕	✕	✕	✕	✕	✕
Jumping and landing	✕	✕	✕	✕	✕	✕	✕
Transferring weight	✕	✕	✕	✕	✕	✕	✕
Manipulative							
Throwing, underhand	✕	✕	✕	✕			
Throwing, overhand		✕	✕	✕	✕	✕	✕
Catching	✕	✕	✕	✕	✕	✕	✕
Bouncing	✕	✕	✕	✕	✕		
Rolling			✕	✕	✕		
Kicking	✕	✕	✕	✕	✕		
Trapping			✕	✕	✕	✕	✕
Volleying			✕	✕	✕	✕	✕
Striking with rackets and paddles		✕	✕	✕	✕	✕	✕
Striking with long-handled implements			✕	✕	✕	✕	✕
Fitness concepts							
Effects of exercise on pulse rate			✕	✕	✕		
Strength				✕	✕	✕	✕
Flexibility				✕	✕	✕	✕
Cardiorespiratory endurance				✕	✕	✕	✕
Muscular endurance					✕	✕	✕
Body composition					✕	✕	✕
Health-related fitness tests			✕	✕	✕	✕	✕

the school year. Discussing yearlong plans with other teachers will give you a sense of timing. This process will help you select the skills, content areas, or units of study that will link your program to another in the school.

SELECT CONTENT

Once you have reviewed the curriculum guides, you are ready to select the content of the interdisciplinary learning experience. Choose the knowledge and skills you want to teach rather than falling into the trap of using activities that may, at best, result in a superficial or contrived connection. Begin with one lesson or a part of a lesson focused on a specific topic or single idea. Set reasonable objectives for the learning experience, and move to the next step of gathering content information and materials. Try to develop an awareness of natural relationships between subjects. When the ideas flow and they make sense, use them—this is a powerful way to teach. When there is no natural match, don't try to force the issue. Forcing connections makes for poor teaching of both subject areas.

GATHER CONTENT INFORMATION

It is essential to research information and gather materials before teaching an integrated learning experience. Your success is largely based on accurate information that is relevant, current, and age appropriate. You can effectively integrate multiple subject areas when you are familiar with the concepts and skills taught in the subject areas you have chosen to integrate.

The school or community library is a valuable place to search for information. You may find books on a specific topic or reference books that lead to additional sources. Your colleagues will have access to additional information in files, in classroom texts, or possibly in their personal collection of books, materials, or computer programs. You can also access information regarding specific subject areas, themes, or topics in a variety of sources as outlined in table 2.3.

You can place a call for materials in a district or professional association newsletter, make an announcement at a professional meeting, or contact parents through a flyer. As you begin to ask for information, you will also have the oppor-

Table 2.3

Accessing Information Sources

Read broadly in journals, texts, or newsletters of other disciplines.
Visit a bookstore.
Use key words on an Internet search engine, such as "interdisciplinary," "curriculum standards," or "integrated curricula."
Draw on your own experiences, for example, travel, personal collections, pictures.
Build a resource library of books, posters, or videos.
Enroll in a class for your professional growth and to increase your knowledge and awareness.
Attend a poetry reading.
Visit museums and exhibits, science centers, aquariums, zoos.
Attend theater, dance, or music performances.
Visit classrooms and learning centers.
Participate in a music, art, or math lesson.
Interview students about what they are learning.
View hallway displays or exhibits.
Observe the strategies used in the classroom to teach other disciplines.
Reach out to the community to find experts, places, or sources for thematic activities.

tunity to inform others of your plans to integrate your curriculum with other subject areas. The reward for your efforts will be increased dialogue with colleagues or interested individuals seeking opportunities to collaborate, as well as a wealth of information and materials.

Planning the Delivery

Collaboration with colleagues frequently occurs as a result of a school or district planning session or simply as a result of informal conversations during lunch. Be proactive and let others know you are interested in working on an interdisciplinary learning experience. You should start small, select a class or group of students for whom you think success is possible, and keep planning and implementation manageable.

SELECT A MODEL

Chapter 1 describes three interdisciplinary teaching models that can help you decide the extent to which you will pursue an interdisciplinary learning experience. Your decision will determine the type of collaboration and the amount of planning time needed for successful implementation of an interdisciplinary learning experience.

The connected model provides a place to begin interdisciplinary teaching. This model allows you to plan independently, select content from another subject area (one you may find personally interesting or have experience in), and integrate it at a time that fits your plans. You can also consult with another person for resources on a topic. For example, if you are teaching a dance lesson focused on changing levels, you can use the scientific concept of evaporation as an image of water rising from the earth to the sky. In preparation for teaching this lesson, review the process of evaporation to ensure accuracy in your lesson.

As you gain confidence, you can expand the depth of content integration in your program by using the shared model or the partnership model. Take the initiative and schedule a meeting with another teacher (figure 2.1). Review the two subject areas and the respective standards; give some thought to the area(s) of content you would like to pursue. Remember to consider your colleague's teaching approach. Again, begin small and allow your collaboration efforts to grow.

As you can see, success requires creativity, commitment, and flexibility on the part of each teacher. Once you have taken the initial, small step with one colleague, you may decide to pursue a more inclusive effort to increase the number of opportunities to integrate the curriculum. This can lead to a conversation with a group of teachers or participation in a thematic event involving the entire school. Working with a group calls for teamwork and an understanding of group processes. Respect the group process—learn to negotiate and be sensitive to interpersonal issues. After all, the process will involve professionals with different teaching styles, viewpoints, perspectives, and approaches to solving problems.

CREATE LESSON PLANS AND ADDRESS LOGISTICS

You are now ready to get down to specifics. If you are working with a colleague, this is a good time to take a moment to brainstorm activities you can use in meeting the lesson's objectives. As you design the lesson, keep in mind that the students should feel that the activities are fun and exciting and see meaningful links between the subject areas.

You will need to determine whether the activities can fit into your current schedule, whether an adjustment can take place between colleagues, or whether a change is needed schoolwide. Identify the materials and equipment you will need, and discuss the type of space required for a successful experience. Finally, plan how you will organize students to work (individually or in groups), how you will attend to individual needs and learning styles, and how you will ensure that everyone is actively involved.

Assessment of Interdisciplinary Learning

The integrated curriculum is dynamic, interactive, situational, and creative. There is no single model; thus there cannot be a single model for evaluating success. Assessment of interdisciplinary learning experiences requires us to move beyond the conventional approaches to assessment. Planning for assessment is an integral part of planning for instruction. Objectives, learning activities, and assessment procedures are closely interrelated and cannot be designed independently. Select those most relevant to your students' learning.

LINK ASSESSMENT TO LEARNING

Past attempts at evaluation and assessment have largely been linked to grading. Too often discrete tasks alone (such as multiple-choice or true-false paper-and-pencil tests and product scores in physical education, or time for the

Figure 2.1   Meeting with another teacher is the first step in planning to use a shared or partnership model.

50-meter dash or distance in feet and inches for a throw) have been used for the purpose of determining a student's grade. In physical education, standardized tests for assessing physical fitness, sport skills, knowledge, and psychosocial characteristics have often been used as norm- or criterion-referenced measures to compare students to national standards. From a practitioner's point of view, these types of tests tend to be impractical and often fail to measure the instructional objectives of interest to teachers (National Association for Sport and Physical Education, 2003). These factors have contributed to inappropriate assessment practices and poor instruction in general. As a result, reform in education has refocused the goal of assessment on the enhancement of learning rather than simply the documentation of learning. When seen from this viewpoint, assessment becomes more formative. It focuses on the process of learning. It becomes more informal, authentic, practical, and expedient.

ALTERNATIVE ASSESSMENT STRATEGIES

A number of alternative assessment strategies have emerged from the educational reform movement. They are particularly appropriate because they emphasize outcomes-based education, integrated learning, and critical thinking skills, each of which is central to reform in education. Examples of alternative assessment include student portfolios, projects, logs, journals, interviews, debates, observation, self-assessment, role-playing, event tasks, anecdotal records, checklists, rating scales, and video analysis. Most of these alternative assessment techniques use defined criteria to judge student performance. Rubrics describe the range of possible student performances or responses based on a defined set of criteria. The criteria should be written by teachers before instruction begins and are shared with students as a unit of work is explained. When students are aware of the criteria for performance, they understand the quality their work should exhibit. Clearly defined criteria allow you and your students to provide meaningful feedback during instruction.

You are encouraged to develop your own assessment instruments to document student

learning in an interdisciplinary lesson. Consider the following concepts when developing assessment instruments:

- The assessment instrument must be consistent with the objectives.
- Assessments must enable students to demonstrate learning.
- Assessments must be reliable and consistent over time.
- Assessments must be understood by students, parents, and administrators.

There are a wide variety of alternative assessment options; choose an assessment instrument that is most relevant.

EXAMPLES OF ASSESSMENT INSTRUMENTS

This section presents three examples of assessment instruments for the three interdisciplinary teaching models introduced in chapter 1. The examples include the content areas, suggested grade level, description of activity, and assessment instruments.

Physical Education and Science Using the Connected Model

Content Areas: Physical education—overhand throw for distance; science—third-class levers

Suggested Grade Level: 2 and 3

Description: In this learning experience the teacher has instructed the students on how to perform a mature overhand throw for distance. The instruction includes an explanation of how an overhand throw uses the principles of a third-class lever system. The science principle is included to illustrate the biomechanical operation of the arm in a throw. The student can see how a science principle is used in a practical situation. The instruction is followed by time for the students to practice the overhand throw. The teacher emphasizes the following performance criteria during instruction: side to target, step with opposite foot, elbow out and back, and follow-through.

Assessment Instruments: The teacher uses a performance checklist to score how well students use mature form when performing the overhand throw for distance. The assessment will show the teacher how many students have mastered the skill and how many need more practice and instruction.

To assess the students' understanding of the connection between the physical skill of the overhand throw and the science principle of third-class levers, the students write in their physical education journal about how an overhand throw uses the principles of a third-class lever. The teacher reads the journal entries and comments to each student on his or her description. As a result of this assessment, the teacher learns about the students' knowledge of levers and their application to the overhand throw.

Physical Education and Mathematics Using the Shared Model

Content Areas: The physical education teacher and the fifth grade teacher introduce the concepts of symmetry and asymmetry during the same week. In the physical education program the concepts are taught using shapes and balances in gymnastics; in the mathematics program they are taught in a geometry lesson focused on dividing the space within triangles, squares, and rectangles.

Suggested Grade Level: 4 through 6

Description: In the physical education class, partners create a gymnastics routine using three different static balances that demonstrate symmetrical and asymmetrical shapes. Together they explore making various symmetrical and asymmetrical balanced shapes with their bodies at low, medium, and high levels and then select three shapes for the routine, one at each level. In the geometry lesson the mathematics teacher asks students to find different ways to symmetrically and asymmetrically divide the space of a triangle, square, and rectangle.

Assessment Instruments: The gymnastics lesson is completed using a peer assessment. Each pair of students observes another set of partners performing their gymnastics routine and scores the routine based on a set of criteria and a scoring rubric that has been developed by the teacher and students at the beginning of the lesson. The following is an example of a rubric for this lesson:

Excellent: Partners include symmetrical and asymmetrical shapes in their routine. They can

hold all three balances for a count of three and move smoothly from one balance to another.

Good: Partners include symmetrical and asymmetrical shapes in their routine. They hold two balances for a count of three or hesitate when moving from one balance to another.

Needs improvement: Partners do not include both symmetrical and asymmetrical shapes in their routine or hold only one balance for a count of three.

For assessment of the geometry lesson, each student draws his or her solutions demonstrating how a triangle, a square, and a rectangle can be divided into three symmetrical and three asymmetrical shapes. The scoring rubric identifies the number of accurate drawings needed for each level of achievement, for example:

Outstanding: 16 to 18 accurate drawings

Very good: 13 to 15 accurate drawings

Satisfactory: 10 to 12 accurate drawings

Needs extra help: 9 or fewer accurate drawings

After each lesson is assessed, the scores for each child from the gymnastics lesson and the geometry lesson are collated to evaluate the student's understanding of the concept of symmetry and asymmetry in different situations.

Physical Education, Language Arts, and Music Using the Partnership Model

Content Areas: The physical education teacher, the music teacher, and the language arts teacher plan and team-teach a learning experience to meet the objective that students will develop collaborative skills contributing to successful friendships.

Suggested Grade Level: 4 through 6

Description: All three teachers present activities in which the students write poetry on the theme of collaboration in friendship and then use the poems as inspiration for creating instrumental music and dances. Collaboration is the focus for all activities during the creative process as well as when students present the final products. The learning experience concludes with a performance that entails a choral reading of the poems, an instrumental music piece composed and played by a small group of students, and a dance performed to the music piece.

Assessment Instruments: The teachers have developed several instruments for evaluating the students' understanding of the concept of collaboration; these include student self-assessment, teacher assessment, and peer assessment.

Self-assessment: Before the learning experience, students complete a set of questions about their understanding of the meaning of collaboration and when it appears in their daily life. At the end of the learning experience, they complete a similar set of questions that prompt them to describe how collaboration was used in the activities and to comment on their personal feelings about collaboration during the learning experience. The teachers review the responses with each student in a personal conference.

Teacher assessment: The teachers identify the collaborative behaviors they want to see exhibited by the students during the creation of the music composition and the dance choreography. They develop a checklist and record which behaviors they observe and how many times the behaviors appear. Each teacher takes a turn observing and assessing a student group while the other two teachers work with the students.

Peer assessment: Students view a videotape of the performance and write or draw a picture to describe a part of the performance in which collaboration is used.

Developing a Successful Support Network

The development and success of an interdisciplinary curriculum are often determined by the support you receive from school administrators, parents, students, and colleagues. It is important to include these individuals in the early planning stages and keep them informed as the process unfolds.

ADMINISTRATORS

Gaining your administrator's support for interdisciplinary teaching is an important step toward achieving success. The administrator can be an advocate with the school board and parents. He or she can be an ally when you want to expand the interdisciplinary program to include more students and teachers or to continue it for extended periods of time. Your administrator will also be helpful when scheduling changes are necessary, when coordinated planning time is needed, or when materials and equipment require school funds.

> Enlightened administrators will have established a school culture that supports innovation and risk taking. As you plan your curriculum, seek the participation of the administrator. He or she need not be part of the team meetings but should receive progress reports on the planning. His or her ideas for support or reallocation of resources can enhance implementation. If you feel that the administrator will not support the integrated unit outright, discuss among yourselves ways of introducing him or her to your more general goals and beliefs. Copying an article on integrated curriculum to share with the administrator may start the support process. Another method is to find a colleague in another school who is active in implementing integrated curricula. Ask if that school's administrator can call your own administrator to discuss the advantages of the integrated approach. (Maurer, 1994, pp. 31-32)

STUDENTS

Success in any interdisciplinary learning experience depends on the enthusiasm with which your students participate in the activities. Selecting and planning lessons that are interesting and relevant is certainly necessary; however, you may need to explain to your students the purpose for integrating one or more subjects and the benefits that will result from the lesson. Students may at first be skeptical and ask, "Why are we doing math in physical education?" You can help them make the transfer of skills and knowledge from one subject to another through planning meaningful activities that invite inquiry, challenge, and ultimately success for the student.

COLLEAGUES

Once you have completed an initial collaborative effort with a colleague, look for ways to maintain the relationship that will lead to additional opportunities for integration. Remember, you are learning not only about how to integrate curriculum, but also about how to work together.

Here are ways you can develop collaborative efforts with colleagues:

- Pursue long-term goals for a project by planning in collaboration with other teachers. As the units are designed, you can plan yours to complement, lead into, or follow the unit in the classroom.

- Initiate brief exchanges about the area the students are studying. When a teacher drops off a class for physical education, ask what books the students are reading or what they are currently studying in science.

- Provide colleagues with information about what you are currently teaching. They may be able to use the topic in a writing lesson, use it as the focus in a mathematical problem-solving situation, or use the words you have emphasized in your class as spelling words.

- Attend curriculum meetings in other content areas to stay current with content and practices. These meetings may take place in your school or may be held on a district-wide basis.

- Attend grade-level meetings to gain an understanding of specific issues and program direction.

- Invite other teachers to observe a part of your class to see how you have integrated an idea. Ask them for additional suggestions or assistance. Teachers will be pleased to see that you have an interest in their discipline or grade level.

- Invite teachers to participate in the physical education class. Even if it is not feasible for them to attend the entire class, they will appreciate the invitation and may be able to observe or listen to a portion of the class.

- Set up a weekly or monthly meeting time with colleagues to maintain the interest and continue to informally share ideas. Having someone with whom to brainstorm ideas is a huge help.

- Ask teachers to place a note in your mailbox about upcoming units of study. Leave them notes to keep them up to date with what you are doing.

Successful collegial collaborations are characterized by sharing responsibilities, cooperating to assure positive relationships, supporting one another, communicating with one another, recognizing one another's strengths, and developing an environment that promotes trust (Chen, Cone, and Cone, 2005). The experience will not only benefit you but will also influence your students. What they see is what they will model.

PARENTS

Parents can play a key role in supporting interdisciplinary learning experiences. For many parents, the concept of integrating subjects may be unfamiliar and they will welcome information on the objectives and activities so they can reinforce your efforts at home. "A letter home or an attractive flyer announcing the unit would also alert them that some new activity is about to start. It is hoped that the child's enthusiasm will also reinforce your message. If there is a culminating activity at the end of the unit, such as a presentation, skit, or simulation, invite the parents" (Maurer, 1994, p. 29).

Summary

Interdisciplinary teaching offers an opportunity to deliver knowledge and skills from a new perspective. It maintains the integrity of the subject areas and benefits from clearly defined objectives and performance expectations. This approach to teaching is initiated through a review of the scope and sequence in current curriculum guides before a specific content area is selected for integration. The next step is to gather information from a variety of sources. Begin the journey by reflecting on your own experiences; seek out your colleagues, review texts from other subjects, or visit classrooms. Select the interdisciplinary teaching model that is appropriate for meeting the lesson or unit objective. You can use the connected model individually as you link one subject with another. The shared model expands the depth of content integration with another teacher, and the partnership model requires meeting with colleagues to plan and team-teach. During the planning process, consider the logistics of implementation, including schedule changes, facilities, materials and equipment, and the organization of students. Start with a topic or skill you feel comfortable with, be sure to keep it small and manageable, and build on those accomplishments.

Planning for and implementing an interdisciplinary learning experience should always include a means of assessing the objectives of the lesson. Various forms of assessment can be used, including self-assessment, peer assessment, teacher assessment, portfolios, journals, video analysis, checklists, and written responses to questions.

Efforts to integrate subject areas are more likely to succeed when you communicate your plans and gain support from administrators, parents, and students, in addition to developing relationships with your colleagues. Don't underestimate the value of an administrative advocate, one who can speak knowledgeably about your program and who can provide support in the decision-making process.

Making It Work: Practical Applications

" YOU MUST BE THE CHANGE YOU WISH TO SEE IN THE WORLD. "

Mahatma Gandhi

The second part of the book includes five chapters that provide practical applications for integrating the content of language arts, mathematics, science, social studies, music, theater arts, and visual arts with the content of physical education in an active learning experience.

The purpose of these chapters is to provide both classroom and physical education teachers with many practical ideas on how to use experiences based in movement to enhance the presentation of content from other subjects to children in elementary school. Chapter 3 focuses on the language arts abilities of reading, writing, speaking, listening, and viewing. Chapter 4 addresses the mathematical concepts and skills related to numbers, measuring and graphing, geometry, patterns and functions, probability and statistics, logic, and algebra. Chapter 5 contains information on science concepts from the biological and life sciences, earth and space sciences, and physical sciences. Chapter 6 presents the areas of relationships within families, school and community, citizenship, character education, history, mapping and globe skills, national identity and culture, and geography in the social studies discipline. The final chapter addresses music, theater arts, and visual arts. In addition, each chapter contains an introduction describing the impact that the discipline has on a child's education and the value that is gained when the skills and concepts are reinforced using movement. For each chapter you will also find a sample scope and sequence of discipline content that provides an overview of the skills, concepts, or processes that teachers use to develop curricula and lessons.

Twenty-four examples of complete learning experiences are presented to offer a practical approach to interdisciplinary teaching. You can use each learning experience, as written, as a teaching model, or the examples may be an inspiration for you to develop your own learning experiences. They provide actual language for the teacher to use with the students when presenting the tasks. Each learning experience illustrates one of the interdisciplinary teaching models described in chapter 1 and provides an example of real-life implementation. These learning experiences can also serve as the basis for a conversation with a colleague about how two or more disciplines can be linked together to provide an enriched lesson or unit of study for your students. You will also find over 185 additional ideas for developing active learning experiences that may serve as a stimulus for creating your own interdisciplinary endeavors. In addition, to each chapter we have added a section on ongoing interdisciplinary strategies for the physical education classroom.

Finally, appendix B presents an example that integrates multiple disciplines. Because of its interdisciplinary nature, this subject matter can easily address combinations of physical education with language arts, mathematics, science, or social studies–geography or more than one of these.

Explore, experiment, and enjoy using the learning experiences. They are for you, your colleagues, and your students to share as you discover new ways of using an interdisciplinary approach to teaching and learning.

Integrating Physical Education With Language Arts

One January morning while Mr. Mann, a fifth grade teacher, and Mrs. McWilliams, the physical education teacher, were talking about the cold weather, they mentioned what they were planning to teach during February to bring excitement and challenge to the cold winter month ahead. Mr. Mann mentioned developing a poetry festival featuring poems about friendship, the heart, love, and the color red, while Mrs. McWilliams discussed presenting a unit on cardiorespiratory endurance using jump rope skills. The two teachers joked about how students could jump rope to the rhythm of a poem and also write poems about jumping rope with friends. A casual conversation on a cold January morning eventually developed into a shared interdisciplinary learning experience for both the teachers and their students.

The language arts are an integral part of education at the elementary level. "They are the means through which one is able to receive information; think logically and creatively; express ideas; understand and participate meaningfully in spoken, written, and nonverbal communications; formulate and answer questions; and search for, organize, evaluate, and apply information" (New Jersey Department of Education, 2004, p. C-1). A comprehensive language arts program is characterized by an integration of the skills and concepts in reading, writing, speaking, listening, and viewing (figure 3.1). These skills and concepts are essential for communication and learning in all disciplines.

The descriptions in the scope and sequence section of this chapter are a summary of information gathered from various state standards documents, the *National Standards for the English Language Arts* (National Council of Teachers of English and International Reading Association, 1996), curriculum guides, and program activities. You may find a slightly different version in your state or school district, one that has been designed to consider local perspectives and needs.

You can provide opportunities in the physical education class that support learning language arts skills and concepts and that incorporate the physical education experiences as part of the learning experience in the classroom (Cone and Cone, 2001). Connor-Kuntz and Dummer (1996) reported that students who were taught language skills during physical education activities showed improvement in language abilities. The study also showed that it is easy to implement language skills in physical education classes without sacrificing the physical skills being taught or requiring additional time. Remember as you develop interdisciplinary experiences that the activities should enhance children's educational experience in both disciplines.

When children make the shapes of letters using their bodies in an alphabet dance, they reinforce the development of letter formation gained through a handwriting exercise. They may also use an action of the body to increase understanding of word meanings, such as *around the corner, bend over backward,* or *climb to the top.* The content in a physical education program offers experiences that can be used as inspiration for writing stories, reflective pieces, news articles, poems, or reports. Students also find enjoyment in reading novels, stories, and poems that

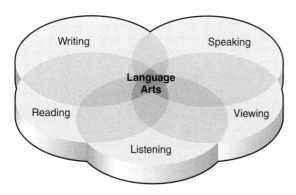

Figure 3.1   The components of language arts.

highlight a physical activity they may have experienced. These readings may also inspire students to create dances, games, and movements that represent the ideas, events, and characters portrayed in the literature (see appendix A for using children's literature in physical education and dance).

Speaking and listening skills are reinforced when students give or receive directions for an activity, explain and discuss a game strategy, or share feedback with a classmate. As part of all learning experiences, students gain valuable information by viewing presentations by the teacher, observing others as they perform skills, or looking at videos or visual displays.

Scope and Sequence for Language Arts

The language arts curriculum content is composed of five basic academic competencies. This section defines the areas of reading, writing, speaking, listening, and viewing. The matrix in table 3.1 indicates the grade in which specific language arts skills and concepts are presented. Some skills and concepts introduced during the primary grades are continued during the intermediate grades at higher levels and with more complexity.

Table 3.1

Scope and Sequence of Language Arts Concepts Taught in Elementary Schools

CONCEPT	GRADE						
Reading	K	1	2	3	4	5	6
Reading for different purposes	✖	✖	✖	✖	✖	✖	✖
Literature study	✖	✖	✖	✖	✖	✖	✖
Conventions of language	✖	✖	✖	✖	✖	✖	✖
Vocabulary	✖	✖	✖	✖	✖	✖	✖
Comprehension	✖	✖	✖	✖	✖	✖	✖
Reading strategies	✖	✖	✖	✖	✖	✖	✖
Story structures	✖	✖	✖	✖	✖	✖	✖
Writing							
Writing for a variety of purposes	✖	✖	✖	✖	✖	✖	✖
Composition	✖	✖	✖	✖	✖	✖	✖
Handwriting	✖	✖	✖	✖	✖	✖	✖
Spelling	✖	✖	✖	✖	✖	✖	✖
Mechanics	✖	✖	✖	✖	✖	✖	✖

(continued)

Table 3.1 *(continued)*

CONCEPT	GRADE						
Speaking	K	1	2	3	4	5	6
Speaking for different purposes and audiences	✗	✗	✗	✗	✗	✗	✗
Questions and answers	✗	✗	✗	✗	✗	✗	✗
Oral presentations					✗	✗	✗
Group discussions	✗	✗	✗	✗	✗	✗	
Directions or instructions	✗	✗	✗	✗	✗	✗	✗
Listening							
Listening for a variety of purposes	✗	✗	✗	✗	✗	✗	✗
Oral directions	✗	✗	✗	✗	✗	✗	✗
Questions and answers	✗	✗	✗	✗	✗	✗	✗
Note taking					✗	✗	✗
Music and sounds	✗	✗	✗	✗	✗	✗	✗
Critical listening			✗	✗	✗	✗	✗
Viewing							
Viewing for a variety of purposes	✗	✗	✗	✗	✗	✗	✗
Personal interactions, live performances	✗	✗	✗	✗	✗	✗	✗
Visual arts involving oral or written language	✗	✗	✗	✗	✗	✗	✗
Print media	✗	✗	✗	✗	✗	✗	✗
Electronic media	✗	✗	✗	✗	✗	✗	✗
Fact and fictional representations	✗	✗	✗	✗	✗	✗	✗

PRIMARY-GRADE LANGUAGE ARTS SKILLS AND CONCEPTS

Most children experience many rich and valuable life experiences before their arrival at school. Experiences such as watching television, listening to music, drawing pictures, communicating through speaking, and being introduced to books provide a readiness that will enhance the formal learning process that begins in kindergarten. In kindergarten and first grade, students learn about letters, listen to stories and poems, and develop a sight vocabulary. They are encouraged to speak about their experiences and describe them through drawings, words, or simple sentences. At this level, children are introduced to different types of literature and enjoy sharing stories and their writing with peers and adults.

The language arts program in the second and third grades continues to focus on the development of a solid foundation of the basic skills and concepts. These skills and concepts are needed to acquire information, communicate ideas, and ultimately provide the means for the student to enjoy success. Students learn to apply reading strategies for decoding and comprehension, expand their vocabulary, organize thoughts, and write for a variety of purposes. Their speaking abilities are enhanced as they give brief oral presentations, participate in group discussions, learn to summarize information, and practice giving clear directions. Listening skills are developed through activities that use a hands-on approach to interpret information from a variety of sources. Children become better at following a series of oral directions, asking relevant questions, listening critically, and restating what others say. They develop strategies to gain meaning from visual experience and become skilled at using visual media to support their reading, writing, and speaking.

INTERMEDIATE-GRADE LANGUAGE ARTS SKILLS AND CONCEPTS

The intermediate grade level is characterized by a refining of the language arts skills and concepts and the further integration of these skills and concepts with learning in the other disciplines. Students read novels and stories that directly relate to social studies and science units. Research and note-taking skills are introduced, and the editing process becomes common practice in students' writing. Students have internalized the skills and strategies necessary to read text, make the connections between what is read and their own experiences, and understand the components of a story. The study of literature at this level includes nonfiction, fiction, poetry, and dramatic works representing a diversity of cultures and authors. Students increase proficiency in speaking by delivering oral presentations based on research, learning to use body language, effectively using the voice, increasing eye contact, and participating in collaborative speaking activities. Through active listening, students increase comprehension of oral reports, discussions, interviews, and lectures and are able to restate, interpret, respond to, and evaluate increasingly complex information. Students use viewing to respond thoughtfully and critically to both print and nonprint visual messages. Intermediate students view and use simple charts, graphs, and diagrams to report data, and respond to and evaluate the use of illustrations to support text. They learn about different media forms and how these forms contribute to communication.

When students learn to read, write, speak, listen, and view critically, strategically, and creatively and when they learn to use these arts individually and in groups, they have the literacy skills they need to discover personal and shared meaning throughout their lives. The language arts are valuable not only in and of themselves but also as supporting skills for students' learning in all other subjects. Students can best develop language competencies, like other competencies, through meaningful activities and settings.

Learning Experiences

Each of the five learning experiences (table 3.2) demonstrates one of the interdisciplinary teaching models presented in chapter 1. The learning experiences have been designed to include skills and concepts from physical education and language arts. For each learning experience we include a name, a suggested grade level, an interdisciplinary teaching model, objectives, equipment, organization, a complete description of the lesson, and assessment suggestions. In addition, tips on what to look for in student responses, suggestions for ways you can change or modify the lesson, and ideas for teachable moments provide further insights into each learning experience.

Table 3.2

Language Arts Learning Experience Index

Skills and concepts	Name	Suggested grade level	Interdisciplinary teaching model
Language arts: listening and responding to a story through movement; comprehension of word meaning Physical education: traveling movements, level, and tempo; creating a dance; observing a dance	The Rumpus Dance	K-3	Connected
Language arts: letter recognition and reproduction Physical education: traveling movements and balances	Alphabet Gymnastics	K-1	Shared
Language arts: writing descriptive information and speaking before a group Physical education: using throwing and catching skills in a game	Create-a-Game	4-6	Partnership
Language arts: reading comprehension and writing descriptive information Physical education: applying fitness concepts; creating and performing movement sequences	Sport Words in Action	3-6	Shared
Language arts: effective speaking using body language, inflection, enunciation, eye contact, and intonation Physical education: creating a conversation dance using the call-and-response form	A Moving Conversation	4-6	Shared

The Rumpus Dance

Suggested Grade Level

Primary (K through 3)

Interdisciplinary Teaching Model

Connected

Children listen to a reading of Maurice Sendak's *Where the Wild Things Are* as part of an author-of-the-month program and create a dance expressing the feeling of being at the wild rumpus.

Language Arts

Listening and responding to a story through movement; demonstrating comprehension of word meaning; increasing vocabulary

Physical Education

Performing locomotor movements using change of direction, level, and tempo that express the meaning of a word; creating a dance that has three movements; observing and responding to a dance performed by another student

Objectives

As a result of participating in this learning experience, children will

- discuss and create a written list of words to define the word *rumpus* from Maurice Sendak's *Where the Wild Things Are;*
- explore different movements that express the descriptive words for *rumpus;* and
- create a rumpus dance using changes of level, direction, and tempo.

Equipment

Where the Wild Things Are by Maurice Sendak, fast-tempo music, chalkboard or chart paper, chalk or markers

Organization

Students create and perform movements individually and then work with partners to observe each other's dances.

Description

"You have just heard the story *Where the Wild Things Are.* This is an exciting story about the adventures of Max as he visits a strange land where the Wild Things live. Now you are going to create a dance about the wild *rumpus* that happened in the story."

▶ Write the word *rumpus* on the top or in the center of the chalkboard or chart.

"Do you remember when the rumpus happened in the story? Let's look at the pages in the book and see how the Wild Things and Max are moving during the rumpus."

▶ Show students the pages in the book.

"What kinds of movements are they doing at the rumpus?" Students respond, for example, "hopping, jumping, skipping, turning, hanging, swinging, stretching, marching."

▶ Write the words on the chalkboard or chart paper (figure 3.2).

▶ Tell the students that they will try these movements as part of their warm-up today.

▶ First, have each student find his or her own space and begin hopping in forward, backward, and sideways directions. Remind students to give each foot a turn. Ask them if they can hop four times on one foot in one direction and four times on the other foot in another direction.

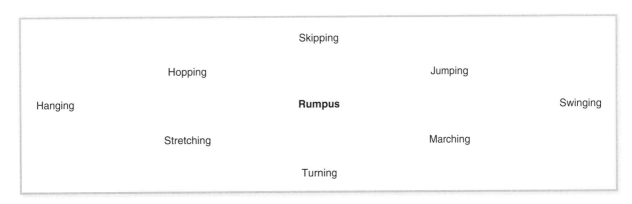

Figure 3.2   **Rumpus movements.**

▶ Next, encourage them to try big skips that lift them up off the floor. Ask them to find a way to add a turn while they are skipping.

▶ Now have them combine jumping and stretching together. "Jump and stretch to the right, then jump and stretch to the left." Repeat the movement to the right and left several times.

▶ Tell them that they will not be using swinging today, but they will use swinging the next time they use the gymnastics apparatus.

"Now we are going to create our own rumpus movements. Tell me some words that describe a rumpus." Students answer, "wild party, going crazy, being very excited." You respond, "What movements can you do to express the meaning of the word *rumpus* that we did not do in the warm-up?" Students answer, "roll on the floor, spin around fast, shake your body, kick your legs up."

▶ Add these words to the rumpus words already on the chalkboard or chart paper (figure 3.3).

Wild party		**Going crazy**		**Being excited**
	Rolling	Skipping		
	Hopping		Jumping	
	Spinning	**Rumpus**		**Kicking**
Hanging		**Shaking**		Swinging
	Stretching		Marching	
		Turning		

Figure 3.3   Student-suggested rumpus movements.

"Each person, choose one movement from the list of words on the chalkboard. Andrew, what word did you choose?" Andrew responds, "marching." "Now find a space and practice your movement using a forward, backward, and sideways direction. I will play the music while you are practicing."

▶ Move through the class and ask students to identify their movement and demonstrate it in the three directions.

"Everyone stop and return to the chalkboard. Now choose a second movement from the list, find a space, and practice doing this movement changing from low to high and high to low. Again, I will play the music while you practice."

▶ After a brief practice time, have the students stop, then ask them to put the two movements together in a sequence.

"Be sure to move smoothly from one movement to the other. See if you can find a way to blend the end of one movement into the beginning of the second movement."

▶ Walk around and observe how children are moving from the first movement to the second.

"Now stop, return to the chalkboard, and choose a third different movement from the list. Practice the movement using strong and fast energy that becomes slower and slower until you stop in a still shape. Can someone demonstrate how he or she can make a movement start strong and fast and let it become slower and slower until the movement stops in a still shape? I see Meredith would like to demonstrate. What movement are you going to use?" Meredith responds, "I'm going to spin around and wave my arms up and down to show how I go crazy and then get tired at my rumpus." "That sounds great. Let's watch Meredith to see how the tempo of her spinning movement becomes slower and slower until she stops in a still shape."

▶ Meredith demonstrates for the class.

"Thank you, Meredith."

▶ Write the sequence on the chalkboard or chart paper (figure 3.4).

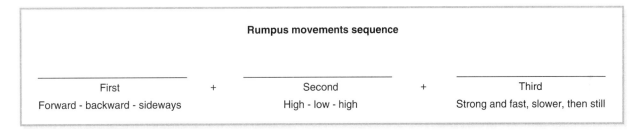

Figure 3.4   Sequence of rumpus movements.

"Now practice putting all three movements you have chosen from the chalkboard in a sequence. Remember, the first one uses three different directions, the second one changes levels, and the third one starts fast and strong and ends in a still shape. The music will be playing while you practice."

▶ While all the students are practicing, approach individual students and ask them to explain their sequence and to demonstrate the movements.

"Now let's show each other the rumpus dances we have created. I would like half the class to sit and observe while the other half demonstrates their rumpus dance. Perform your dance once, then hold your still shape until everyone in the group has finished. I will play the music while you are performing."

▶ Each group performs their rumpus dance while the music is playing. Lower the music volume as the students begin to stop in their still shapes.

"The second time you perform I will assign a person to observe your rumpus dance. When you are finished, your observer will tell you what movements he or she observed. Then you will switch places." (See figure 3.5.)

Assessment Suggestions

▪ Use the partner conversation at the end of the learning experience as one type of peer assessment.

▪ Figure 3.6 shows a sample self-assessment. The student writes the first, second, and third movements of his or her rumpus dance on each line. Children can also add a drawing or comments about their feelings as they performed the dance.

▪ You can videotape small groups of students performing their rumpus dance. Have the students observe their performance and match the words they have written describing the dance to the movements they perform in their dance.

Figure 3.5   Assign observers to comment on each other's movements.

Look For

■ Clear changes of direction, level, and tempo and ending the dance in a still shape.

■ Smooth transitions from one movement to another. Do the children blend the end of one movement with the beginning of the next?

How Can I Change This?

■ Emphasize other elements of movement such as size (big or small) or pathways, or develop a specific rhythm for each movement.

shake spin Jump

SPIN ON 1 foot

my Jump

I liked the spin best.

Figure 3.6   Sample assessment of rumpus dance.

- Have the children perform three movements using a pattern, such as first movement, fast and strong; second movement, slow and strong; third movement, fast and strong.
- Use other words or phrases from the story.
- Have students work in pairs or groups of three to select the words and develop the three movements of the dance. They can practice and perform in unison.

Teachable Moments

- Emphasize proper technique for performing movements, such as safe landings from a jump, using balance and strength to make smooth transitions from one movement to another, or using the correct rhythm for a skip.
- Encourage experimentation with the sequence of movements in the dance.

Alphabet Gymnastics

Suggested Grade Level

Primary (K and 1)

Interdisciplinary Teaching Model

Shared

In the classroom the students learn to identify and form letter shapes, and in physical education they learn to make shapes in gymnastics.

Language Arts

Letter recognition and reproduction

Physical Education

Locomotor movements and balances

Objectives

As a result of participating in this lesson, the student will

- identify different letters of the alphabet,
- use his or her body to make the shapes of letters,
- practice writing the letters,
- practice balances using different body parts,
- travel in different directions (forward, backward, sideways), and
- create a sequence of movements using three letters.

Equipment

Mats, chalkboard or chart paper, chalk or markers, 8½- × 11-inch paper, crayons

Organization

Partners or small groups share a mat.

Description

"Today's lesson is called Alphabet Gymnastics. You are going to make your body into the shape of different letters and find a way to hold it still in a balanced position. Then you will find different ways to make the letter travel in the space."

▶ After a brief, running warm-up, assign students to a mat.

"We are going to continue to warm up our bodies using stretching letters. Everyone sit on your mat, legs straight and in front, sit up tall, and stretch your arms to the ceiling. What letter did you make?" Students respond, "a capital L." "Now slowly reach forward, curving your arms, head, and back to make the letter C. Slowly stretch back into the L shape. Let's try slowly moving a couple times from the L to the C so we can warm up our bodies."

▶ You can do the movements with the students.

"Next, stand up on your mat with your feet together and arms stretched out to the side. What letter does this shape look like?" Students respond, "a small t." "Slowly twist your arms to the right, then slowly to the left. Let's try this movement a couple more times."

▶ Students can follow you or try the stretch on their own time.

"We are going to do one more stretch using the letter *t* shape. Standing on the mat or the floor, slowly raise your heels, stretching your ankles, and then slowly lower your heels. Remember to keep your ankles straight so you are not leaning on the outside of your feet. Rise up and down five times slowly, keeping your stomach muscles tight to help you balance."

▶ Have the students assemble with you near the chalkboard for the next section of the lesson.

"I would like someone to write a letter from his or her name on the chalkboard. I see Timothy has his hand up. Timothy, choose a letter from your name and write it on the board."

▶ Timothy writes an uppercase *Y.*

"That's great, Timothy. Class, what letter did he write?"

▶ A student recognizes the letter and tells the class.

"How can you make a *Y* with your body? Lisa, can you show us your idea? I see Lisa is making a standing *Y.* Is there another way to make a *Y?* Yes, Raquib is lying on his back. I want you to return to your mat and try the ways Lisa and Raquib used to make a *Y.* Then try to make a *Y* using your own idea." (See figure 3.7.)

▶ Students return to their mats and begin to practice.

"Everyone stop now and think of the letters in your name. Choose one of these letters and make your letter using a high, medium, and low level. Ask the other students at your mat to guess what letter you are making."

▶ Students take turns making letters and guessing the letters formed by the other students on the mat.

Figure 3.7 **Students using shapes to form letters.**

▷ Next, write a letter on the chalkboard or chart and prompt the students for each new letter with the following directions.

"Now, you are going to make letters using a still balance. Make the letter *P* while balancing on one foot. Can you balance and say the alphabet until you come to the letter *P?*

"Make the letter *V* with your legs in the air as you lie on your back. Can you make your letter *V* a little wider?

"Make the letter *K* as you balance on your right foot. Make a *K* while balancing on your left foot.

"Choose another letter and find a way to make it balance. Hold your body still while you are balancing. What body part are you balancing on? Ask someone on your mat to guess what letter you are using for your balance.

"Now, two or three people get together and make a letter. What body parts are you using to balance on? Let's stop and look at some of the letters people made and see if we can guess the letter and name the body parts they are using to balance on."

▷ Call on each group of students to demonstrate their letter, and have a student from another group write the letter on the chalkboard or chart.

"Next, we are going to make traveling letters. You will find different ways to take a trip around the mat with your body in the shape of a letter. Let's start with everyone in a standing position making the shape of the letter *X*."

▷ Draw a large *X* on the chalkboard or chart.

"Great *X*s! I see your arms are apart and reaching up to make the top of the *X* and your feet are apart to form the bottom of the *X*. Using your letter *X*, begin to walk forward around the mat. Keep the spaces between your arms and legs. Try making the *X* walk backward. Tilt the *X* onto one foot and balance for a moment.

"Now try a jumping lowercase *i*. Can someone tell the class what an *i* looks like?" Ishmael has his hand up and responds, "It looks like this. You make a straight line and put a dot on the top."

▷ Ishmael draws the letter in the air using his hand as he verbally describes the letter.

"That's a good way to describe the letter *i*."

▷ Ask another student to draw a lowercase *i* on the chalkboard or chart.

"Everyone draw the letter *i* in the air. Now draw a very big *i* so you have to jump up in the air to put the dot on the top. Make sure you land on your feet at the end of the big jump."

▷ Students practice making the letter. Encourage the students to reach as high and low as they can to make the long, vertical portion of the *i*. Then have them jump as high as they can to dot the *i* with their hand.

"Now, before you draw your letter *i*, I want you to take three little jumps moving forward. The order is jump, jump, jump, draw the straight part of the *i*, and take another big jump to make the dot. Practice the jumping *i* a couple more times.

"Choose a letter and find a way to make the letter travel in the space. You can use your feet or other parts of your body, and try moving forward, backward, and sideways."

▷ As the students practice different letters traveling in the space, you or other students guess the letters. You may also ask students to demonstrate their letter for others.

"Next, you are going to choose three letters and write them on a piece of paper using a crayon. You may choose which letter will be first, second, and third. Your first letter will be a still balance, your second letter will travel in the space, and your third letter will be a still balance. Now choose your letters, write them down, and practice. I will be walking around to see how you are doing."

> ▶ As the students practice, observe the letters the students have printed and how they are using their bodies to make the shapes. Ask the students to demonstrate for others who are sharing the mat.

Assessment Suggestions

▪ Students are in pairs or groups of three. One student makes a letter with his or her body in a still, balanced position. The other students in the group write down the letter they see the student make. The students then discuss whether the letters written down on paper correspond to the letter the student made with his or her body.

▪ Students identify the parts of the body that are used to make the different parts of the letter.

Look For

▪ Slow stretching without straining or bouncing.

▪ Straight ankles during the toe rises, with the body weight distributed evenly on all toes.

▪ Controlled movement in and out of balances. Students should not fall out of the balances.

▪ The different ways students use their body and its parts to make letters. Some students may use their whole body, while others may emphasize the shape of the letter with only their arms or legs.

▪ Accuracy with which students draw the letter on paper.

How Can I Change This?

▪ Create balances from the letters that make up the word *balance.*

▪ Use the letters in a word that describes a traveling movement, such as *hop, jump,* or *run* (e.g., a running letter *r,* then *u,* and finally *n*).

▪ Use letters that have only straight or curved lines.

▪ Use only uppercase or lowercase letters.

▪ Have the entire class form a letter.

Teachable Moment

Students can trade their three-letter gymnastics sequence with other students and try to reproduce the letters selected by the other students.

Create-a-Game

Suggested Grade Level

Intermediate (4 through 6)

Interdisciplinary Teaching Model

Partnership

You and the other teacher present a learning experience covering the process of developing and recording a game. Students create a game based on throwing and catching skills and write a description of the game; they then give an oral presentation on the game to their classmates.

Language Arts

Writing descriptive information and speaking before a group

Physical Education

Using throwing and catching skills in a game

Objectives

As result of participating in this lesson, students will

- practice throwing and catching skills while stationary;
- practice throwing and catching skills while moving;
- work collaboratively to create a game emphasizing throwing and catching;
- compose a description of their game listing the skills, directions, roles of the players, and rules and draw a diagram of the space; and
- teach their game to another group of students through an oral presentation.

Equipment

Bases or floor markers, balls of various sizes, empty boxes of various sizes, wall targets (12- × 17-inch colored construction paper), tape for wall targets, practice task cards (figure 3.8)

Organization

Students work in pairs or small groups.

Description

"In the past several lessons you have learned and practiced the techniques for the overhand throw, underhand throw, and catch. You practiced these skills from stationary and moving positions, individually and with others. Today you are going to apply these skills in a game that you create. Before you begin your game, you will have a chance to practice throwing and catching using the task cards I will give you [see figure 3.8].

Throwing and Catching Practice Task Card

You may practice the tasks in any order.

- **Underhand throws.** Throw the ball high to your partner so he or she can catch the ball above the head. Decide how many successful throws and catches you and your partner will accomplish before moving to another task. You need to complete a minimum of five.

- **Overhand throws.** The catcher makes a target with his or her hands, either high or low or right or left. Decide how many successful catches you and your partner will accomplish before moving to another task. You need to complete a minimum of five.

- **Your choice of throws.** Toss and catch to your partner using either the underhand or overhand throw as you move through the space. Decide how many successful catches you and your partner will accomplish before moving to another task. You need to complete a minimum of five.

Figure 3.8 Throwing and catching practice task card.

I have assigned students to work together. Please look at the chart on the wall to see whom you will be working with. Find your partner, choose a ball, take a card, and begin to practice."

▶ Observe students and provide feedback.

"Stop and please join me by the poster. As you can see, I have listed the parts of a game you will need to include as you design your game. (See figure 3.9) As you begin your planning, I want you to use the guidelines for the game I have listed on the chalkboard." (See figure 3.10)

Parts of a Game

Name of the game: _____

Skills: _____

Equipment: _____

Number of players: _____

How is the game played? _____

_____

Rules: _____

_____

Draw a diagram of the space:

Figure 3.9   Parts of a game.

Guidelines for Creating a Game

- All players must be involved in the game. No one is eliminated.

- Throwing and catching skills must be used.

- Players cannot be targets. Use a piece of equipment, the wall, the floor, or a piece of paper if you decide to use a target.

- You may use a point system or you may decide not to keep score.

- Share the space and equipment with others. You can select from the available balls, boxes, paper, wall targets, bases, and floor markers.

Figure 3.10   Guidelines for creating a game.

▶ Read the guidelines from the chalkboard.

"Creating a game is similar to the writing process. You gather your ideas, compose a draft, revise it, edit, and then share and publish your final piece. Your game may change several times as you try out different ideas. Once you have completed your game, write a description that includes all the parts listed on the poster. You may begin your planning."

▶ Students begin to work on their ideas. Circulate among the groups and offer suggestions if needed.

"Take your descriptions with you so you can continue to work on them in the classroom. The next time we get together, please bring your game description so you can make adjustments and changes to your game. Once you have finished creating and recording your game, you will have the chance to teach it to the rest of the class."

▶ Students may need several sessions to complete the process. After coming up with an initial idea, they may try different ways to play the game, make adjustments, reach agreement on a final form, and ultimately teach the game to others in the class.

Assessment Suggestions

- The assessment is based on the completion of a written description of the game and an oral presentation of the game to the rest of the class. The game must follow the guidelines.

- Students write about what worked well in their game and what changes they made so that it would be successful.

Look For

- How throwing and catching skills are used in the game.

- Games that include all players.

- Games that are challenging yet enjoyable.

- Partners who are having difficulty generating an idea or working cooperatively in the planning and implementation of the game. Provide the partners with strategies to help them work together and solve problems.

How Can I Change This?

- Include a different manipulative skill, such as kicking, volleying, or striking with an implement.
- Have all students use the same quantity and type of equipment.
- Assign partners or groups a specific space, such as a corner of the gym; a large square, circle, triangle, or a rectangle taped on the floor; or a space that includes a wall.

Teachable Moments

- Discuss the skills needed to work cooperatively with others.
- Talk about a personal experience you had of writing a story, or have the other teacher or one of the students do so. Draw parallels between the process of writing and the process of designing a game.

Sport Words in Action

Suggested Grade Level

Intermediate (3 through 6)

Interdisciplinary Teaching Model

Shared

Students use reading and writing skills to record sport actions sequences and to identify corresponding fitness concepts.

Language Arts

Reading, writing

Physical Education

Fitness skills and knowledge

Objectives

As a result of participating in this learning experience, students will

- increase their understanding of fitness concepts;
- improve cardiorespiratory endurance and strength;
- reflect on their fitness progress through journal writing;
- read and write words related to specific sport actions; and
- develop a fitness routine using sport actions, identifying which actions emphasize strength and which emphasize cardiorespiratory endurance.

Equipment

Paper and pencils for each student to record sport fitness words; dictionary

Organization

As a class, students follow you as you lead a fitness routine; they then collaborate in groups of three or four to create their own fitness routine.

Description

"Today, I will lead you in a fitness warm-up that uses actions from different sports. I have listed the sport and the action on the chart paper. Together, let's read the sport and the action."

▷ Ask students to read out loud together from the list on the chart (figure 3.11).

Volleyball overhead pass

Soccer dribble

Basketball dribble

Baseball base running

Figure 3.11 **Sport exercise routine chart.**

"Ready? Stand up, find your personal space, and face me. Here we go:
Four overhead volleys, one, two, three, four.
Repeat four times reaching to the right.
Now four times reaching to the left.
Now alternate right, left, right, left."

▷ Demonstrate and lead this sequence several times until the students can easily follow.

"Next, 16 soccer dribbles in place, alternating right and left.
Now try 16 soccer dribbles while turning in a circle to the right.
Now facing front again for 16 dribbles.
And repeat 16 dribbles circling to the left."

▷ Lead students through this sequence, encouraging continuous movement.

"Now, three basketball dribbles forward and take a jump shot. Get up off the floor on the jump.
Now, move backward using three basketball dribbles and shoot.
Repeat forward again, now backward."

▷ Ask students to practice this sequence after you demonstrate. When students can remember the sequence, add the next section.

"Let's try one more sport action using baseball, running the bases.
Run to your right for eight counts.
Now to the left for eight counts.
Repeat to the right and the left."

▷ Practice the running with the students.

"Now, let's perform the routine again without any stops between sports. I will call out the sport and the counts while you follow me."

▷ Repeat the sport action fitness routine two times and then discuss how the movements focus on arm and leg strength and cardiorespiratory endurance.

"Now, I will organize you into groups of three or four, and each of you, on your own paper, should write a sport and then an action and the number of times you want to do the action. Write next to your sport action whether it is for building strength or for developing cardiorespiratory endurance. Look at the actions your group has selected and make sure they are all different. Then place the papers in a sequence and practice the routine together. Be sure to check for correct spelling. If you need help, I have two dictionaries available."

▶ Rotate from one group to another to check on student progress. When students have agreed on the order of their routine, ask each student to write the order on the back of his or her paper.

"I noticed that every group cooperated and stayed focused on creating their fitness routine. I want you to memorize your routine so you can perform it without the paper. When you are ready, I will ask you to show it to another group."

Assessment Suggestions

■ Use a checklist to record your observation of the routines. Did students include a strength and a cardiorespiratory movement in their routine? Was the group able to perform the routine in unison with a smooth transition between sport actions?

■ Students complete a journal entry in response to the following question: What part of the routine did you like best and why?

Look For

Check to make sure students are choosing appropriate exercises and performing the exercises using correct technique to avoid injury.

How Can I Change This?

■ Ask each group to choose a specific sport and use actions from that sport in their routine.

■ Use pictures of sport actions instead of written words to develop the routine.

■ Add pedometers to calculate the number of steps.

■ Add heart rate monitors to determine whether children are exercising in their target heart rate zone.

Teachable Moments

■ Ask students to teach their exercise routine to another group.

■ Students can read another group's written exercise routine directions and then try to perform the routine.

A Moving Conversation

Suggested Grade Level

Intermediate (4 through 6)

Interdisciplinary Teaching Model

Shared

The students are currently learning to convey a message effectively. During a dance lesson, students create a conversation with another student using movement.

Language Arts

Effective speaking using body language, inflection, enunciation, eye contact, and intonation

Physical Education

Creating a conversation dance using the call-and-response form

Objectives

As result of participating in this lesson, students will

- understand the similarity between how movement is used to communicate feelings and ideas and how body language, inflection, enunciation, eye contact, and intonation are used in speaking; and
- understand how the call-and-response form is used as a way of relating to a partner through movement.

Equipment

Chalkboard

Organization

Students work in pairs or groups of three.

Description

"Today we are going to have a conversation with a partner, using movements instead of words to express our thoughts. Let's begin to warm up our bodies so we will be ready to move in many different ways. Follow me for all the warm-up movements."

▶ Perform a series of warm-up movements that include moving the head, shoulders, arms, back, legs, ankles, and feet using bending, stretching, twisting, and rotating body parts.

"Now, you will create movements using a body part to express a thought. Instead of using words to tell someone your thoughts, you will use a movement. Let me demonstrate with a partner."

▶ Have a student stand facing you for the demonstration.

"I will begin moving my arms and hands in a shaking motion. Andrew, I want you to watch me, and after I stop, you should respond to me by moving your hands in a different way. That's great. What we have just done is use the call-and-response form as a way for two people to move together. The *call* means that one person starts the conversation, and the *response* is the other person's answer to the call. Then the first person continues with another statement and waits for a response. This pattern continues, just as when you have a conversation with a friend. All right, now let's use different body parts and movements each time we want to say something to each other, just as we use different words in a conversation."

▶ You and Andrew continue to converse using movements of the head, shoulders, feet, and back.

"You can see that our movements are not exact representations of our thoughts. They are a mixture of gestures and many different movements that may or may not have any specific meaning. When I shake my hands like this, I'm saying hello or 'Watch out, you shouldn't do that.' Now I'll assign partners, and you will choose who will begin the movement conversation. Be sure to wait until the person who is moving has stopped before you move and respond. It's like a conversation: One person speaks, and when that person is finished the other person responds. Do not interrupt each other in the middle of speaking with movements. Watch to see what movements your partner is using; they may determine how you will respond to your partner."

▶ As the conversations begin, circulate among the students, reinforcing the behavior of waiting until the first partner stops moving before the second partner begins his or her movement response.

"Can someone demonstrate how he or she might ask a question using movement? Okay, Jim, give it a try!"

▶ Jim creates a short movement sequence and demonstrates it to the class.

"That's great! Eileen, can you answer that question with a movement?"

▶ Eileen answers Jim by spinning around three times.

"What about a question that uses only one word, such as *why*? How would you express that thought in movement?"

▶ Another student demonstrates a short, quick movement of the hands and shoulders.

"Now let's add some long and short questions to the movement conversations—questions that can be expressed using a sequence of movements or maybe using only one movement. Try to respond with another question or an answer that may be one word, or try one answer with a long sentence."

▶ Students continue to create movements that reflect questions and answers using long and short sentences.

"Next, you will change the intensity of your movement conversations. You can make the movements small and light to express a whisper or talking softly to someone. You can make the movement big and strong to express yelling or shouting to get your message across. Also, consider how fast or how slowly you want to speak to someone. Are you a fast talker, or do you want to speak slowly? Your personality still plays a role."

▶ The students continue their movement conversations with an emphasis on the amount of force they use in the movements.

"The last part of this lesson will allow you to have different movement conversations with other people in the class. Use long and short statements, ask questions, use soft and loud or fast and slow statements, and carefully watch the other person to see how you will choose to respond. Sometimes use just a body part and sometimes use your whole body. Now find a different partner and begin your movement conversation. I will signal you when to stop and find another partner."

▶ The students find new partners and use the call-and-response relationship in a variety of different ways, similar to improvised dance.

Assessment Suggestions

▪ Students can write a list of several movements they used in their conversation and describe how they were performed. Were they fast, slow, big, small, strong, or light? What did the movements communicate? For example, a student may write, "I waved my hands very fast using a lot of strong movements. It was like I was trying to tell someone to get away from me."

▪ Students can describe a movement their partner made and how they chose to respond.

▪ Students can describe what type of movements dominated their conversations.

Look For

■ Students who may need ideas for movement. They may feel uncomfortable expressing themselves through creating movements. Have these students begin with frequently used hand gestures—those they normally use when talking—and have them make the gestures bigger, smaller, faster, or slower.

■ Students in groups of three may need to decide whether they will take part in the conversation in a predetermined order or whether the conversation will be random.

How Can I Change This?

Add different types of music, and have the students relate their conversation to the tempo, style, and volume of the music.

Teachable Moment

The students can write a conversation and recreate the conversation using only movement.

Additional Ideas for Developing Learning Experiences

This section offers additional learning experiences to develop the language arts skills identified in table 3.1: reading, writing, speaking, listening, and viewing. In addition, these skills influence world language learning, and sample experiences are included. Curricular areas, suggested grade level, and a brief description are provided for each activity. These activities are intended to inspire additional ideas for interdisciplinary work between classroom and physical education teachers. We encourage you to develop these ideas more completely. Sometimes the connected model will be most appropriate; other times the shared or partnership model may be useful. Your main concern should be to meet the developmental levels and needs of your students; you can adapt activities to accommodate your teaching schedule, equipment, and available space.

READING SKILLS

Alphabet in the Air

Language Arts

Letter recognition and formation

Physical Education

Body-part identification

Grade Level

K and 1

Students draw the shapes of the alphabet in the air using different body parts. They can imagine that a body part is covered with paint. The students paint the letter above their head or behind their body, reaching high and low, going as slow or as fast as they can, going from small to big, using different locomotor movements, making a letter with their right and left hands at the same time, or using two different body parts at the same time.

The Alphabet Children

Language Arts

Letter recognition and formation

Physical Education

Locomotor and nonlocomotor movements

Grade Level

K and 1
Students move in the following sequence with their bodies in the shape of a letter. All the letters are sleeping on the floor. They slowly begin to wake up by stretching and slowly rise to their feet. The letters go out to play and skip, run, jump, or use other traveling movements. The letters also try to twist, bend, swing, or use other nonlocomotor movements. Then they become very tired and slowly sink to the floor and go back to sleep.

Alphabet Freeze Tag

Language Arts

Letter recognition and formation

Physical Education

Running, dodging, and matching shapes

Grade Level

2 and 3
The game is similar to the traditional Freeze Tag. However, in this game, students freeze in the shape of a letter when tagged. Frozen players become unfrozen when another runner mirrors their letter shape.

Letter Targets

Language Arts

Letter recognition and formation

Physical Education

Throwing underhand or overhand for accuracy

Grade Level

K through 3
Using large letters printed on 8½- × 11-inch or 11- × 17-inch paper as wall or floor targets, children practice throwing beanbags or balls underhand or overhand at a letter. They identify the letter they are aiming at, identify the letter they hit, and write the letter on paper or the chalkboard.

Alphabet Activities and Sports

Language Arts

Letter recognition and beginning letter of a word

Physical Education

Identifying physical activities and sports that are part of an active lifestyle

Grade Level

K through 3
Create a bulletin board using the letters of the alphabet. Place on the bulletin board words for physical activities, sports, or skills that begin with the various letters, as well as pictures if you wish.

Sports News

Language Arts

Increasing vocabulary; word meaning and use

Physical Education

Identifying sport movements and skills

Grade Level

4 through 6
With the students, clip movement phrases used by sportswriters from articles on the sports pages. Have students discuss the phrases and demonstrate their meaning through movement.

Syllables

Language Arts

Determining the number of syllables in a word

Physical Education

Developing rhythmic patterns of locomotor and nonlocomotor actions

Grade Level

K through 3

Use people's names, nursery rhymes, or children's poetry with themes such as Halloween, Sesame Street, or Dr. Seuss to break words down into syllables. Match the syllables into eighth, quarter, half, and whole notes to develop basic rhythm patterns that are repeatable. Students clap hands, stamp feet, shake hips and head, or take walking, jumping, or hopping steps to match the rhythms created.

Bounce-a-Word

Language Arts

Spelling

Physical Education

Bouncing a ball

Grade Level

2 through 6

The students bounce a ball and spell a word, one bounce for each letter of the word.

Rhyming Movements

Language Arts

Rhyming words

Physical Education

Locomotor and nonlocomotor movements

Grade Level

2 through 4

Have the students create movement sequences or dances that reflect a series of rhymed words, for example the words *ball, small, fall,* and *tall.*

Opposite Pairs

Language Arts

Antonyms

Physical Education

Locomotor and nonlocomotor movements; shapes

Grade Level

2 through 6

Develop, or have students develop, a list of antonyms such as *high* and *low, big* and *small, fast* and *slow, over* and *under, open* and *close,* or *push* and *pull.* The students work individually or with a partner. They choose a set of antonyms and create a movement or still shape to express each word.

Mother Goose

Language Arts

Reading nursery rhymes

Physical Education

Creating movement sequences to interpret action words within nursery rhymes

Grade Level

K through 2

Use nursery rhymes to create movement sequences with children. Select nursery rhymes that depict actions, such as "Jack Be Nimble," "Humpty-Dumpty," "Jack and Jill," and "Eensy-Weensy Spider."

Dancing Books

Language Arts

Understanding story sequences and characters

Physical Education

Creating movements and shapes

Grade Level

K through 6

Choose, or ask a student to choose, a story or a character from a story. The student then creates movements that reflect a sequence of events and demonstrate the way the character moves.

Poetry in Motion

Language Arts

Expressing meaning through movement

Physical Education

Creating movements and shapes

Grade Level

4 through 6

Students in small groups create a dance using a poem. Each student is assigned one line of the poem and creates movements that reflect the meaning of the words.

Weather Report Gymnastics

Language Arts

Reading

Physical Education

Making shapes; rocking and jumping

Grade Level

2 through 4

Students read a weather report printed in the newspaper and create movements that represent the weather words. Examples are *sunny*—make the shape of the sun by stretching the whole body, or stretch the arms up toward the sun; *windy*—rock forward, backward, and sideways on different parts of the body; *rain*—jump into and over puddles; *ice storm*—freeze in different shapes; *cloudy*—make the shapes of clouds with the body and travel in the space.

The Greedy Python

Language Arts

Action verbs and adverbs

Physical Education

Locomotor and nonlocomotor movements

Grade Level

1 through 3

Read *The Greedy Python* by Richard Buckley. Talk about action words (verbs) and their modifiers (adverbs). Give several examples, such as *scamper to and fro, wind back and forth and in between, jump up from below, swim a bit too slow,* and *fly a bit too low.* Create a movement sequence based on the selected words. Have the children create their own action-word sequences based on verbs and adverbs they select.

Moving Adverbs

Language Arts

Action verbs and adverbs

Physical Education

Throwing, kicking, striking; locomotor and nonlocomotor movements

Grade Level

3 through 6
Develop a list of adverbs currently being used or studied by the students. The students change the way they throw, kick, strike, or use locomotor and nonlocomotor movements as they apply an adverb to the action—for example, throw softly, kick quickly, or strike smoothly.

Direction Words

Language Arts

Reading and identifying words

Physical Education

Traveling over, under, and between pieces of apparatus using locomotor movements

Grade Level

2 through 4
Attach movement and directional phrases to different pieces of apparatus, such as *jump over, crawl under, walk between, step over,* or *roll under sideways.* Students make the movements indicated.

Letter Lineup

Language Arts

Letter recognition

Physical Education

Organization for lines, teams, or issuing equipment

Grade Level

K through 4
Students form groups or lines based on the letters in their first or last name. Students can be organized using the first letter, the last letter, or any other letter in their name.

Toss-a-Word

Language Arts

Spelling

Physical Education

Tossing a ball

Grade Level

2 through 6

A single student tosses a ball into the air. With each toss, he or she calls out a letter and completes the spelling of the word with additional tosses. Partners can toss a ball to each other and spell a word with each successive toss.

Action Pictures

Language Arts

Nouns, verbs, and adjectives

Physical Education

Identifying activities that demonstrate and promote active lifestyles

Grade Level

3 through 6

Children cut out pictures from magazines of people participating in active lifestyles. Ask children to study the pictures and list nouns, verbs, and adjectives that their pictures suggest.

Dessert Dance

Language Arts

Reading, speaking

Physical Education

Locomotor and nonlocomotor movements performed to a rhythm

Grade Level

K through 3

As students suggest a list of their favorite desserts, record the list on chart paper. Together with students, create locomotor or nonlocomotor movements that reflect the rhythm of the syllables in each dessert word. For example, for coconut cake, the students can jump in a different direction on each syllable: *co-co-nut-cake.*

Muscle Mania

Language Arts

Reading, vocabulary, comprehension, writing, composition, drawing

Physical Education

Identifying muscles and performing fitness exercises for each muscle

Grade Level

3 through 6

Students are in small groups, each at a muscle station. They read a card that lists the muscle identified at the station and then create an exercise for that muscle. Students also write a description of the exercise and draw a picture. In the next class, the exercise descriptions and drawings are posted at the stations for a circuit workout.

Vocabulary Circle

Language Arts

Increasing vocabulary

Physical Education

Hand-eye coordination, ball toss and catch

Grade Level

2 through 6

A small group of students stands in a circle with one person in the middle holding a ball. The student holding the ball tosses it to a player in the circle and calls out a letter. The player who catches the ball passes it to the right so that it travels around the circle. The player in the middle must name five words that begin with the called letter before the ball gets back to the player who caught it initially. A player who cannot call out five words in time remains in the middle of the circle, passes the ball to a different player, calls out a new letter, and so on.

WRITING SKILLS

Body Spell

Language Arts

Letter formation and spelling

Physical Education

Making shapes

Grade Level

K through 6
Each student can individually spell words by making each letter with his or her body in the correct sequence. Or a group of students can spell words: Each student in the group forms a letter using his or her body, and the group members then arrange themselves to spell a word.

Gymnastics Sentences

Language Arts

Writing sentences

Physical Education

Rolling, turning, and balance

Grade Level

2 through 6
Students create a gymnastics sequence using rolling, turning, and balances. They record the sequence by writing a sentence that describes the movement.

Action-Word Poetry

Language Arts

Writing poetry with an emphasis on using prepositions, verbs, and adverbs

Physical Education

Developing movement sequences that interpret action words in poetry

Grade Level

3 through 6
Students write and perform action-word poetry as part of their language arts experience or during physical education. Use prepositions, verbs, and adverbs as an emphasis.

Provide examples to get them started; have them write their own poetry and then develop creative movement sequences based on the poems. Students can work individually, with a partner, or in a small group. These are some sample poems (Boorman, 1973):

Over, under, around and through
Backwards, forwards, where I greet you.

Spin, turn, churn
Twirl round and round
Run, leap, jump
Then gently touch the ground.

Feet are stamping everywhere
Knees are flying, poking through the air.
Hands are threading gently through space.
Every body part explodes. Stop. What a face.

The fog crept in lingering, surrounding
It hovered over the building
Then, silently it scattered, floating away.

Do You Haiku?

Language Arts

Learning about and writing haiku poetry

Physical Education

Developing movement sequences to interpret haiku poetry

Grade Level

4 through 6

A haiku is a 17-syllable, unrhymed verse of Japanese origin that may be used as a stimulus for creative writing and movement experiences. Each poem has three lines: five syllables in the first line, seven in the second, and five in the third. Often the poetry is about nature or the environment and has a surprise ending. Seasons of the year, weather, animals, birds, and trees are good topics. To begin, students may develop movement sequences to one or more of the following poems. Then they can write their own poetry and develop their own movement sequences. These are examples of haiku (Peter Werner):

Clouds softly floating
White feathers in the bright sky
Silently past us.

Rain softly falling
Summer crops soak up the wet
Grow delicious fruit.

Grassy river bank
Unexpected frog goes splash
Scared almost to death!

One fallen flower
Returning to tender branch
Oh no— butterfly.

The Jump Rope Rhyme

Language Arts
Writing rhymes

Physical Education
Jumping rope

Grade Level
3 through 6
The students create a rhyme to be used when jumping rope.

Name It

Language Arts
Writing words and identifying them with objects

Physical Education
Identifying the names of pieces of equipment

Grade Level
2 through 4
Students write labels for the equipment used in the gym, such as playground balls, jump ropes, softballs, Frisbees, vaulting horses, and scooters. The labels can be used at stations or to mark places for storage.

Drawing Pathways

Language Arts
Writing and spelling

Physical Education
Pathways; locomotor and nonlocomotor movements

Grade Level
2 through 6
Students draw a pathway on a piece of paper using straight and curved lines and create movements to perform while traveling on the pathway. The names of the movements are written on the path.

Writing a Warm-Up

Language Arts

Writing

Physical Education

Games, sports, gymnastics, or dance

Grade Level

4 through 6
Students write a list of warm-up exercises that can be used in a gymnastics, dance, game, or sport lesson. They can describe how to do the exercise through writing, drawing pictures, or speaking.

Base of Support Detective

Language Arts

Writing, spelling, viewing

Physical Education

Creating and controlling balances using different bases of support

Grade Level

3 through 6
Students are organized into small groups or partners. One person makes a balance shape using different body parts as the base of support. The observer identifies and writes the body-part name used as the support.

Words That Rock

Language Arts

Writing, increasing vocabulary

Physical Education

Developing cooperation and respecting others

Grade Level

K through 6
Locate a place in the gym or classroom to list vocabulary words related to the content presented in the lesson. During a rock-climbing unit, the word wall can display terms such as *handholds, grip, flexibility, ready to climb, respect, cooperation,* and *traverse,* or a series of positive phrases that partners exchange when working together such as *great job, you're awesome, excellent climb,* or *terrific move.*

Go for the Goal

Language Arts

Writing, drawing

Physical Education

Setting a goal for skill achievement

Grade Level

3 through 6
Students are asked in the beginning of a unit or lesson to identify a goal they want to achieve. They write the goal and include a picture of themselves performing the skill. During a unit on striking skills in badminton, students may write, "I want to volley the shuttle five times in a row," or "I will use the backhand stroke in every game."

SPEAKING, LISTENING, AND VIEWING SKILLS

Onomatopoeia: It's Just Fun to Say

Language Arts

Speaking words that suggest sounds

Physical Education

Developing movement sequences to interpret words that suggest sounds

Grade Level

2 through 4
Onomatopoetic words suggest sounds. Each sound may suggest a different energy based on time, force, or flow. By placing three to five words together, one can develop movement sequences. Combine words that show contrast to make the movement sequences more interesting or exciting. Students can say the words (exaggerating the sounds) or make a recording to accompany their performance of the movements. Examples of onomatopoetic words include the following:

bam	boom	tick-tock	hum	whir	zoom
sigh	sizzle	ding-dong	honk	zap	hiccup
gurgle	whoosh	glug-glug	sip	bang	sniffle
pop	swish	beep-beep	plunk	plop	fizzle

Sample movement sequences might include bam-whir-fizzle-plop and sip-gurgle-drip-hiccup.

Word Categories

Language Arts

Listening for a word category and responding by saying a word from that category

Physical Education

Chasing, fleeing, and tagging

Grade Level

2 through 4

Children play a game of Freeze Tag. When a player is tagged, he or she must freeze. While players are frozen they can call out a category of words—noun, verb, adjective. Other players can come by and say a word from that category, for example noun—*table,* verb—*run,* or adjective—*blue.* If the answer is correct, the frozen person can become active in the game again. Reverse the game and have an active person visit a frozen person and say a category. If the frozen person responds with an appropriate word, he or she can become active in the game again.

Scooter Maze

Language Arts

Speaking and giving directions

Physical Education

Demonstrating understanding of directions, such as right, left, around, backward, forward, stop, and go

Grade Level

2 through 4

Students work in pairs; one partner moves on a scooter while the other partner gives directions to move through a scooter maze. The person on the scooter can move only when he or she receives a verbal direction.

Long or Short?

Language Arts

Listening for long or short vowel sounds in words

Physical Education

Participating in a running and tagging game

Grade Level

1 through 3

Students participate in a running and tagging game similar to Crows and Cranes. Students start the game facing each other in two opposing lines, 5 to 8 feet (1.5 to 2.4

meters) apart. Use a large open space with end lines (goal line) away from walls. One line should be designated as the long-vowel line and the other as the short-vowel line. When a word is called out that has a long vowel sound, the long vowels chase the short vowels toward the end line. Anyone who is caught becomes a member of the long-vowel line and the game continues. When a short vowel is called out, the short vowels chase the long vowels to their end line. Anyone who is caught becomes a member of the short-vowel line. Ask the language arts teacher what vowel sounds the children are learning, and do only one vowel at a time.

A *Sounds*

Long: table, label, able, fable, maybe, ape, tape, skate, scale

Short: cat, sat, hat, mat, lack, bat, granny, salad, rap, apple

E *Sounds*

Long: even, elastic, event, tree

Short: elephant, effort, egg, treasure

I *Sounds*

Long: ivory, Iowa, ideal, triangle

Short: impala, wimp, whimsy, triple

O *Sounds*

Long: hotel, motel, open, close

Short: hop, stop, shop, top, mop

U *Sounds*

Long: ukulele, union, universe, unite, unit, uranium, use

Short: up, under, umbrella, ugly, ulcer, ulna, umpire, uncle

Word Hopscotch

Language Arts

Reading, writing, speaking, and identifying vocabulary words currently used in the classroom or physical education lesson

Physical Education

Hopping and jumping patterns

Grade Level

2 through 4

Using chalk, students draw a hopscotch pattern on the sidewalk. Instead of numbers, they write words and call out the words as they hop or jump. Rhyming words or other categories—such as nouns, verbs, adverbs, prepositions, or contractions—can also be used.

Listen Before You Speak

Language Arts

Speaking and listening

Physical Education

Teaching a skill

Grade Level

3 through 6

Make an oral presentation describing how to perform a skill such as the badminton forehand overhead stroke. During the same class or in the next session, a student restates the information to the class. In pairs, each student can restate the information to a partner.

Seeing Is Knowing

Language Arts

Viewing to gain information

Physical Education

Teaching a skill

Grade Level

3 through 6

Present a video or charts describing a skill, such as a technique for jumping rope. The students view the visual information and then perform the skill. Rely on the video or chart to provide the information instead of using oral directions.

WORLD LANGUAGE SKILLS

Hablar Español en Educacion Fisica (Speak Spanish in Physical Education)

World Language

Spanish

Physical Education

Locomotor, nonlocomotor, and manipulative activities

Grade Level

K through 6

Using the words presented in tables 3.3, 3.4, and 3.5, incorporate Spanish words into any of the following physical education activities.

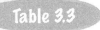

Table 3.3

Action Words

Traveling actions	
run	correr
skip	un paso y salto a la vez
creep	arrastrarse lentamente
rush	apresurar
flee	huir
slither	deslizarse
hop	brincar en un pie
gallop	galopar, deslizarse hacia al frente
dart	salir disparado

Vibratory actions	
shiver	escalofrio
quiver	estremecer
wobble	tambalear
patter	golpear
shake	sacudir
tremble	temblar
vibrate	vibrar
shudder	estremecer

Turning actions	
spin	vuelta
twirl	dar vueltas
swivel	girar
whirl	hacer girar
whip	batir

Rising actions	
lift	elevar
rise	subir, crecer, ascender

Stopping actions	
freeze	congelar
perch	posarse
anchor	ancla
settle	asentar
hold	sostener
grip	agarre
pause	pausa

Expanding actions	
grow	crecer
release	relajar
spread	extender
reach	alcanzar
open	abrir

Jumping actions	
leap	saltar
toss	tirar
prance	encabritar
soar	elevar
hurl	arrojar
bound	rodear
bounce	hacer (re)botar
fly	volar

Contracting actions	
shrink	incoger
close	cerrar
shrivel	marchitar
narrow	angosto

Percussive actions	
stamp	dar patada en el suelo
explode	explotar
patter	golpear
punch	picar/perforar
pound	azotar

Sinking actions	
collapse	desplomar
lower	bajar
fall	caer
sink	hundir
drip	gotear

Table 3.4

BSER Movement Framework

BODY		SPACE		EFFORT		RELATIONSHIPS	
Actions of the body		**Areas**		**Time**		**Body parts**	
Curl	Enroscar	General	General	Fast	Rapido	Above–below	Encima–debajo
Bend	Doblar	Personal	Personal	Accelerating	Acelerado	Apart–together	Separado–junto
Twist	Torcer			Sudden	Repentino	Behind–in front of	Detras–al frente de
Swing	Columpiarse			Decelerating	Reducir velocidad	Meeting–parting	Encuentro–separacion
				Sustained	Sostenido	Near–far	Cerca–lejos
						Over–under	Encima–debajo
Actions of body parts		**Directions**		**Slow force (weight)**		**Individuals and groups**	
Support body weight	Sostener peso del cuerpo	Forward	Hacia adelante	Firm	Firme	Mirroring–matching	El movimiento contrario–el mismo movimiento
Lead action	Primera accion, guia	Backward	Hacia atras	Strong	Fuerte	Contrasting	Contraste
Receive weight/force	Recibir peso/fuerza	Sideward	De lado	Fine	Fino	Successive–alternating	Sucesivo–alternado
Apply force	Aplicar fuerza	Upward	Hacia arriba	Light	Sutil–delicado	Questioning–answering	Pregunta–respuesta
		Downward	Hacia abajo			Acting–reacting	Accion–reaccion
						Following–copying	Sequir–copiar
						Lifting–being lifted	Levantar–dejarse levantar
						Supporting–being supported	Sostener–ser sostenido
Activities of the body		**Pathways**		**Space**		**Apparatus and equipment**	
Locomotor	Locomotor	Straight	Rector	Direct	Directo	Over–under	Encima–debajo
Nonlocomotor	No locomotor	Curved	Curvo	Indirect	Indirecto	Near–far	Eerco–lejos
Manipulative	Manipulativo	Zigzag	Zigzag	Flexible	Flexible	Above–below–alongside	Encima–debajo–al lado
		Twisted	Torcido			Behind–in front of	Detras–al frente de
						Arriving on–dismounting	Llegar–arribar a–desmontar

BODY		SPACE		EFFORT		RELATIONSHIPS	
Body shapes		**Planes**		**Flow**		**Other types**	
Straight	Recto	Saggital	Sagital	Bound	Con conciertos limites	Goals and boundaries	Metas y limites
Wide	Ancho	Frontal	Frontal	Stoppable	Deteniendose	Music and sound	Musica y sonidos
Round	Redondo	Horizontal	Horizontal	Jerky	Entrecortado	Poems, stories, and words	Poemas, cuentos, y palabras
Twisted	Torcido			Free	Libre	Beats and patterns	Toca (el tambor) y patrones
Symmetry	Simetrico			Ongoing	Continuo	Art and artifacts	Arte y artefactos
Asymmetry	Asimetrico			Smooth	Suave		
		Extensions					
		Large	Grande				
		Small	Pequena				

Table 3.5

Word Poster

Directions	Body parts	Numbers	Physical education things	Physical education commands
on—sobre	arm—brazo	one—uno	ball—pelota	run—corre
under—abajo	leg—pierna	five—cinco	hoop—aro	jog—corre despacio
over—encina	head—cabeza	ten—diez	rope—cuerda	walk—camina
around—alrededor	knees—rodillas	times—veces	parachute—paracaidas	jump—brinca
through—atraves	hand—mano		scoop—paleta	gallop—galope
forward—adelante	foot—pie		mat—estera	skip—skip
backward—atras	shoulder—hombro		glove—guante	hop—salta
slow—despacio	fingers—dedos		beanbag—saco de frijoles	toss—tira
fast—rapido	toes—dedos de los pies		yarn ball—pelota de lana	throw—lanza
top—arriba			racket—raqueta	catch—coge
front—enfrente			exercise—ejercicio	kick—patea
right—derecha			bat—batea	roll—enrolla
left—izquierda			basket—cesta	bounce—rebota
bottom—fondo			room—cuarto	spin—gira
in—en				
out—entre				
stop—quita				
go—be vete				

- Call out in Spanish different ways students can travel and stop in general space (i.e., *correr* = run; *un paso y salto a la vez* = skip; *congelar* = freeze). Encourage students to change pathways (i.e., *recto* = straight; *zigzag* = zigzag), directions (i.e., *hacia atras* = backward; *delado* = sideward), or the level (i.e., *bajo* = low; *alto* = high) at which they travel or change more than one of these at the same time.
- Make signs for an obstacle course through which students must travel: *encima* = over; *debajo* = under; *alrededor de* = around; *atraves* = through.
- Place Spanish directions on activity cards. Depending on the size of the cards/signs they can be laid on the floor or attached to a cone for children to read and perform accordingly. As such they can be thought of as stations to visit.
    1. *Salta sobre una pie cinco veces.* (Hop on one foot five times.)
    2. *Brinca la cuerda cinco veces.* (Jump rope five times.)
    3. *Lanza y coge la pelota diez veces.* (Throw and catch a ball 10 times.)
    4. *Tira la pelota de lana en la cesta.* (Toss a yarn ball in the basket.)
    5. *Gira sobre tu fondo.* (Spin on your bottom.)
    6. *Una enfrente enrolla sobre la estera.* (Do a front roll on the mat.)
- Have students write their gymnastics routines in Spanish, for example, *nivel alto, rodada hacia adelante, nivel bajo* = balance at a high level, roll forward, balance at a low level.
- Have students create and dance an action-word sequence in Spanish, for example, *correr, saltar, congelar, vuelta, dar vueltas, asentar* = run, leap, freeze, spin, twirl, settle.

Ongoing Strategies for the Physical Education Classroom

- Present cues for teaching motor skills in written form on a poster.
- List class learning behaviors or game rules on posters for reading and viewing.
- Label equipment. Place signs on or near equipment to help students learn how words are spelled, or have students place the signs.
- Write an outline of your lesson on a poster or on whiteboard or chalkboard. This way students can read the sequence of activities and learn new terminology presented in the lesson.
- Develop a word wall to reinforce reading and writing and help students identify terms used in the physical education curriculum.
- Display writing or drawings that children have completed in response to an in-class or homework assignment.
- Ask questions that require students to explain their answers. Then ask other students to add to the explanation. This verbal response helps students use their speaking skills to describe an event or describe how to do a motor skill.
- Use written directions at stations or for explaining games. This strategy provides students with practice in using reading skills to interpret directions.
- Use physical demonstrations, posters, video or DVD, or Internet or other visual media to focus students' viewing skills as a means of learning a skill or learning about a topic.

■ Create assessments that require reading questions and writing answers. Students apply basic reading and writing skills within the context of physical education content.

Summary

The integration of five basic academic abilities—reading, writing, speaking, listening, and viewing—forms the K through 6 language arts curriculum. It is through language arts that students acquire knowledge, shape experience, and respond to their own particular needs and goals. The language arts are valuable not only in and of themselves but also as supporting skills for students' learning in all other subjects. Students can best develop language competencies through meaningful activities and settings. It is through the physical education program that students gain the essential kinesthetic learning experiences that will enhance their ability to communicate effectively through both movement and the language arts.

The learning experiences described in this chapter illustrate how a favorite children's book becomes the inspiration for a dance, how the letters of the alphabet come alive in a gymnastics sequence, how the use of throwing and catching skills in a game provides the opportunity to refine students' writing and speaking skills, and how movement and language share similarities when one is communicating feelings or ideas. The additional ideas can be used as a springboard to develop your own learning experiences in the language arts and in physical education.

chapter 4

Integrating Physical Education With Mathematics

During a lesson on geometric shapes with a group of second grade children, we were working on circles, squares, triangles, rectangles, and so on. We used air pathways to make the shapes, with selected body parts tracing the shapes in the air. We used floor pathways and jumping and hopping to trace the patterns on the floor. We stayed in self-space and made the shapes with our bodies. We made the geometric body shapes as individuals and with partners. At one point, I saw Alex just standing there with a puzzled look on his face, seemingly wiggling his nose in the air. Confused, I went over to Alex and asked if he had a problem. "No," he said. "I'm making Os or circles with my nose [nostrils]." I just had to laugh. He certainly knew the concept of roundness.

The film *The Mirror Has Two Faces,* starring Barbra Streisand and Jeff Bridges, depicts a modern love story. The main characters are both Columbia University professors, she in literature and he in mathematics. A wonderful subplot woven into the story is that she is an incredibly successful teacher who ties themes from the classics—which otherwise could seem boring and outdated—to everyday life. Students flock to her classes, often staying after to ask questions. He is a brilliant mathematician who has published books and is in demand on a European lecture circuit. The courses he teaches, however, are stale. Students rarely ask questions, often fall asleep in class, and are ready to leave before class time is over. At one point in the story, he asks her for some help on becoming a better teacher. She teaches him to use practical applications from everyday life to bring his subject alive. He finally catches on and uses a baseball game to help illustrate calculating ball velocity and the distance a hit ball will travel. Students become excited. They ask a lot of questions. They stay after class to continue discussions. This is a powerful example of the relevance of interdisciplinary integration and of tying theory to practice.

In much the same manner, play experiences and game situations are often used in mathematics textbooks to enhance the presentation of mathematical concepts and problems to children in the elementary school. In fact, instructional practices call for mathematics teachers to develop concepts concretely and then abstractly, to develop problem situations from other content areas and from everyday experiences, and to give attention to connections between mathematics and other content areas.

Whitin and Wilde (1992), two of the leading authors of elementary mathematics education textbooks, have documented how children's literature provides a meaningful context for mathematics. Their book cites numerous children's stories that serve as a springboard for mathematical investigations. The authors describe selected books to illustrate how children learn about classification, place value and numeration systems, counting, arithmetic operations, fractions, estimations, big numbers, geometry, and measurement. Whitin, Mills, and O'Keefe (1991) use children's interests in dinosaurs, eggs, losing teeth, bicycles, pancakes, animals, and speed to further illustrate how mathematics develops out of human experience and to restore an aesthetic and affective dimension to mathematical learning. Classroom teachers also often use physical education activities and play experiences such as team scores, practice attempts, and batting averages to teach mathematics more effectively to their students.

A number of studies have been conducted to determine the effectiveness of the integration of mathematics with physical education. Ashlock and Humphrey (1976), Cratty (1985), Gilbert (1977), Humphrey (1974), and Werner and Burton (1979) have published books presenting research and practical implementation ideas for integrating physical education activities with mathematical content ranging from the simple mathematics concepts such as whole numbers (figure 4.1) and counting to mathematics set theory. Other studies advocating integration of mathematics concepts with physical education evolved in a series of lessons combining the two subjects. Memmel (1953) illustrated lessons in which rope jumping, team games, throwing, kicking, marching, rhythms, and shooting baskets were integrated with mathematics concepts. Jensen (1971) suggested the use of jump ropes for solving simple arithmetic problems and designing geometrical patterns through physical education. More recently, Werner, Bowling, and Simmons (1989) designed physical education experiences to enhance children's understanding of geometric shapes, angles, numbers, and addition and subtraction. Lessons for the teaching of number concepts, addition, subtraction, multiplication, division, averages, linear measures, time, geometric forms, and the metric

Figure 4.1 Simple mathematical concepts such as whole numbers can be taught through movement activities.

system have also been presented by various other authors. All authors indicated a positive response by the children to the active learning experiences.

Scope and Sequence for Mathematics

If children are to be taught mathematical concepts in physical education, teachers should be aware of the mathematical concepts that are presented at the various grade levels. Review of several mathematics textbook series and mathematics projects such as the School Mathematics Study Group, Stanford Project, and Minnesota Mathematics and Science Project indicates that the following mathematics concepts are taught at the elementary school level: numbers, measurement, geometry, patterns and functions, probability and statistics, logic, and algebra (table 4.1).

PRIMARY-GRADE MATHEMATICAL SKILLS AND CONCEPTS

During the primary grades, concepts taught within the major category of numbers are the meaning of numbers through 100,000; computation using addition and subtraction; modeling the fractions 1/2, 1/4, 1/3, 1/10, and 1/16; recognizing money and making change; and comparing numbers using the less than (<) and greater than (>) symbols. Measurement topics at the primary level include comparing nonstandard and standard units of measure; identifying time in terms of days, weeks, months, yesterday, today, tomorrow; telling time; sequencing seasons; measuring temperature; using customary and metric measures; and finding areas of simple geometric figures. While studying geometry in the primary years, children learn to model, recognize, and name simple geometric figures; to understand terminology regarding position and spatial orientation such as *over, under, around,* and *through;* to recognize symmetrical patterns; to find and compare sides and angles of polygons; to recognize and find right angles in everyday life; and to show congruency by flipping, sliding, and turning figures. While studying about patterns and functions at the primary level, children learn to find patterns in everyday life; to identify missing objects in a pattern; to identify objects that do not fit a pattern; to translate and describe patterns from one medium to another; to order objects into a specific pattern such as from large to small; to recognize regularities in events, shapes, designs, and sets of numbers; to skip-count forward and backward; to classify numbers as odd and even; and to identify rules of a given pattern. While studying about probability and statistics, primary-grade children learn concepts related to judging everyday events as certain, possible, or impossible; reading and summarizing pictographs and bar graphs to describe more, fewer, and same; and predicting outcomes of events using terms such as *more, all, none, most likely, probably,* and *definitely.* With respect to logic, primary-grade children learn to sort objects by attributes such as color, shape, or size; to place items in logical sequences; and to speculate and draw conclusions about everyday situations using terminology such as *all, and, every, some, none, or, many,* and *not.*

INTERMEDIATE-GRADE MATHEMATICAL SKILLS AND CONCEPTS

At the intermediate level, children learn more complex concepts in each of the mathematics categories. With respect to numbers, they learn to read and write numbers through 1,000,000; to demonstrate a working knowledge of multiplication and division problems based on everyday life; to compare, order, and sequence decimals and fractions; to model and explain exponents; and to write and solve percentage problems based on everyday life. Measurement concepts at the intermediate level

Table 4.1

Scope and Sequence of Mathematical Concepts Taught in Elementary Schools

CONCEPT	GRADE						
	K	1	2	3	4	5	6
Numbers	✖	✖	✖	✖	✖	✖	✖
Meaning of numbers 1 through 12	✖						
Meaning of numbers through 99		✖					
Meaning of numbers through 999			✖				
Meaning of addition and subtraction		✖					
Addition and subtraction computation			✖				
Meaning of numbers through 100,000				✖			
Meaning of multiplication and division				✖			
Meaning of numbers through 1,000,000					✖		
Multiplication and division computation					✖		
Meaning of decimals through hundredths					✖		
Meaning of decimals through thousandths						✖	
Meaning of addition and subtraction of fractions and decimals						✖	
Number theory						✖	
Meaning of multiplication of fractions and decimals							✖
Integers and ratios							✖
Percents							✖
Measuring and graphing	✖	✖	✖	✖	✖	✖	✖
Geometry	✖	✖	✖	✖	✖	✖	✖
Patterns and functions	✖	✖	✖	✖	✖	✖	✖
Probability and statistics	✖	✖	✖	✖	✖	✖	✖
Logic		✖	✖	✖	✖	✖	✖
Algebra			✖	✖	✖	✖	✖

include finding elapsed time based on problems of everyday life; solving and explaining problems involving time; using linear measurement to the nearest fraction and in metric units; modeling standard and metric units of measure; and converting measurements between the metric and customary systems when given conversion charts. Topics about geometry that are taught to children at the intermediate level include modeling more complex geometric figures; classifying triangles based on their properties; identifying, drawing, and defining acute, right, and obtuse angles; using compasses and protractors to draw and measure geometric figures; and drawing front, side, and top views of concrete objects. Concepts regarding patterns and functions that are taught at the intermediate level include classifying patterns as repeating patterns or growing patterns; using a constant function on a calculator to create a pattern; translating numbers in a function table to a graph; and using powers of 10 to create patterns. Probability and statistics concepts at this level involve finding means; interpreting and summarizing graphs; conducting experiments relating to dependent and independent events; comparing predictions of results with actual results; and using sampling to predict the composition of the whole population. Children learn to construct flowcharts to show the steps involved in completing a task; use the process of elimination to justify conclusions; use inductive and deductive reasoning to justify conclusions; and demonstrate *if and only if* statements using examples from everyday life while studying about logic. Topics in algebra studied at the intermediate level entail demonstrating the field properties of commutation, association, identity, and zero with multiplication and division; using and explaining formulas for the area of simple geometric figures; and graphing number sentences.

Learning Experiences

Each of the four learning experiences (table 4.2) demonstrates one of the interdisciplinary teaching models presented in chapter 1. The learning experiences have been designed to include skills and concepts from physical education and mathematics. For each learning experience we include a name, suggested grade level, interdisciplinary teaching model, objectives, equipment, organization, complete description of the lesson, and assessment suggestions. In addition, tips on what to look for in student responses, suggestions for ways you can change or modify the lesson, and ideas for teachable moments provide further insights into each learning experience.

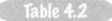

Table 4.2

Mathematics Learning Experiences Index

Skills and concepts	Name	Suggested grade level	Interdisciplinary teaching model
Mathematics: whole numbers, counting, addition, subtraction Physical education: balancing, steplike weight transfer	I'm Counting on You	K-2	Connected
Mathematics: repeating and growing patterns Physical education: axial gestures (clap, snap, tap) and locomotor patterns (hop, jump, step)	Pete and Repeat	1-3	Shared
Mathematics: geometric shapes, commutative and associated properties Physical education: balance, locomotor patterns (walk, hop, jump)	Playing the Field	3-5	Connected
Mathematics: measuring and graphing Physical education: locomotor patterns (hop, jump, leap)	Measuring Sticks	3-5	Partnership

I'm Counting on You

Suggested Grade Level

Primary (K through 2)

Interdisciplinary Teaching Model

Connected

In mathematics during the early elementary years, children learn to recognize and count whole numbers and to perform simple operations such as adding and subtracting. For this learning experience you can refer to counting books such as *Moja Means One* (Feelings, 1971) and *Count and See* (Hoban, 1972) to connect number concepts to physical education with a focus on balancing and traveling actions.

Mathematics

Whole numbers, counting, addition, subtraction

Physical Education

Balancing, steplike weight transfer

Objectives

As a result of participating in this learning experience, children will improve their ability to

- balance on different numbers of body parts with a focus on stillness and good principles of stability;
- travel in different pathways and directions using a variety of locomotor patterns;
- count using whole numbers to 100 and solve simple addition and subtraction problems;
- count and perform simple mathematical operations using selected foreign languages; and
- use another number system, such as Roman numerals, to represent the same number concepts.

Equipment

Mats are spread out in scattered formation. In the absence of mats the children could safely attempt their balances on the floor.

Organization

Throughout this lesson the children will work by themselves, spread out in general space.

Description

"Hello, girls and boys. Have a seat. See these two books I have today? They are about counting, and I know from talking to Mr. [Ms.] _____ that you are learning about counting [or adding or subtracting] in your math classes. Well, today we are going to use some ideas from counting, adding, or subtracting to help us move. Let's look at a few pictures first. See, here there is one what? [Fire hydrant.] Yes, one fire hydrant. Here's what? [Two friends.] Now what? [Three school buses.] What about here? [Eight windows.] How many on the bottom? [Five.] Top? [Three.] Right. Well, 5 +

3 = 8. This next book is about counting in a different language called Swahili. [It could just as easily be French, Spanish, or German.] Let's see how to count in Swahili. See this picture? It is of one mountain—the highest one in Africa. This mountain is called Kilimanjaro. "One" in Swahili is *moja* (mo' * jah). So we see *moja* mountain and *moja* what else? *Moja* sun. Right, one sun. Here we see two friends playing a game. "Two" in Swahili is *mbili* (m * bee' * lee). So we see *mbili* friends. Here we see *tatu* (ta' * too), or three, coffee trees. Coffee is grown in Africa. Here are *nane* (nah' * nay), or eight, market stalls. How many on one page? *Tano* (tah' * no), or five. How many on the other page? *Tatu* (ta' * too), or three. Guess what? *Tano* plus *tatu* equals *nane*.

"With those ideas in mind, let's start to move. While you are still sitting there, use just your fingers, hands, or arms and show me how you can make the shape of a one, or *moja*. How about a three, *tatu*? A four, *nne* (n' * nay)? Okay, get up and let's spread out into an open space. Show me with your whole body how you can make a six, *sita* (see' * tah); an eight, *nane* (nah' * nay); a nine, *tisa* (tee' * sah); a seven, *saba* (sab' * bah); and a five, *tano* (tah' * no). Can you make a 10, *kumi* (koo' * mee)? Perhaps make a one followed by a zero.

"Now let's make the task a little harder. I will say a number, and I want you to balance like a gymnast on that number of body parts. Are you ready? Two. Oh, that's too easy. I see a lot of people standing on two feet. Do two again, but this time use other body parts. Great, Susie, a foot and a hand, belly to the sky. Nice, Demetria, an elbow and a knee. Way to go, Saudah, a seat and a hand. Now you're thinking. I'm seeing a good variety of balances, each with two body parts touching the floor. One more point. Remember that when we are trying to be gymnasts, for each balance that we choose we want to hold very still for 5 seconds. You could even count to yourself silently. Stay with two body parts, but change your level. Low, medium, high. Can you balance on two body parts and be wide? Narrow? Symmetrical? Asymmetrical? Let's try balancing on *nne* (four) body parts. [Repeat the preceding variations.] How about *moja*? [See figure 4.2.] *Tatu*?

"Next we will do some locomotor actions while we use our counting skills. For starters, let's count together to 10 as we jump in place. Ready, 1, 2, 3. . . . Let's do the same but count in Swahili. We'll jump slowly so you have time to think of what number comes next. Ready? *Moja, mbili, tatu.* . . . Let's count backward from 10 while

Figure 4.2   **Balance on *moja* body part.**

we take backward steps. Ready? Ten, nine, eight . . . . Backward in Swahili while taking backward steps. Ready? *Kumi, tisa, nane.* . . . Rather than staying in one place, begin to travel somewhere with your locomotor actions. Try hopping forward three times. Slide sideways eight times. Take four big jumps forward, then two tiny jumps backward. Do *tisa* gallops with one foot forward and then *saba* gallops with the other foot forward."

▶ It is up to you as the teacher to create additional tasks according to your students' ability levels. Combine simple locomotor actions with a focus on a specific number of steps in a specific direction or pathway. If the children are ready for it, try simple addition or subtraction problems. For example, two hops plus three hops equals how many hops? Nine jumps minus five jumps equals how many jumps?

Assessment Suggestions

■ Have children call out, using corresponding foreign numbers, or solve simple addition or subtraction problems as they engage in movement experiences in physical education. For example, balance on *ein* body part; jump *dos* times; skip *dix* times. Observe children's responses for correctness.

■ Simple paper-and-pencil quizzes can check students' knowledge.

Look For

■ Good-quality balances are important to this experience. The children should be able to keep their center of gravity over their base of support and hold their chosen balances for 5 seconds without falling or wobbling all over the place. In addition, good lines and angles without sagging body parts are important.

■ Watch locomotor actions with mature patterns in mind. Jumps should use a two-footed takeoff and a two-footed landing. A good arm swing and body lean are also important to initiating a good jump. Hopping actions should use one foot and stay under control. The arms should be used for balance and to help attain some elevation. The free foot should be held up behind the hopping leg. Skipping should be done on alternating sides: step, hop, step, hop.

■ Watch the children's responses very carefully to notice whether they understand the number concepts. When three is the correct answer, are they balancing on three body parts? When five is the correct answer, are they jumping five times and stopping?

How Can I Change This?

■ Include counting in various foreign languages such as Spanish, French, or German (table 4.3).

■ Combine static balances and locomotor actions into a sequence, for example, jump three times, then balance on four body parts.

■ Increase the level of mathematics to include two, three, or four operations in one problem. For example, balance on the number of body parts that is the solution to this problem: $4 + 3 - 5 + 2 =$ _____.

Teachable Moments

■ Use task cards placed at stations around the floor that require children to read a math problem, figure out the solution, and perform the corresponding number of balances or locomotor actions. This will enable children to see interrelationships among reading, mathematics, and movement.

■ Introduce another number system, such as the Roman numeral system, to teach the same lesson. Children profit from learning multiple ways to represent the same concepts.

Table 4.3

Numbers From One to Ten in Selected Foreign Languages

English	French	Spanish	German	Swahili
one	un	uno	eins	moja
two	deux	dos	zwei	mbili
three	trois	tres	drei	tatu
four	quatre	cuatro	vier	nne
five	cinq	cinco	fünf	tano
six	six	seis	sechs	sita
seven	sept	siete	seiben	saba
eight	huit	ocho	acht	nane
nine	neuf	nueve	neun	tisa
ten	dix	diez	zehn	kumi

Pete and Repeat

Suggested Grade Level

Primary (1 through 3)

Interdisciplinary Teaching Model

Shared

As children learn about repeating (*,#,*,#) and growing (1, 2, 3, 5, 8, 13, 21—Fibonacci pattern) patterns in mathematics, repeating themes (ABAB, ABAC, etc.) in music, and repeating lines and patterns in art, they can simultaneously learn these concepts in physical education through a coordinated effort with the classroom teacher. In this sample lesson, the ideas for movement focus on axial and nonlocomotor gestures, such as snap, clap, tap, bend, stretch, twist, and on locomotor actions such as step, hop, and jump.

Mathematics

Repeating and growing patterns

Physical Education

Axial gestures (clap, snap, tap) and locomotor patterns (hop, jump, step)

Objectives

As a result of participating in this learning experience, children will improve their ability to

■ perform simple axial gestures such as bending, stretching, tapping, snapping, and clapping in sequence;

- perform simple locomotor actions such as stepping, hopping, and jumping in sequence;
- copy repeated and growing patterns using axial and locomotor actions after observing and listening to patterns you have established; and
- develop their own repeated and growing patterns using axial and locomotor actions with and without musical accompaniment.

Suggested references: *Clap, Snap, Tap* (Brazelton, 1975), *Only Just Begun* (Brazelton, 1977), *Modern Rhythm Band Tunes* (Palmer, 1969), *Simplified Lummi Stick Activities PK-2* (Johnson, 1976), *Rhythmically Moving* (Weikart, 1989), *Music* (Silver Burdett, 1974).

Equipment

A record player and one or more of the suggested records are used during the lesson. In addition, children may use small percussive instruments such as drums, sandpaper blocks, maracas, wooden (lummi) sticks, or triangles to develop and play their own repeated patterns. Children will write patterns on 3- × 5-inch index cards.

Organization

During the first part of the lesson, the children will work individually, spread out through the work space, listening to, observing, and copying patterns you have established. For the second half of the lesson, the children will work in pairs or small groups to design their own repeating and growing patterns. The pairs or groups are spread out through the work space as well.

Description

"As you come in today, watch what I'm doing, and as soon as you figure it out, begin to join me."

▸ Perform a repeating pattern of groups of four sounds or actions, for example, clap, clap, clap, clap, snap, snap, snap, snap, or touch one hand to head four times and then one hand to knee four times. You may choose to have music in 4/4 time as an accompaniment. To begin, keep the pattern simple, ABAB.

"Well, I'm impressed. You sure picked that up in a hurry! Who can tell me what we were doing? Any guesses? Tana?" Tana answers, "Warming up." "Yes, that's part of what we are doing. Kelly?" Kelly responds, "Doing things in groups of four." "You're right, too. As a matter of fact, not only were we doing things in groups of four, but we were repeating the patterns over and over: four claps, four snaps, four claps, four snaps, and so on [or four heads, four knees, four heads, four knees, and so on]. We could call that an ABAB pattern. Are you learning about patterns in any of your other classes? Jenny?" Jenny answers, "When we had music last week, we learned about repeating melodies in songs." "You're quite right. Peter?" Peter says, "Ms. Bauer is teaching us about repeating patterns in math." "Great. It may be a surprise to you, but I've been talking to your teachers, and we all planned together that we would teach you about recurring patterns that happen in all subjects and in everyday life. So what we are going to do in physical education today is first copy some patterns that I will do with you. Then I will give you a chance to invent some of your own patterns and share your patterns with a partner.

"When I say 'go,' I want you to get up and spread out so that you have your own personal space to work in. Our boundaries today are the four cones you see set up. Remember to stay inside them so we can stay away from the walls and be safe. As you find your space, I want you to stop and look at me so I know you are paying attention. Go. . . . Freeze. First, we want to work on different types of repeating patterns. A repeating pattern is set up and then is done over and over again. When you came in, we were doing repeating patterns. Let's do some more, but think of types of patterns we can do. One pattern is called unilateral, meaning that we do something on one side of our body. Let's all do bend, stretch, bend, stretch with one arm. Ready, go. . . . Stop. Can you think of another body part we can bend and stretch? Barclay?" Barclay says, "Leg."

"Let's try it. This is a 1, 2, 1, 2 repeating pattern because it counts the number of axial gestures. Let's do some more. With one hand, touch your ear, shoulder, hip, knee, and foot on the same side. Keep repeating the pattern. This is a 1, 2, 3, 4, 5 pattern because it has five actions. It is also a unilateral pattern because all actions are on the same side of the body. Another pattern might be called bilateral. The syllable 'bi' means two, as in the word 'bicycle' (two wheels). Let's use both sides of our body to clap, clap, clap, tap [on thighs], tap, tap. Ready, go. . . . Stop. Some more bilateral patterns might be bend, stretch, bend, stretch with both arms or both legs or use both hands at the same time to touch both ears, shoulders, hips, knees, feet."

▶ We encourage you to invent your own additional bilateral patterns.

"Another pattern is called alternating. For example, we could do something right, left, right, left. Ready, tap right hand to right thigh, left hand to left thigh, right, left. . . . Stop. Now snap right fingers, left fingers, right, left. . . . Stop.

"I'm getting tired of just sitting or standing and doing these patterns. How about you? We could do some of the unilateral, bilateral, and alternating patterns by using our traveling actions. First, let's hop four times on one foot, then four times on our other foot. Ready, go: One, one, one, one, other, other, other, other. . . . Stop. We could jump with our feet close together, then wide apart. What kind of pattern is it when we use two sides at the same time? Remember the 'bi' word? Alden?" "Bilateral." "Very good. You have a good memory. Ready, follow me. Close, close, wide, close, close, wide. . . . Stop. Let's change that a little and jump short, short, short, long. Ready, follow me. Short, short, short, long, short, short, short, long. . . . Stop. What about some alternating patterns? The easiest is walking. Everyone with me, ready, go. Step, step, step, step, step. . . . Stop. What about step, hop, step, hop, step, hop, step, hop? Does anyone know what that is called? Tim?" "Skipping." "Way to go! Let's all do it. Ready, go: Step, hop, step, hop. . . . Stop. I can see that almost everyone is a good skipper, but a few are not. We'll work on getting better at that pattern another time.

"Next we'll try to mix up some of the patterns a little. We don't have to do only nonlocomotor actions (clapping, snapping, touching body parts) or locomotor actions (walking, hopping, jumping, skipping) in separate patterns. We could put them together. These are some examples. How about clap, clap, clap, step, clap, clap, clap, step; clap, step, snap, step, clap, step, snap, step; hop, hop, touch tummy, hop, hop, touch; step, step, step, tap thigh, step, step, step, tap. We could even change the size, time, or force of our patterns. For example, while jumping, we could go short, short, short, long. While hopping, we could go slow, quick, quick. While stepping, we could go light, heavy, heavy, light, heavy."

▶ Develop additional repeated mixed patterns of your own. We encourage you to use one or more of the suggested records at this time. Each record presents a variety of activities that include repeated patterns, using, for example, lummi sticks, simple percussive instruments, axial gestures such as clapping and snapping, and locomotor actions to both double and triple time. Each record comes with a simple teacher's guide and has both a narrative and an instrumental side to allow you and students the option of following a scripted pattern or inventing one to accompany the music.

"So far we have been working on repeated patterns that you have been learning about in your classes in mathematics, music, and art. There is another kind of pattern that we can create. Does anyone remember the name of that pattern? No one? Well, that's okay. It is a hard one to remember. It is called a growing pattern. I'll give you an example to help you remember. If I snap my fingers [snap], then clap my hands [clap], snap, clap, clap, snap, clap, clap, clap, snap, . . . , what do you think comes next? Jawan." "Four claps." "Awesome! You paid attention to the fact that first there was one clap, then two, then three. That is an example of a growing pattern. Let's do some more. What about hop, hop, jump, hop, hop, jump, jump, hop, hop, jump, jump, jump, . . . ; tap thighs, clap hands, jump, tap, tap, clap, clap, jump, jump, . . . ; step, hop, step, step, hop, step, step, step, hop, . . . ; touch head, touch shoulders, quick jump, slow walk, head, shoulders, jump, jump, walk, head, shoulders, jump, jump, jump, walk. . . . You really catch on quickly to all of my patterns.

"You're so good, in fact, that I'm going to challenge you to make up some of your very own patterns. First, you need some time to experiment with your ideas. Remember the types of patterns that we have already tried. You don't have to invent a pattern that no one has ever done before. However, I am asking that you combine some of the nonlocomotor gestures and locomotor actions in ways that we haven't tried yet. Think of all of the types of patterns we have tried [unilateral; bilateral; alternating; 1212; 123123; 12341234; patterns that include changes in size, time, or force; growing patterns]. I'm going to give each of you three index cards and a pencil. After you experiment with a pattern and develop one you like, I want you to write it down using one-word cues so that you can remember it. I'll give you an example. If I did touch nose, touch elbow, slap bottom, long jump, hop, hop, I might write, 'nose, elbow, slap, jump, hop, hop.' Get the idea?" A student responds, "Yes, but why do we get three cards?" "I'm giving you three cards because I want you to make up three different patterns. All right, then. Everyone get started. Raise your hand if you need some help, and I'll listen to your ideas."

▶ Allow several minutes for the children to develop their ideas and write them down.

"Okay, stop. On the count of three, find a partner and sit down together. One, two, three. What I want you to do now is to share with your partner. I want one partner to perform one of his or her patterns and the other partner to watch. If you are the partner who is moving, you can use the card that shows the pattern to help you remember. Then as soon as possible I want the observer to say what he or she thinks the pattern is and get up and do the pattern alongside his or her partner. How about an example? Anyone want to show us one of his or her patterns? All right, Gabrielle. [Open mouth, close mouth, arms out to side, arms down, hop, hop, long jump.] Good work. That pattern includes both gestures and locomotion and was a 1, 2, 3, 4, 5, 5, 6 repetition. Everyone share your patterns with your partners now. . . . Stop.

"Get a new partner. One, two, three. The last thing that I want you to do is share one of your cards with your new partner. Your new partner will see if he or she can read the pattern on the card and, with no demonstration, do the pattern. Then I want the two of you to talk to decide if the pattern was right. If not, demonstrate the pattern, and then the two of you do it together. Finally, talk with each other and see if you can describe in words the type of pattern it is."

Assessment Suggestions

▪ As children develop different repeating and growing patterns in movements, have them record their patterns in writing as journal entries.

▪ Assign partners after children create a pattern, and have the observing child orally identify or write out the pattern he or she sees the moving partner perform. Also encourage children to compare their responses to other patterns in art and music.

Look For

▪ Some children have trouble with transitions from one movement to another. Try to help these children move smoothly during transitions in whatever pattern they are having trouble with.

▪ Sequential memory is an essential skill for performing repeating or growing patterns well. This includes both auditory and visual sequential memory. Make sure you start with simple patterns, and move to more difficult patterns only when the children are successful with the easy ones. Pair those who have trouble remembering the patterns with a buddy who catches on readily.

▪ When the children work on developing their own patterns, a few may lack the confidence to think up their own or may not feel that they can work independently. Work closely with these children. Use their ideas to develop a pattern, and say "See, you can do that. I'll bet you have more ideas just like that." Or allow them to work with a friend to get started.

How Can I Change This?

▪ Include other activities using equipment such as bouncing balls, streamers, jump ropes, and so on to develop patterns, for example, bounce, catch, toss, catch (with a ball) or four clockwise circles overhead, four figure eights in front of body, four clockwise circles to the right side, four clockwise circles to the left side (with a streamer).

▪ Use simple aerobic dance or step aerobics actions to develop patterns with the children. Include music in the background to enhance the experience, and perform the pattern to a steady beat.

▪ Make music patterns an integral part of the experience by using the concepts of measures; whole, half, quarter, and eighth notes; tempo; pitch; and dynamics. The children can perform nonlocomotor gestures and locomotor actions to music that they create.

Teachable Moments

▪ Help children become aware of the patterns in their everyday lives. Even a routine of getting up, eating breakfast, and going to school is a pattern. Days of the week, months of the year, seasons, and so on are patterns as well. How many other life patterns can you and the children think of?

▪ Listen to music or sing familiar songs (e.g., "Old MacDonald," "The Hokey Pokey," "The Twelve Days of Christmas"), and analyze the types of patterns they contain.

▪ Bring in some famous paintings, and look for repeating lines or patterns.

▪ Help children recognize patterns in fence posts, bridge designs, windows in buildings, basketry, clothes, and other everyday objects and places.

Playing the Field

Suggested Grade Level
Intermediate (3 through 5)

Interdisciplinary Teaching Model

Connected
As children travel from marker to marker and create balance shapes, they can understand in a practical sense the relationships among body shapes and angles and geometric shapes and angles, and the commutative and associative rules of mathematics.

Mathematics
Geometric shapes, commutative and associative properties

Physical Education
Balance, locomotor patterns (walk, hop, jump)

Objectives
As a result of participating in this learning experience, children will improve their abilities to

■ make body shapes;
■ balance on a variety of large and small body parts, using characteristics of good form;
■ balance in a variety of selected symmetrical and asymmetrical shapes;
■ use their feet to travel by exploring each of the five basic steplike actions;
■ relate body shapes to basic geometric shapes and angles; and
■ understand the commutative field property of addition in mathematics.

Equipment
A half sheet of newspaper for each student

Organization
A large, open space is needed for this activity. A hard surface or gym floor is preferred. Students work individually in scattered formation.

Description
"Hello, girls and boys. As you come into the gym today, you will see that I have several stacks of half sheets of newspaper spread about the space. When I say 'go,' you are to get a piece of newspaper, take it to a personal space, lay it down on the floor, and sit on top of it. I'll know you are ready when everyone is sitting, looking at me. Go. . . . Thanks. You sure did that quickly, and you selected good personal spaces. Everyone is spread out nicely. That will be important for today's lesson because we are going to do a lot of traveling (running, hopping, jumping, skipping, and sliding) and balancing. While we are moving and balancing, we will also relate what we are doing to some concepts you are learning about in math.

"As we begin, I want you to imagine that the newspapers you are sitting on are houses or buildings and that you are all superpeople—superwomen and supermen. You have the power to leap over a building in a single bound. Let's start with your own home. Stand up and step outside. Have the front of your body face the front of your house. Now jump over your house: a two-footed takeoff and a two-footed landing. Do that several times. Remember to swing your arms and reach for the sky as you jump. Also crouch and explode with your legs. Then land softly—squash. Good, Kim. That was a powerful jump and a soft landing. Can you jump backward over your house as well? Sideways? Backward and sideways are harder, so remember to keep a two-footed takeoff and a powerful, explosive leg action. Still try to swing your arms to help you get lift. Can you try a hop over your house—from one foot to the same foot? What about a leap, one foot to the other? One foot to two? Two feet to one? Great, Rodney, Juaquin, Jolene. You can jump over your house in a variety of ways. Stop. Sit down in your home.

"You're getting good at bounding (hopping, jumping, leaping) over your own building, so now we are going to take a trip. First, look where you are right now. That is your home and neighborhood. To help you remember, look all around. Where is your home in this gym? What lines or walls is your home near? Who are your neighbors to your front? Side? Back? We'll take a short trip first. When I say 'go,' travel (run, hop, jump) to another house and jump over it, then return to your own home by traveling in a different way, and balance in it on three body parts. Watch. [Demonstrate as you explain.] I'm going to leave my home and hop. As I get to Susan's home, I'll jump over it, then return to my own home by skipping, and end by balancing on three body parts in a shape that I choose. I'll know everyone is finished when I see everyone balancing very still with three body parts touching the floor. Who can tell me what you are supposed to do? Shandria. Yes, good. Go. . . . Whoops. One or two people got a little lost. Remember to go to only one house, then return home. If you are not sure, don't travel too far before returning home. If you are confident, you might want to travel way across the gym, and then find your way home. Let's try that again. Go. . . . Much better that time. Everyone found their way back without getting lost.

"Now we're going to make the task even more difficult. This time when I say 'go,' I want you to keep traveling, and when you get to a house, jump over it. Keep traveling to another house and another, each time jumping over the house in a different way. When you hear my signal of a drumbeat, go to your home as quickly as you can, and balance on four body parts in a shape of your choice. Who can tell me what they are going to do? . . . Good remembering, Johnny. Travel, jump, travel, jump, and so on, drum, return home, and balance on four body parts. Go. . . . Great! I see some people skipping, others sliding, others jogging while traveling. Good jumps, too. Some frontward, some sideways, some from one foot to two feet, some from two feet to two feet. Good variety. [Drum.] Wow. Everyone still remembered where home was. [Repeat several times.] Stop. Gather in front of me. Sit down and listen.

"What we are going to do next is a little bit complicated, but I know you can do it. We are going to travel and visit some other homes. While you are at those homes, you will balance inside them for 5 seconds. To help you remember, our balances will concentrate on the idea of shapes. Think of the geometric shapes you have learned about in math. Round or curved body shapes are like circles, spheres, or curved lines. Pointed body shapes with bends at the elbows, knees, hips, and the like can remind us of the corners or joints in triangles, squares, rectangles, and so on. Straight shapes can remind us of long extended lines."

▶ Balances can also focus on symmetry or asymmetry or acute, right, and obtuse angles.

"Your first balance in the first house you visit will be round or curved. Watch me. I'll start at my house and travel any way I like to the house of anyone I choose—let's say Peter's house (Peter won't be there because he will be busy visiting someone else's home). When I arrive at this house, I will balance in it for how many seconds? Five. Good listening, Sam. It will be important for you to remember the house you visit, so while you are balancing, take a look around at where you are. What lines or walls are close? Also remember the balance you do in that house: round or curved. After balancing for 5 seconds, I will return to my own home and sit down. So the task is to travel, do a round or curved balance, travel home, sit down. Ready, go. . . . Can you remember where you went and the balance you did? Try it again. Go to the same place and do the same balance. Go. . . . Excellent. Everyone is seated, which tells me that you are back home.

"Now comes the tricky part. We are going to add a second house. You will start from your home and travel to your first house. What type of balance do you do there? Round or curved, right! Then you will go on to a second house and balance with a shape that has a lot of points (elbows, knees, hips, and so on bent at angles). Hold that balance for 5 seconds, look where you are, then travel home, and sit down. Watch Lauren demonstrate. Let's tell her what to do as she is doing it. Travel, do a round or curved balance, travel, do a pointed-shape balance, travel home, sit down. Thanks, Lauren. Everyone try it. Go. . . . I'm noticing that almost all of you are doing your balances while on your feet. I'm going to give you one chance to change your balances, and I ask that you try to balance on different body parts and still be rounded or have pointed shapes. Still remember the houses you are balancing in. Go. Travel, balance, travel, balance, home, sit down. Very good. I saw some excellent rounded or curved and pointed balances on different body parts that time. Do you think you could remember your travel route if you did it backward? What I mean is go to your second house first and do your pointed balance, then go to your first house and do your round or curved balance. Let's try. Go. . . . Stop. A couple of people got confused, but most did real well. Let's try again. Travel, pointed balance, travel, round or curved balance, travel home, sit down. That's it, much better. While you are sitting, I would like to talk about what you are learning in mathematics for a minute. When you are adding numbers—say 1 and 2—does it make any difference what order you add them in? No. 1 + 2 = 2 + 1. That is called the commutative property of math. Well, we just did that in our balances. We reversed the process. The order changed, but we still did the same two balances. Pretty tricky, right?

"Let's see if we can make our sequence even harder. Let's add a third balance. The third balance will be straight or stretched. I want to see good extensions, arms and legs straight. You can do these straight or stretched shapes while balancing on different body parts. Let's rehearse. Travel, rounded or curved balance, travel, pointed balance, travel, straight or stretched balance [figure 4.3], travel home, sit down. Go. . . . Good work. Do it again. . . . You seem to have mastered it. Now do it in reverse. I'll talk you through it. Travel, straight or stretched balance, travel, pointed balance, travel, rounded or curved balance, travel home, sit down. Well done. Do it on your own. Go. . . . Stop. Gather in here. Remember when we talked about the commutative property of math? Well, your movement sequence was an example of the commutative property of mathematics. You have been learning that if you add 1 + 2 + 3, you get the same sum as if you add 3 + 2 + 1. That is also called the commutative property of mathematics. It works in physical education too. Even if we reverse the sequence of our balances (round, pointed, straight = straight, pointed, round), we balance the same number of times (three). Can you think of any other situations in which you might use the commutative properties of math? Very good. Yes, we could take turns in a different order. We could listen to the tunes on a CD in a different order. There are a lot of ways we could use these properties. It's time to leave class now. Good-bye for now."

Figure 4.3   Children travel, then create a straight or stretched body shape.

Assessment Suggestion

As children travel to different "homes," check for the correctness of their responses. Are the shapes round, pointed, or straight when they are supposed to be? Can the children name objects in the real world that are round, pointed with lots of angles, or straight? Can they reverse their balance sequences? To assess their knowledge of the commutative properties of mathematics, have them write a simple mathematics or movement problem to illustrate their understanding.

Look For

■ Children should focus on quality traveling actions. This is not a race. Look for a change in their method of traveling after visiting each "house." Also encourage variety in their choices of direction, pathway, and speed: They should not always travel forward, straight, and fast.

■ Quality in the children's balances is also important. Stillness while holding shapes, well-defined lines and angles of body parts and joints, and a concentrated focus of intent are key to producing definitive work.

■ Some children may get lost after visiting another "home" and returning to their own. Suggest that these children not travel as far away (e.g., go next door and return) or that they travel to easily located houses (e.g., one in the center circle of the basketball court) to help them remember. Or they could travel with a friend.

How Can I Change This?

■ For more advanced students, add a fourth and fifth balance to further develop sequential memory skills.

■ Include mapping as a skill in this lesson. Children could draw a map of their route, including their pathway to each stop on the route, their method of travel, and the type of balance at each house visited. This process may be compared to making an itinerary or a travel plan.

- Do the same lesson, but focus the balance shapes on symmetry and asymmetry or on acute, right, and obtuse angles.
- Use a map and compass, and turn this into an orienteering experience. From their own "home," children could move five paces at 30 degrees, for example.

Teachable Moments

- Use this lesson to reinforce spatial awareness and body awareness concepts such as front, back, side, inside, outside, over, and so on.
- Teach the compass directions north, south, east, and west.
- Talk about finding your way. Concepts such as street signs, familiar landmarks, travel routes, and maps are topics that can be used to enhance this lesson.
- The topic of neighborhoods from social studies can also be included. Examples are the amount of space people need to live; what a neighborhood consists of, such as close friends, stores, churches, and open spaces for play; and urban, suburban, and rural communities.
- The concept of motorways—interstate highways, city streets, and back roads or blue highways—provides a model that children can associate with this physical education lesson. Sometimes they can travel fast and go mostly straight ahead. At other times they have more traffic, smaller roads, and regulated speeds. On the back roads they must travel slowly, make many sharp turns, and change gears often.

Measuring Sticks

Suggested Grade Level

Intermediate (3 through 5)

Interdisciplinary Teaching Model

Partnership

You and the classroom teacher can work as a team during this learning experience. As children learn how to measure using different units in mathematics, they can use this learning experience for practical application of this information in physical education by measuring and graphing the distances of their traveling actions.

Mathematics

Measuring and graphing

Physical Education

Locomotor patterns (hop, jump, leap)

Objectives

As a result of participating in this learning experience, children will improve their abilities to

- use good body mechanics to hop, jump, and leap;
- combine basic locomotor actions into a sequence (e.g., hop, step, jump);

▪ measure and record their performances on scoring sheets; and

▪ diagram their performances on charts and make decisions about which efforts produce the best results.

Equipment

A ruler, yardstick, newspaper wand, bat, or stick with which to measure; a score sheet or histogram chart and pencil to record results; markers to mark jump length (popsicle sticks, tape, pencil line, etc.)

Organization

Students will work in pairs in an indoor or outdoor space.

Description

"Good morning, boys and girls! Are you ready to do some exciting jumping today? What I have in mind for us is to do different styles of jumping and to see which ones allow us to jump the farthest. In addition to jumping today, the most important thing we are going to learn is how to measure our jumps, record our scores, and graph our performances.

"First, get a partner and stand back to back. Go. . . . If you don't have a partner yet, raise your hand, and I'll help you find one. Good. Now let's warm up. Play follow the leader with your partner, trying to stay close to each other. Vary the way you travel—sometimes jogging, sometimes hopping, jumping, skipping, and so on. Remember to change directions, pathways, and speeds. Perhaps take long and short steps, heavy and light steps. Stop. . . . Change leaders. Repeat. . . . Stop. Now let's do a few stretching exercises especially for our legs because we are going to use them a lot today."

▶ Have children perform exercises of your choice, but make sure that they stretch hamstring, quadriceps, and calf muscles.

"Stop. Quickly come here in front of me. Sit down. I'm going to hand out score sheets, graphs, measuring sticks, and pencils to each of you. [Distribute materials.] When I say 'go,' you and your partner will find or make a [chalk] line within our space. This will be your jumping line. Each time you jump, you will start with your toes on, but not over, the line. [Demonstrate.] That is important because you will use that line for measuring every jump. After placing your toes on the line, you will make your jump. Your partner will mark your jump by putting a marker where your heels land or, if you fall backward, the part of your body that touches nearest the takeoff line." [Demonstrate.]

▶ Note that children's abilities to measure accurately differ. Depending on the level of the child, crude measurements may be used, such as the number of lengths of a shoe, folded newspaper, book, or forearm (figure 4.4). Children who have more advanced measuring abilities may use more accurate measures, such as the nearest yard, foot, inch, or centimeter. Work with the classroom teacher on measurement skills.

"Each time you make a jump, measure it with your partner and record it on your score sheet. [Demonstrate.] Spread out and find a good jumping space with your partner. Go. . . . Stop. Good, I see that you are spread out and that your jumps will not interfere with each other. You have also chosen or made good lines from which to jump. For your first jump, I want you to place your toes on the line and jump. Use a two-footed takeoff. Don't swing your arms much or bend your legs. Just an easy jump. [Demonstrate.] Measure and record it on your score sheet. Take turns with your partner.

Go. . . . Stop. On your next jump, try swinging your arms back and then forward and up (reach for the sky). [Demonstrate.]

"Make three jumps, and record your best jump. Go. . . . Yes, way to go, Lauren. Good arm swing. I like the way Tom and Tyron are cooperating by taking turns jumping and then measuring. Remember to measure accurately, then record the score on your sheet. Stop. Now, let's try crouching and exploding in addition to the arm swing. [Demonstrate.] Swing, crouch, explode. Try three more jumps each, and record your best score. Remember to take turns, and help each other mark the jump and measure. Go. . . . Wow! What an explosive jump, Daniel. Super, Sharon and Devon, I see that you are recording your scores in the right places on your sheets. Does anyone need any help with the score sheets or with measuring? Okay, Sharon and Devon, would you go and help Amy and Liz for a little while? Answer the questions they have about measuring or scoring. Thanks. . . . Stop. Do you think it makes any difference if we lean forward (45 degrees) as we jump? [Demonstrate.] Swing, crouch, lean, explode! Try three more jumps, and record your best score. Go. . . . Stop.

Figure 4.4 Children measure their jumps with a bat, book, shoe, or other object.

"Let's graph what we have so far [figure 4.5]. On the horizontal graph line (X axis), indicate the type of jump. On the vertical line (Y axis), mark the distance of your jump. [Demonstrate.]

"Everyone, graph each of your best jumps. Use the scores from your score sheets. Work with your partner, and help each other. Make sure you get each jump recorded correctly. Raise your hand if you need any help. . . . Okay, look at your graph. What type of jump gave you the best results? Yes. As you added body parts (arm swing, leg explosion, trunk lean), you were able to jump farther. In science this is called using a summation of forces to get better results. Can you think of any other type of physical activity in which you use a summation of forces to get better results? Yes, when we throw or kick, we use our whole body in our effort to throw or kick a far distance.

"Now let's try some other types of locomotor skills and see how far we travel through the air. What about a hop (one-footed takeoff, same-foot landing)? Try three hops and record your best score. Go. . . . Stop. Now try a leap (one foot to the other). Try three leaps, and record your best score. Now graph those performances and compare them with your jumping performances. Were you able to travel farther with a jump, hop, or leap?

"Finally, move back from the takeoff line. What I want you to do now is to take several steps before you jump so that you have forward momentum as you go into your jump. It will be important to plant your takeoff foot or feet on, but not over, your measuring line. [Demonstrate.] As in the rules for track and field, any takeoffs that go over the line do not count. Make several tries at jumping with a walking approach. Work out your steps to get them just right.

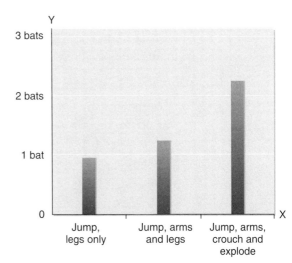

Figure 4.5 Children graph the distance of their jumps.

Try a one-footed takeoff (hurdle step) and a two-footed takeoff. [Demonstrate.] Always land on two feet. Remember to still swing your arms and explode with your legs at takeoff. As you land, rock forward from heels to balls of your feet and lean forward. Go. . . . Your toes went a few inches over the takeoff line that time, Leigh. Correct the error by starting back about 6 inches [15 centimeters] from your present mark. Then you will plant your toes right on the line at takeoff. Yes! That's it. Very good that time. Stop. Now that you have your steps down, choose your best way of jumping and make three tries. Measure each attempt. Record your best score. Place the score for your moving jump on the graph. Go. I can see that you have learned to measure accurately, Brent and Riley. You measure from the takeoff line to the point of impact nearest the line each time. Each score is to the nearest inch [or foot, book, stick]. Your graphs are giving you an accurate picture of your results. Stop. Everyone come in here and sit down. Let's talk about jumping and what your scores and graphs are telling you. Were you able to jump as far or farther using a moving jump? What does this tell us about momentum and the sum of forces? Thanks. You worked hard today. You are learning a lot, not only about how to jump better, but also about how mathematics and science can help us understand how our bodies move."

Assessment Suggestion

In addition to the graph in figure 4.5, have the children graph the distances of other traveling actions, such as a hop, leap, and moving long jump. Also give them an oral or written test on their understanding of the concepts of momentum and summation of forces.

Look For

■ Children need to use good mechanics to get optimal results. A good arm swing, explosive leg action, and leaning at a 45-degree angle are key to successful results. Timing is also a key. Some children will swing their arms, then stop and jump. Others will crouch, then stand up straight and jump up. Placing a barrier (a towel or small hurdle to jump over) sometimes helps.

■ Children are often confused about measuring. Be clear about the unit of measurement. Start with crude measurements. It is easier to understand "five books" or "five sticks" than inches as a fraction of a foot or yard. Also be clear about where to start the measurement and how far to measure.

■ Converting scores to graphs is not an easy task. Work with the classroom teacher on this task and on helping the children understand the meaning of the results. Analysis and interpretation require higher-level thinking skills.

How Can I Change This?

■ Combine locomotor skills into a sequence. How far can children jump using a step or leap (from one foot to the other), then a hop (from one foot to the same foot)? Three jumps in a row (two feet to two feet)? A hop, then jump? A hop, step, jump?

■ Measure and graph high-jumping skills.

■ Measure and graph throwing or kicking efforts.

■ Measure and graph heart rate after different types of exercise of different durations and levels of intensity.

Teachable Moment

Although this lesson is about learning to jump better, it is also about learning in a very practical way how to use mathematics and science. Rather than measuring lines in a book to the nearest fraction of an inch or centimeter, the children are actually doing an experiment in human performance. They are learning to measure and graph real attempts and can see which attempts produce better results. They can also readily see that by using certain scientific principles, such as summing body forces and using momentum, their performances will improve.

Additional Ideas for Developing Learning Experiences

This section offers additional learning experiences to develop children's understanding of the mathematics concepts identified in table 4.1: numbers, measuring and graphing, geometry, patterns and functions, probability and statistics, logic, and algebra. Curricular areas, suggested grade level, and a brief description are provided for each activity. These activities are intended to inspire additional ideas for interdisciplinary work between classroom and physical education teachers. We encourage you to develop these ideas more completely. Sometimes the connected model will be most appropriate, while other times the shared or partnership model may be used. Your main concern should be to meet the developmental levels and needs of your students; you can adapt activities to accommodate your teaching schedule, equipment, and available space.

NUMBERS

Whole-Number Designs

Mathematics
Number recognition and formation

Physical Education
Body shapes, use of air and floor pathways

Grade Level
K and 1

▪ Written numbers are made of straight, curved, or diagonal lines. Categorize each of the numbers by discussing the composition of each number. Categories may vary, depending on how the children are taught to form the numbers. Have children make the shape of each of the numbers using different body parts or the whole body.

Straight line: 1, 4, 9
Curved line: 0, 2, 3, 6, 8, 9
Diagonal line: 4, 7
Straight and curved: 2, 3, 5, 9
Straight and diagonal: 4, 7

▪ "Can you make the shape of a number from 0 to 9 using your whole body? . . . What other numbers can you make using your whole body? . . . Can you make number shapes using different body parts? . . . Can you make the same number shapes while changing your body level? . . . Can you stand, kneel, or lie on the floor to make your body shapes? . . . What numbers can you make with a partner or small group? . . . Can people in a partnership or small group combine to make one number, or can each make a separate digit of a bigger number [0-9,999]?" (See figure 4.6.)

Figure 4.6   Children create a pattern of body shapes.

▪ Have children use air or floor pathways to trace number patterns. "Can you hop or skip and make a 3 or 7? Can you use your elbow, knee, or head to trace an 8 in the air?" Ask children to use two or three different body parts to trace the same number simultaneously.

▪ Make a line grid on the floor or pavement, as in figure 4.7, or have the students draw the grid. Then have the children jump, hop, walk, slide, or skip along the lines on the grid to make the numbers from 0 to 9. Have them move forward, backward, or sideways to make the numbers or move fast or slowly while making the numbers.

▪ "I am going to call out a number. When I do, put that same number of body parts on the floor and create a balance. When I say 'three,' you should touch three body parts to the floor. Can you use your hands, wrists, elbows, shoulders, tummy, seat, side, shins, thighs, knees, feet? Ready? Four. That's it. I see two knees and two elbows. Four again, but use four different body parts."

▪ Construct beanbags in the shapes of numbers, or have a parent support group stitch the beanbags. The children are playing catch with a partner. They each have several

Figure 4.7   Traveling along the lines on the grid to trace each whole number.

beanbags. They choose a beanbag from their pile, crumple it up in their hand, use a kind (looped) toss to their partner. While the beanbag is in the air, the catching partner visually identifies and calls out the number of the beanbag they are about to catch.

■ "Make the shape of a number with a jump rope on the floor. Walk, hop, slide, or jump as you trace the number along the floor. Jump or hop from side to side or into and out of the empty spaces of the number you chose. Move backward or sideways to trace along the number."

Rhythmical Addition

Mathematics

Addition

Physical Education

Rhythmic patterns, body coordination

Grade level

2 through 6

■ Students will use body movements designated by point values to complete a mathematical problem. A hand clap is worth 1, a foot stomp is worth 5, and a knee slap is worth 10.

■ Ask students to use a combination of body movements to calculate the number 50. Possible solutions: 5 hand claps, 5 foot stomps, and 2 knee slaps; or 10 hand claps, 2 foot stomps, and 3 knee slaps.

■ Change the number or ask students to suggest new numbers. Change the point value for each body movement.

Count on Me

Mathematics

Counting

Physical Education

A variety of locomotor, balancing, and manipulative experiences and exercises

Grade Level

1 through 3

■ "As I call out a number, I want you to take that many steps in one direction or pathway. Ready? Five steps forward. Eight steps backward. Six slides sideways. Ten skips in a curved pathway. Seven hops in a straight pathway."

■ "As I clap my hands, silently count the number of claps to yourself. Then make the shape of the number you counted with your body." Have children do additional counting problems by snapping fingers, tapping thighs, clucking tongues, and stamping feet. Each time the children make a body shape of the number counted.

■ "While doing exercises, count the number you perform." Have the children count from 1 up, or count down to zero.

■ Have the students count exercises in sets. For example, they may count four repetitions of a two-count exercise, such as a toe touch or sit-up, as 1, 2; 2, 2; 3, 2; 4, 2, or count a four-count exercise by fours (1, 2, 3, 4; 2, 2, 3, 4; 3, 2, 3, 4; 4, 2, 3, 4). Have them count the measures in a piece of music using the same procedure, then make up an aerobic dance routine or dance sequence to represent actions for each of the measures.

■ Have the children use their counting abilities to keep score in games such as hopscotch or shuffleboard, or use their counting abilities to keep score in a game that they make up.

■ "Count the number of throws and catches you and your partner can make without dropping the ball. . . . Count the number of consecutive forearm passes you can make to yourself in volleyball without making a mistake. . . . Count the number of consecutive forehand strokes you can make against a wall from a distance of 20 feet [6 meters] without losing control of the ball."

■ Have the children play a game starting with a certain number of points and count down to zero by 1s, 2s, 3s, and so on.

■ "Count the number of times you can jump a rope in a minute. Count by 1s, 2s, 3s, and so on."

■ "Count the number of times you can bounce a ball or throw a ball in 10 seconds." Use different time trials, and have students use addition or subtraction to compare the sums or differences between trials.

■ In certain types of games, such as line games in which a certain number of children are caught, children can count the number of players caught. The number of children not caught and the total number of children in the class can be used in addition and subtraction problems.

■ Using a children's counting book (e.g., Feelings, 1971; Hoban, 1972), hold up a picture with a number of objects in it. Have the children form the shape of the number they counted with their bodies.

■ Hold up a number card (1-20) or point to a number on a chart. Have the children bounce a ball, twirl a hoop, or jump rope that number of times.

■ While working with partners, children hop, jump, skip, or slide a self-chosen number of times. The observing partner should count the number of tries and then orally express the total, for example, "I saw you skip five times."

■ Create number lines from 1 to 100 across the floor. Ask the children to move and count the numbers by 2s, 3s, 4s, 5s. Have them jump to 10 counting by 2s or skip to 50 counting by 5s. For each of the sums or products, have them shape the answer with their bodies.

Odd and Even Tag

Mathematics

Odd and even numbers

Physical Education

Tag game; chasing and fleeing

Grade Level

1 through 3

This activity is modeled after the traditional game of Crows and Cranes, in which two teams form parallel lines (one line represents crows, the other represents cranes). When you call out "crows," the crow line chases the cranes to their end line. When you call out "cranes," the crane line chases the crows to their end line. Anyone who is caught joins the opposite team. You also may call out names as distracters such as "Christmas," "crickets," and "crumpets," at which time neither line moves.

■ In another version of this activity, the two lines are the odd line and the even line. Call out an odd number, and the odd line chases the even line to their end line. Call out an even number, and the even line chases the odd line to their end line.

■ Call out an addition problem ($3 + 1$, $2 + 3$, etc.). If the solution is even, the even line chases the odd line to their end line. If the solution is odd, the odd line chases the even line to their end line.

■ Call out a subtraction problem ($3 - 1$, $4 - 3$, etc.). If the solution is even, the even line chases the odd line to their end line. If the solution is odd, the odd line chases the even line to their end line.

■ Play the same game using multiplication and division problems.

You're a Real Operator

Mathematics

Addition, subtraction, multiplication, division, fractions

Physical Education

Body shape, locomotor actions

Grade Level

2 through 4

■ Construct a 5 × 5 or 6 × 6 number grid of all the single-digit numbers (from 0 to 9) on the floor or pavement. (Figure 4.8 shows a sample grid.) Then, have the children jump or hop into each of the sequential numbers from 0 to 9, hopping into the odd numbers and jumping into the even numbers.

Figure 4.8 Children jump or hop into the odd and even numbers.

■ Using the same number grid, have children perform simple addition and subtraction problems from their math class (e.g., 1 + 4 = 5) as they jump or hop into the appropriate numbers.

■ Using the same number grid, have children perform more complex math problems of multiplication and division. For example, for 4 × 6 = 24, they hop from the 4 to the

6 and finish by jumping and landing with one foot in a 2 and the other in a 4. "Try 35 ÷ 5 = 7. What other math problems can you solve?"

■ "Let's use our bodies to calculate some math problems. First, we'll use body shapes. Someone choose a shape. Oh, that's good—balancing on two knees and one hand. Now, if we had three more people copy that shape, how many total people would be balancing in that shape? That's right, four. So let's do that by making a math sentence: 1 + 3 = 4. We'll need one person each to make the plus and minus signs, and enough people to do the balances for each number. Now, we'll do some more problems: 2 + 4 = 6; 5 – 2 = 3; 4 – 4 = 0. Can you think of other balances for each of the problems?"

■ "This time we'll do body-number computation. Who can make his or her body into the shape of a 3? We'll need someone to be a plus sign. Lauren, can you make a 4? Brian, be the equal sign. Who can form the answer? That's right. It is a 7 (3 + 4 = 7)." Have children get into groups of five and calculate several math problems. (They can also do multiplication or division problems if they are capable.)

■ "Using nonlocomotor actions, do the following in sequence. One twist, two punches, three swings, four stretches, five presses, six bends, seven turns, eight shakes, nine pulls. . . . Can you think of a way to do a locomotor sequence?"

■ Have children try doing a sequence of activities in one order, then reverse the order of the sequence. An example is one hop, two jumps, three slides, four ball bounces, then four ball bounces, three slides, and so on.

■ Set up a sequence of stations (figure 4.9). Each station should have an ordinal number of objects. Give each child a task card with a list of tasks to accomplish. To avoid children's waiting in line, vary the station and ordinal position of equipment each child uses. For example, while one child skips around the fourth hoop, then jumps over

Figure 4.9   Setting up an ordinal or sequential obstacle course.

the fifth wand, another might bounce the second ball 10 times, then do a forward roll on the first mat.

■ "Think about how you could divide your body in half. You could have a top half and bottom half or a right half and a left half. Can you bend your body parts on the right half and stretch your body parts on your left half? What about twisting the top half of your body while leaving the bottom half straight? How else can you divide your body in halves?"

■ "Let's divide the room into fourths. Can you run through one-fourth the distance of the room fast, then walk slowly across the remaining three-fourths? . . . What about skipping for the first half of the distance, then walking the next fourth, then again skipping the last fourth? . . . Using walking, skipping, leaping, hopping, jumping, sliding, and crawling, what other fractions can you illustrate while moving across the floor?"

■ "In groups of six to eight, make a geometric shape while lying on the floor. Then divide that shape into halves, thirds, or fourths using your bodies to create lines to make the correct fractions."

■ Have children answer the following questions about fractions by jumping, hopping, skipping, or leaping the correct number of times. What is 1/5 of 15? What is 1/4 of 16? What is 3/4 of 8? What is 1/2 of 10? What is 2/3 of 24?

■ Have the children throw or kick a ball at a target 10, 15, or 20 times and then count the number of successful tries. Then, they can calculate the percentage of successful tries. For example, 7 out of 10 tries is .70 or 70 percent.

■ "Let's see if we can remember the rules for whether number computations result in odd or even numbers when we are adding, subtracting, multiplying, and dividing. If the answer is even, make an *E* shape with your body, or balance on an even number of body parts. If the answer is odd, make an *O* shape with your body, or balance on an odd number of body parts. Ready? Even + Even = Even; Even + Odd = Odd; Odd + Odd = Even. Get the idea? Now you do the rest. Even – Even; Odd – Even; Odd – Odd; Even × Even; Even × Odd; Odd × Odd; Even ÷ Even; Odd ÷ Even; Odd ÷ Odd."

Beanbag Place-Value Toss

Mathematics
Place values

Physical Education
Underhand or overhand tossing for accuracy

Grade Level
3 through 6

■ Place students in groups according to the number of place values: three in a group for 1s, 10s, and 100s, four in a group for 1s, 10s, 100s, and 1000s, and so forth. Assign a place value to each student. Designate a number such as 2,495 or 158 or 25,733 depending on your place-value lesson goal.

■ Each group will have a target for each place value. Use hoops, buckets, or baskets for the targets. Each student will toss to the place value target he or she has been assigned. Upon completion of the appropriate number of successful tosses, the next place-value student begins.

■ You can assign a time limit.

MEASURING AND GRAPHING

I'm This Many

Mathematics

Measuring using nonstandard units

Physical Education

Balancing, locomotor activities

Grade Level

K through 2

Measuring starts as children are taught quantitative concepts using nonstandard units. Even in prekindergarten, children should learn concepts such as big/little, long/short, tall/short, high/low, wide/narrow, many/few, and all/none and positional concepts such as in front, behind, over, under, below, around, between, on, off, and through. The following examples show how children can learn these concepts in physical education and dance:

▪ "Make a big body shape. Can you hold it still? Can you stay in that big shape and move around the room? Make a small shape. Hold it still. Move your small shape around the room." (See figure 4.10.)

▪ "Take short, baby steps to move across the room. Take long, giant steps back the other way. Which way did you take many more steps? Which way took fewer steps? Try jumping and hopping using long and short steps."

▪ "Create a balance position. Can you put your hips higher than your head? Can you put your elbows lower than your knees?"

▪ "Balance your body at a high, medium, or low level. Create different shapes at each level."

▪ "Can you stretch your arms or legs out sideways and make a wide shape at a high or low level? While in that wide shape, can you move across the room? Now pull your arms and legs in to your sides and make a narrow shape. Can you make a narrow shape at a high, medium, or low level? Can you move your narrow shape across the floor? Can you make part of your body narrow and another part of your body wide at the same time? Can you move across the floor in that position?"

Figure 4.10   Making big and small body shapes.

▪ "Hold up one or a few fingers [less than five]. Now hold up many fingers [five or more]. Let's see if we can experiment with many and few. Hop a few steps. Skip, taking many steps. Many children stay standing, while a few sit down. Many children crawl, while a few jump." [Experiment with other ideas, focusing with the children on group awareness and cooperation.]

▪ "Place your hand above your head. Now put your elbow in front of your tummy. Get a partner. One move around the other. Create a balance, one over the other. One partner should make a bridgelike shape, while the other partner goes over and under the bridge like an airplane or ship."

▪ Have the children find ways to move on, off, over, under, through, into, out of, and around a piece of equipment such as a hula hoop, jump rope, wand, box, or bench. Have them balance in front of, beside, and in back of the equipment.

▪ Create situations in physical education in which children are asked to make comparative measurements such as longer than, heavier than, cooler than, and so on. For example, a stamp is heavier than a step. A pressing action is more forceful than a dab. Have children make two different shapes, one longer than the other.

It's Getting Loud in Here

Mathematics

Volume, pitch, tempo

Physical Education

Responding to music qualities

Grade Level

1 through 3

Volume, pitch, and tempo are quantitative mathematical concepts. Experiment with volume, pitch, and tempo concepts using music and dance. Focus on concepts such as loud or soft, high or low, and fast or slow.

▪ Make loud sounds on a drum, triangle, or another percussion instrument, and have the children respond with big, powerful movements. Make soft sounds, and have the children respond with small, light movements. Develop patterns of loud and soft sounds.

▪ Can the children move against the music? Have them move with big, powerful actions when the sound is soft and with small, light actions when the sound is loud.

▪ "Now we'll play some notes on the piano. When the pitch is high, make a high shape or travel at a high level. When the pitch is low, make a low shape or travel at a low level. What about a medium note?"

▪ Change the tempo of the music being played. Have the children move quickly when it is fast and move slowly when the tempo slows. Create patterns of fast and slow tempos.

▪ Find several short pieces of music that contrast the concepts of volume, pitch, and tempo (Boorman, *Pompous Potatoes*). Use pieces with high pitch, fast tempo, and loud volume; low pitch and slow tempo; fast tempo and soft volume; and so on. Have the children respond accordingly.

How Long Will It Take to Get There?

Mathematics

Time awareness

Physical Education

A variety of games and dance and gymnastics experiences

Grade Level

1 through 4

■ Awareness of time sequences starts with focusing on before, now, and after. A good way to demonstrate these concepts is out on the playground at the slide: Children stand at the bottom (before), sit at the top (now), and slide down to the bottom (after). Create a sequence composed of setting a ball up on a batting tee, hitting it off, and having a partner retrieve it and throw it back. Have the children create interpretive movements for "Yesterday it rained" (splash in the puddles) and "Today it is sunny" (play catch, go fishing, jump rope).

■ Use days of the week, seasons of the year, and months of the year as a way to designate positions in a circle on the floor. Then use the positions to group children or sequence the days, seasons, or months. For example, stand on one of the geometric shapes. Now we are all spread out and ready to begin moving. Or, all those standing on a circle will be on one team. Those on a triangle will be on another team. Another scenario would be to have them line up in a group by a day of the week, month of the year, or season. (See figure 4.11.)

■ Use the seasons of the year to develop a movement sequence. Examples: spring—ice melting, flowers blooming; summer—swimming, playing ball, going on a trip; fall—leaves falling, raking leaves, playing football; winter—cold, snow falling, ice skating.

■ Have children make number shapes representing the month they were born, important holidays (day and month), and important days in history (day, month, and year).

■ Have children in groups of three draw a clock face on the floor. Then, by lying on the floor, they show three o'clock, seven o'clock, and so on.

■ "Using the same clock face, stand with your feet at six o'clock. Then place your hands in the center of the clock, kick both feet into the

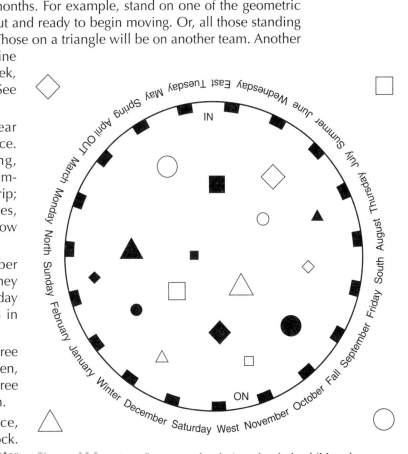

Figure 4.11   Gym floors may be designed to help children learn quantitative concepts.

air, and bring them down together softly at five o'clock, seven o'clock, three o'clock, nine o'clock. Can you start at six o'clock and finish at 12 o'clock? That is a cartwheel."

▪ Divide the children into groups of three. One child represents seconds, one represents minutes, and one represents hours. Use a piece of 4/4 time music. Have the child representing seconds perform a movement (tap, punch, step, jump, bend, etc.) for every quarter note. The child representing minutes should move to every other beat—half as fast, or on beats 1 and 3 or on beats 2 and 4 of each measure—using a different movement. The child representing hours should move to only the first or last beat of the measure using a different movement. If the children have good musical awareness, "seconds" should make one move for every quarter note, "minutes" for every half note, and "hours" for every whole note. Ask children to identify who moves at a fast, medium, and slow pace.

▪ Have children time-sequence work in gymnastics or dance from beginning to end. How many seconds does it take to perform each movement or set of movements?

▪ "Using a stopwatch, keep track of how long you can jump rope, dribble a ball, pass and catch with a partner, or hit forehands continuously against a wall. How many seconds? How many minutes? Record and graph your performances."

▪ Have children run, hop, skip, slide, or gallop various distances. "How long does it take you to go 10, 20, 50 yards [9, 18, 45 meters] doing each? Time, record, and graph your results. Which type of traveling action is your fastest way to travel (which requires least time to cover a given distance)"?

▪ Have students record elapsed time in minutes and seconds for various track events, such as 200-meter, 400-meter, 800-meter, and mile runs. For more sophisticated students,

Figure 4.12 Making a graph that indicates changes in the heart rate.

include tenths and hundredths of a second, especially for shorter distances of 10, 20, and 50 yards (9, 18, and 45 meters). Over trials or between days, have students record and graph performances to show improvement.

■ When working with students on any task, indicate a starting and ending time. Then have them figure out elapsed time. For example, "If you started at 10:12 and ended at 10:27, how much time did you spend practicing? How many practice trials did you do? How many trials per minute does that make? Let's see if we can do better next time." Or, "I'll start you jogging at 11:15. See how long you can go before you care to stop. Shandra, you kept going until 11:20.42. How long was that?"

■ Teach the children where their carotid artery is. Then have them count their resting pulse for 6 seconds and multiply by 10. Have them perform various activities for 10 seconds, 30 seconds, or 1 minute, each time stopping to count pulses, measure, and record the effort. Graph the results (figure 4.12). Work toward the concept of establishing a target heart rate and knowing what types of exercise get the heart working at various levels.

You Weigh a Ton

Mathematics
Weight measurements

Physical Education
Lifting heavy objects

Grade Level
2 through 4

■ "Show me how you would move if you weighed a ton. Even if you are as heavy as an elephant, can you still move fast? Soft? Now you are light as a feather. How will you move now?"

■ Have children use small scales to measure play objects. "How much does a ball, bat, or racket weigh?" Have them record and graph all the data.

■ Have the students lift small, light dumbbells (1 to 5 pounds or 1 to 5 kilograms). Ask them to perform several repetitions of several different exercises. "If you lift 2 pounds [about 1 kilogram] eight times, how much weight have you lifted altogether?"

■ Weigh the children using customary or metric scales. Ask them to support their weight on different body parts (feet, seat, hand and knee, etc.). Ask them which ways are easier and why. (Large muscles of the legs, back, and abdomen are stronger and more capable of supporting weight.) Ask what happens if they support their weight in a push-up position or hang from a chin-up position. (Arms tire quickly.) Have them try supporting someone else's weight partially or completely (figure 4.13).

■ "Now we are going to play a little game. I want you to solve some problems and create your answers by assuming body shapes. How many ounces in a pound? How many grams in a kilogram? How many feet in a yard? How many yards in a mile? This time use your body to make letter shapes, and show me the abbreviations for gram, centimeter, liter, yard, foot, ounce, pound. Finally, use your body to make the shape of the object indicating the correct answer. Which weighs more, a pound of pencils

Figure 4.13   Can a student support someone else's weight partially or completely?

or 12 ounces of chocolates? Which weighs less, 16 ounces of dog food or a pound of feathers? Which weighs more, a pound of cookies or 400 grams of paper clips?" Have the children pair up and create their own brain teasers. One partner creates the question. The second forms the answer using a body shape.

I Went the Farthest

Mathematics

Linear measure

Physical Education

Selected jumping, throwing, and running events

Grade Level

2 through 5

■ Have the children measure the distance of various lines or the results of movement efforts using nonstandard measures. "How many people lying head to toe does it take to go from end to end of the basketball court? The volleyball court? Which takes more? Less? . . . How many hands high is your friend? . . . Lie on the floor, and have your partner mark where your foot starts and head ends, then count how many forearms tall you are. . . . Take three giant steps. How many strings [one foot long] did you go? . . . Take three hops, then three jumps. How many strings for each? What way took you the farthest? . . . Everyone stand side by side and be as wide as you can. How many children does it take to get across the room? . . . Bat a ball off a tee. Then measure how many bats the ball traveled."

■ "Use a foot or yard ruler to measure your walking stride. How far would you go if you took five strides? Hop five times, and measure the distance to the nearest inch, foot, or yard. Jump one to five times, and measure the distance to the nearest inch, foot, or yard. Create a graph showing how far you get using one to five strides, one to five hops, and one to five jumps. Which way do you go the farthest?"

▪ Have children measure various performances in physical education using whole-unit measures of both customary and metric units. They can use inches, feet, yards, centimeters, decimeters, and meters. Ask them how far they can jump or hop. How far can they throw different types of balls? How high can they jump?

▪ While children are learning to high-jump, throw for distance, and so on in a track and field unit, have them measure and graph their best performances each day. They can combine several days' efforts to record improvement in performance.

▪ As children become more sophisticated, make measurements more precise: to the nearest half unit, quarter unit, eighth of an inch, or even millimeter.

▪ During jumping or throwing events, have the children perform math conversions within a measurement system. For example, "Sue just jumped 4 feet, 6 inches. How many total inches is that? John threw the ball 65 feet. How many yards does that make?"

▪ During jumping or throwing events, have the children perform math conversions between customary and metric measurement systems. For example, "Amanda threw the softball 70 feet. How many meters does that make?"

▪ After the children jump or throw various distances that are measured and recorded, have them create graphs of their performances (figure 4.14). Use conversion scales to help interpret results, such as 1 inch = 10 feet, 1 centimeter = 1 meter, and so on. Then

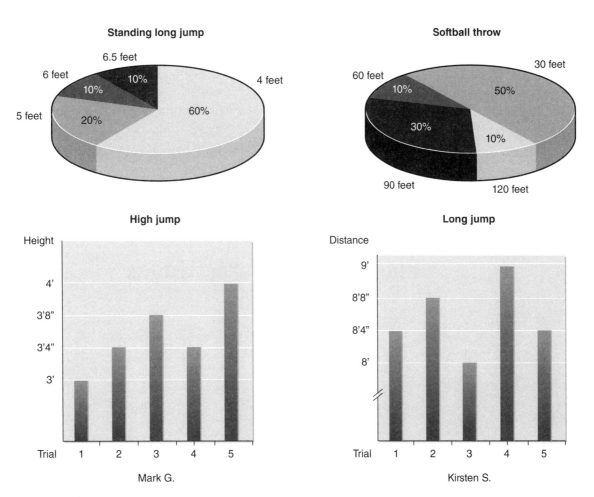

Figure 4.14 Measuring and graphing performance in jumping or throwing events.

have them compare performances (e.g., today's with yesterday's, 10th try with first try) using the graphs they have created. Do they see improvement in their performances?

▪ Many physical education activities require boundaries and certain dimensions. Children can measure and lay out the necessary boundaries and field dimensions and make scale models of the playing areas.

In My Estimation

Mathematics

Estimating distances and times

Physical Education

Running, throwing, and kicking events

Grade Level

4 through 6

▪ Have the students throw a ball. Then have them estimate the distance the ball traveled in yards, feet, meters, or more than one of these units. How close were their estimates? Change the type, weight, or size of the ball and have them perform the same tasks. How close were their estimates this time? Try this several times to see if the students can get more accurate in their estimates.

▪ Have the students use a kickoff style of kicking or a punt style of kicking a football. Partners take turns kicking and measuring the distance of their kicks. Before they kick, have them estimate how far their kick will travel. Or after their kick has landed, have them estimate the distance traveled.

▪ Have students estimate how long it will take them to run a specific distance—20 yards, 50 meters, 100 meters, 400 meters, and so on. Using a stopwatch, time them in the chosen event. How close were the actual times to the estimated times? Graph the results, comparing the estimates with the real times. In general, did the students under- or overestimate their times?

Playing With Percentages

Mathematics

Calculating percentages

Physical Education

Passing and catching a football

Grade Level

4 through 6

▪ Have students work in groups of three. One person acts as the thrower, one as a receiver, and the third as a recorder. Have the receiver go out for a pass. The passer

---

Physical Education: Football Unit

PLAYING WITH PERCENTAGES

Name _____ (passer)

Receiver Only

Passes attempted _____

Passes completed _____

Percentage completed _____

Receiver Against Defender

Passes attempted_____

Passes completed _____

Percentage completed _____

Predict your completion percentage before you start, using your calculator:

1. Enter the number of pass attempts completed with receiver only.
2. Press the divide button.
3. Enter the number of passes attempted with receiver only.
4. Press the equals (=) button.
5. Move the decimal two places to the right (0.75 = 75%).
6. Record that percentage (%).

Repeat the steps for passes against a defender.

_____ Receiver only   _____ Receiver against defender

Figure 4.15   Playing With Percentages worksheet.

counts to three or four and then, using a lead pass concept, attempts to complete the pass. The recorder uses a worksheet (figure 4.15) to record the number of pass attempts and completions. After 10 to 20 turns, players switch roles (passer, receiver, recorder).

▪ Next organize the players into groups of four—passer, receiver, defender, recorder. Players line up. Receiver hikes the ball and runs a route to receive a pass. Passer receives the hike, counts to three, and uses a lead pass to the receiver. Defender starts 3 to 5 yards (3-4.5 meters) off the hiker and defends the pass, trying to deflect the ball or intercept it. No contact is allowed. The recorder uses the worksheet provided and records the number of pass attempts and the number of completions. After 10 to 20 turns, players switch roles (passer, receiver, defender, recorder).

GEOMETRY

Shape Up

Mathematics

Simple geometric shapes

Physical Education

Selected locomotor, manipulative, and gymnastics activities

Grade Level

1 through 3

▪ Have the children find ways to move over, under, in, out of, on, off, in front of, in back of, and beside objects such as hoops, wands, ropes, boxes, benches, or markers on the floor. For instance, they can jump over a rope forward, backward, or sideways; stand beside a box and make a shape; and by placing their hands on a bench find ways to move over it. Find other ways to challenge children's awareness of position in space.

▪ To make an obstacle course, use commercially purchased geometric shapes or shapes cut out from cardboard and supported by slits in 2 × 4s. Have the children crawl through a circle, go through a triangle headfirst, or go feetfirst–belly up through a square. Continue with similar challenges.

▪ Have the children throw yarn balls, sponge balls, or beanbags at a target with openings in the shape of circles, squares, triangles, rectangles, and diamonds. They can call out a shape and try to throw the object through that shape.

▪ Give partners a set of beanbags in the shape of circles, squares, triangles, rectangles, and diamonds. The throwing partner conceals the beanbag before the throw. The catching partner calls out the shape of the beanbag while it is in the air as soon as he or she can, before catching it.

▪ Draw a grid on the floor or outdoor playground with chalk, or have the children do so. Have the children walk, hop, jump, skip, or slide along the lines that make a circle, triangle, square, rectangle, or other shape (figure 4.16).

▪ Children use different body parts to make a circle, square, triangle, or other shape. They can make the same shapes with a partner or in a group of three or four.

▪ Have them make geometric shapes with their body at different levels—a square at a low level, a circle at a high level, a triangle at a medium level.

▪ "I'm going to show you pictures of objects, and it is your job to classify them by properties or characteristics. The first set of pictures will be about size. When you see a large shape, make a big body shape. When you see a medium or small shape, make that size body shape. Next, you'll see the same pictures, but I want you to look at the number of corners the shape has. Then balance on that number of body parts. If you see a triangle, how many parts will you balance on? That's right—three. What about a circle? None. Next we'll characterize the pictures as to whether they roll or don't roll.

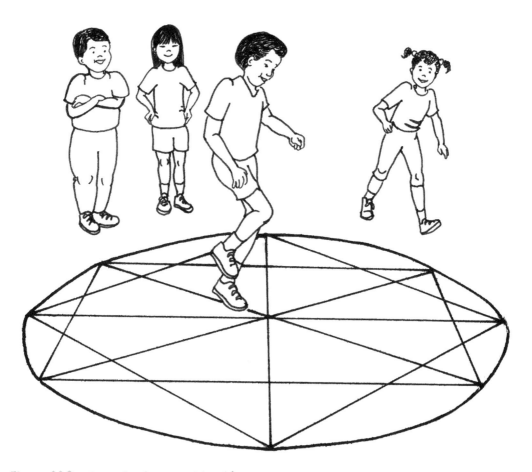

Figure 4.16   Example of a geometric grid.

If you see a picture of something that rolls (circle, sphere, cylinder, ball, pencil, etc.), do a forward roll. If you see a picture that doesn't roll (triangle, square, rectangle, box, cube, etc.), create a balance shape."

■ Have children use air pathways to draw geometric patterns through space. They can try different body parts to trace the patterns in the air.

■ "I will briefly hold a picture up for you [1-10 seconds]. After you see it, walk that pattern on the floor (circle, triangle, square, rectangle, diamond). Try other locomotor actions to trace the shape on the floor."

■ "This time I will hold up a picture of two or three shapes. After you see the shapes, choose one form of locomotion to make one shape and a second form of locomotion to make the second shape." This activity helps develop visual sequential memory.

■ Have children do the preceding activity but use a locomotor action to make one shape and trace the second shape in the air with a body part.

■ While working with a partner, students make shapes that are the same; for instance, both make a circle. Have them keep the same shape but make one large, one small. They can also change shapes (triangle, square, rectangle, and so on), change levels, and make different shapes (one partner makes a circle, the other a triangle). They can make various shapes that are different sizes and then different levels.

It's Getting Complicated

Mathematics

Complex geometric shapes

Physical Education

Body shapes

Grade Level

3 through 5

■ Challenge the children to make various geometric body shapes. Specifically, have them assume shapes that create awareness of the concepts of concave and convex. Can they make concave and convex shapes while lying on the floor (figure 4.17)? Can they make concave and convex bridgelike shapes—back bend (belly up) and angry cat (belly down)—at a medium level? Can they make concave and convex shapes by hanging from rings or parallel bars? Can they make concave and convex shapes at high levels while standing?

■ Have a large group, 10 to 12 children, model a given shape and the parts of that shape. For example, a group assigned to create a circle could make the circumference, center, radius, and diameter. Height, length, depth, diagonal, or perimeter could be represented for a triangle, rectangle, or square.

■ Children create partner shapes that emphasize perpendicular, parallel, and intersecting lines and create these shapes at low, medium, and high levels.

■ While moving with a partner, children show pathway lines that are parallel, then show a different way to move so that their pathways intersect.

Figure 4.17   Making the body assume concave and convex shapes.

Twins

Mathematics

Symmetry

Physical Education

Body shapes

Grade Level

2 through 4

"Let's practice making symmetrical shapes (both sides the same). Show me a symmetrical shape at a low, a medium, and a high level. Then make the two sides different (asymmetrical)." Have students try these shapes at different levels.

- "Work with a partner. One person will make a symmetrical shape. Then the partner will make exactly the same shape. In physical education we might call this mirroring. In mathematics it could be called congruence. Make congruent shapes at different levels."

- Have children, working in groups of three or four, develop ways to make body shapes that show different types of triangles or quadrilaterals. For example, can they make an isosceles, right, obtuse, acute, equiangular, and scalene triangle? Can they make a trapezoid, rhombus, parallelogram, square, and rectangle?

- "Can you make the preceding shapes with one or two people and a piece of equipment such as a bench or rope? You may need to use counterbalances to create your shapes."

You Make Me Flip

Mathematics

Transformations

In mathematics, children learn to do slides and translations, turns and rotations, and flips and reflections.

Art

Tessellations

In art, children explore the same concepts through tessellations. Tessellations are re-creations of patterns such as prints and mosaics.

Physical Education

Body shapes

Grade Level

1 through 3, 3 through 5

- 1 through 3: "Make a shape. Then try to transform that shape by using a flip (reflection or mirror), slide (moving the shape around a flat surface), or turn (rotating around a point). If you kneel down, what would it look like if you were lying on your side or back? Perform a *V-seat*. Then, perform the same shape by putting your hands and feet on the floor with your bottom facing up. Can you create an *X* shape by standing with your arms and legs spread out like spokes in a wheel? Now try the same *X* position by lying down face up or face down. Can you try the same *X* position with one hand and one foot on the floor and the other arm and leg stretched out in the air above you?"

▪ 3 through 5: "Repeated patterns may be accomplished through translation, rotation, or reflection. A translation is a big word for a slide. A rotation is a big word for a turn. A reflection is a big word for a flip." When children perform a balance on the floor and then repeat the balance on a piece of equipment, they are essentially doing a translation. "If you kneel down, what would it look like if you were lying on your side or back? What would a tip-up, tripod, or headstand look like right side up?" Compare other upright and inverted balances. These are also examples of rotations. "When you perform mirroring actions with a partner, you are doing reflections."

Let's Go Angling

Mathematics

Right, acute, and obtuse angles

Physical Education

Body shapes

Grade Level

3 through 5

"Show me a way to make a right angle with your hands. Okay. You can make an *L* by sticking out your thumb from your hand or bending at the knuckles or wrist. Show me a way with your whole body." (Sitting with back straight and legs straight out to the front, standing position with back bent like a table.) "We can also bend at other joints to make right angles. What joints can you bend to make right angles?" (Shoulder, elbow, hip, knee, neck, ankle.) "Can you make your body create a shape with two, three, or four right angles at the same time? Can you move across the floor while you have different body parts bent at right angles?"

▪ "In addition to right angles, we can make our joints bend at acute and obtuse angles. Choose a joint and create an acute angle with it. Change and show me an obtuse angle. Change joints and make acute and obtuse angles. Can you bend one joint and make an acute angle and bend another to make an obtuse angle at the same time? Can you create a symmetrical body shape that emphasizes acute angles? Can you jump into the air and make a body shape with acute or obtuse angles while you are in the air?"

▪ "While you are moving around the room by walking, hopping, jumping, or skipping, I will make three sounds. When you hear a drum, change your pathway at right angles. A triangle means an acute turn. A maraca means an obtuse-angle turn."

Matching Patterns

Mathematics

Growing and repeating patterns

Physical Education

Beat awareness using nonlocomotor and locomotor activities

Grade Level

1 through 4

- Using the *Rhythmically Moving* (Weikart, 1989) series of records or any instrumental music with a strong 4/4 beat (marching music), begin developing patterns of unilateral actions to the beat of the music. Initially focus on the macro beat (first beat of a measure), for example, stretch (one arm up high), 2, 3, 4; bend (same arm pulled in), 2, 3, 4; stretch, 2, 3, 4; bend, 2, 3, 4. Continue with other patterns, for instance, tap (thigh), 2, 3, 4; punch (air), 2, 3, 4; tap, 2, 3, 4; punch, 2, 3, 4. Perform bilateral patterns to a macro beat, such as two-arm stretch, 2, 3, 4; two-arm bend, 2, 3, 4; stretch, 2, 3, 4; bend, 2, 3, 4. Perform these patterns to the micro beat of a piece of music in 4/4 time: stretch, bend, stretch, bend. Point out to the children that you are doing a repeated pattern, ABAB.

- Perform the preceding activity but use locomotor actions to establish patterns, for example, step, hop, step, hop (ABAB) and hop, jump, jump, jump, hop, jump, jump, jump (ABBB).

- Show the children a symbolic pattern (*, #, +, -, *, #, +, - or *, #, *, #) and ask them to develop a movement pattern that reproduces the pattern of the symbols. For example, they could punch, twist, stretch, bend, punch, twist, stretch, bend to the first pattern.

- Using small musical instruments such as drums, shakers, triangles, sand blocks, and so on, beat out a rhythmical pattern, for example, half note, quarter note, quarter note; or quarter note, quarter note, eighth note, eighth note, quarter note. Have the children beat out your rhythm pattern on their instruments. Then have them draw a representation of each pattern using pencil and paper. Have them design their own rhythmical patterns and play these patterns with their instruments. Then, have them perform locomotor or nonlocomotor actions to their rhythmical patterns.

- Perform a specific pattern several times over and have the children observe. Then ask them to use paper and pencil to create a symbolic code for the pattern. For example, "slow movement, slow movement, quick, quick, quick, repeat" might look like —, —, -, -, -, —, —, -, -, -. Next have them take turns with a partner performing a pattern that their partner codes on a piece of paper.

- Require children to observe a repeating pattern, then have them translate and orally describe the pattern they saw. For example, if the pattern is tap thigh, clap hands, snap fingers, tap, clap, snap, they would say "tap, clap, snap, tap, clap, snap." Next have the children choose partners and orally translate patterns that their partner develops.

■ Tap out a pattern on a drum, such as soft, loud, loud, soft, loud, loud, or play high and low notes on another musical instrument. Have the children respond with appropriate movements, for example, a gentle step, a powerful stamp, stamp, step, stamp, stamp.

■ Encourage children to recognize growing patterns, such as *, #; *, #, #; *, #, #, #, by translating them into movement patterns, such as step, hop, step, hop, hop, step, hop, hop, hop; or catch, bounce, catch, bounce, bounce, catch, bounce, bounce, bounce. "What other growing patterns can you think of?"

■ Experiment with a variety of repeating and growing patterns, for example, ABAB, ABACAD, ABBA, *#**#***#. After providing a demonstration, divide the class into pairs, and have them develop nonlocomotor and locomotor sequences in which they recognize, translate into movements, describe, and classify the patterns.

■ Have the children create a series of statue-like poses or balance positions. Then order the poses or balances into a pattern from big to small, wide to narrow, tall to short, and so on (figure 4.18). For example, the sequence front support, tip-up, scale, headstand, handstand progresses from a low level to a high level.

■ Demonstrate a pattern several times using different movements for each repetition, for example, clap, clap, stamp, stamp; or bounce, bounce, strike, strike; or hop, hop, jump, jump. Then have the children describe to you the underlying pattern (AABB). Have them form partnerships and take turns performing patterns and identifying the rules to the patterns.

■ Children skip-count forward and backward by 2s, 3s, 5s, or 10s while jumping rope or playing a game. For example, while jumping rope, they count out 3, 6, 9, 12,

Figure 4.18 Using body shapes to create a pattern of small, medium, and large shapes.

. . . or they strike a balloon up in the air with a body part while counting backward from 100 by 5s.

■ Have the children play a game such as basketball or volleyball and keep score using pattern counting, such as even numbers, odd numbers, by 4s, or by 10s.

■ Perform a pattern two or three times, then perform it again but intentionally leave out or change one part. Ask the children what part of the pattern was left out or changed. For example, perform ABAB, ABAB, then ABAA; or step, step, step, hop; step, step, step, hop; then step, step, step. Ask children to work in pairs. One partner develops a pattern using locomotor, nonlocomotor, or manipulative movements and then intentionally leaves out or changes a part. The other partner watches to recognize and describe the missing or altered part of the pattern.

■ Organize several pieces of physical education equipment into a group related by a common theme or quality, and include one object that does not fit the pattern. For example, group a tennis ball, softball, baseball, and scarf. Obviously, the scarf is the object that does not fit the pattern. What about a tennis ball, softball, baseball, and football? The football does not fit the pattern because it is not round and it is not struck with an implement as it is used. Switch to a focus on physical activities. Group a skip, punch, hop, and jump. The punch does not fit because it is not a locomotor action. Put together three balances at a low level and one at a high level, and try other combinations of physical activities. Once the children get the idea, have them work in pairs; one partner creates his or her own group of actions and the other partner tries to select the movement that does not fit the pattern.

PROBABILITY AND STATISTICS

Take a Guess

Mathematics

Predictions, scientific method, recording data, graphing data

Physical Education

Event records of locomotor and manipulative movement patterns

Grade Level

3 through 5

■ Children should be encouraged early in their physical education experiences to participate in small experiments with one variable. They can use their data to record results; create simple pictographs or bar graphs; describe results; interpret results; and judge events as certain, possible, or impossible. For example, they could step on and off aerobic step benches at heights of 4, 6, or 8 inches (10, 15, or 20 centimeters) as many times as possible in 10 seconds. They could record the number of repetitions for each height. Are these numbers the same or different? They could then create a pictograph or bar graph of their results. They could write a report on their results. On the basis of their results they could predict how many repetitions they might be able to do in 20 or 30 seconds.

■ Later experiments might involve two or three variables: for example, number of bent-knee sit-ups during two trials each in two positions (crossed arms on chest, hands cupped behind head), number of push-ups during two trials each of three positions (regular, hands on bench with feet on floor, feet on bench with hands on the floor), and number of shots made on an 8-inch (20-centimeter) and a 10-inch (25-centimeter) basket from two or three distances in two or three trials. Again, children should organize their data, create graphs, and describe their results using words such as *more, less, fewer, same, all, none, most likely, least likely, probably, definitely.*

■ In their pictographs or bar graphs of data from the preceding experiments, children can use symbols such as body parts, or bar graphs with open, slashed, and blocked bars to graphically represent data for performances in an event such as a rope climb or squat vault (figure 4.19).

■ Using two factors, children should be able to determine possible outcomes of everyday events. What are the possible permutations and combinations of moving at three levels and two speeds?

Figure 4.19 Using pictographs or bar graphs to represent and interpret data.

◾ Give the children a die or a pair of dice, a deck of cards, or a spinner with 6 to 10 numbers on it. Assign a movement task to each number. Have them roll the die, select a card, or spin the needle. They must then do the movement task assigned to the number. With a second die or roll of the die, card, or spin they must do the designated movement the required number of times. What is recorded is only the number of times the designated movement is performed, not the number of repetitions. They should record the number of times they do each task. Using probability, they should predict the results and compare the predictions with the actual results. For example, with use of a single die, there is a 1 in 6 chance of selecting a given task on each roll. Over a large number of trials, it is predictable that each number or task will be rolled approximately the same number of times.

◾ Have the children work individually, tapping a balloon into the air, dribbling a basketball, passing a soccer ball against a wall, striking a forehand against a wall, or hitting consecutive volleyball forearm passes. They should count the number of successful attempts within a specific time (10-30 seconds) and record the results. Tell the children possible ways to improve their performances. Have them conduct several more trials and record the results. After trials are recorded, have them look at all their data and predict how they think they might do on the next trial. Have them perform another try. How close were they to their prediction? Was the number of successful attempts greater or less than the predicted number? Why?

◾ Have the children throw at a target (hula hoop, taped box on the wall) or shoot at a basket from a specific distance. For example, they might throw at a 2-foot-square (0.6-meter-square) target taped on the wall from a distance of 20 feet (6 meters). Have them make 10 tries and record the results, then perform 10 more tries and record the results. Next, have them predict their score on a third set of 10 tries. How accurate were they in their predictions? Move them back to 30 feet (9 meters) from the target, or make the target larger or smaller. Have them predict their results. What were the actual results? Record and compare the data.

◾ Have the children use the data from the preceding experiment to create charts or bar graphs. They then write a report describing the results based on an interpretation of the charts, using words such as *more, less, fewer, same, all, none, most likely, least likely, probably, definitely.*

◾ Over a period of several classes devoted to working on a specific skill (e.g., dribble, pass, shot at target), count the number of successful attempts (e.g., 3 out of 10) or total successful trials over time (e.g., 15 successful attempts in 30 seconds). Keep track of results by recording the data each day. After several days, have the children create a chart or single-line graph. Then have them describe the results (e.g., got better over time, or increased suddenly and then plateaued).

◾ Over a period of several classes devoted to working on a specific skill, have each individual keep track of his or her number of successful attempts or total number of successful trials over time. Then have students calculate their own mean, median, mode, and range of scores.

◾ Collect data on each student's practice trials of a selected skill over a period of several classes. Have the whole class calculate the mean, median, mode, and range of scores for the whole group.

◾ While the children are playing 1 versus 1, 2 versus 2, or 3 versus 3 with players of matched abilities on modified courts in modified games of hockey, soccer, basketball, or another team sport, ask them to predict who will win and state why (e.g., more speed, better passing skills, accurate shots, better defense). After the game, compare results with predictions. What factors entered into the game to bring about specific results?

Are You Average?

Mathematics

Mean, median, mode, range (statistics)

Physical Education

Throwing, kicking, striking, catching, running, jumping

Grade Level

5 and 6

Have each child collect a set of his or her own data on a selected skill, or have the whole class pool their data. For example, students might throw for distance 10 times using a softball, or kick at a target 20 times and keep track of how many times they hit the target, or run 400 meters for time and record the data. Then, have them analyze the data. "What is the range of scores? Subtract the lowest from the highest score. What is the mode or the score that occurs the most often? What is the mean score? Add up all the scores and divide by the number of trials or the number of students. What is the median or the score in the middle?" Use calculators when possible. For advanced mathematics students, introduce standard deviation. After analyzing the data, students should make charts with bar graphs or pie graphs and interpret the data to other students.

LOGIC

Get Real

Mathematics

Classifying, sequencing, inductive and deductive reasoning

Physical Education

Selected balancing and locomotor sequences

Grade Level

2 through 5

 Part of logic is related to a precise interpretation of words such as *all, every, some, none, both, only, many, either, or, and,* and *not.* Movement tasks can be designed to help children understand these words through a variety of practical or concrete experiences. Here are some examples: "All children balance on three body parts. . . . Hop or jump in a forward direction. . . . Many children skip, while some gallop. . . . Can you balance at a low level and be in a symmetrical shape at the same time? . . . While running forward, can you move in either a zigzag pathway or a curved pathway? . . . Every child throw five balls at the target using an overhand pattern. None should use an underhand pattern." You and the students can develop other movement tasks using the key words.

- Develop movement sequences that involve a logical order. For example, in dance you might want to portray the passing of a day, a season of growth, or an occurrence such as a rainstorm. Ask the children, "What comes first, second, third, . . . , last? What is the logical order?" As a movement response, the children can develop appropriate actions to represent getting up, washing, eating, doing daily chores, playing, and finally going to bed at the end of the day. Each piece could be developed separately with appropriate actions and then ordered chronologically.

- Objects are often recognized and sorted by attributes. For example, children can sort blocks by color, shape, size, and so on. Objects can be further sorted (subdivided) by additional attributes. Physical education activities can be sorted by attributes as well. While students are balancing, for example, you can ask the class to look around. "How many children are balancing on two, three, or four body parts? How many shapes are high, medium, or low? How many children are balancing on three body parts at a low level?"

- Have children classify locomotor actions by attributes. While skipping, how many are going fast or slow? How many are going forward or backward? How many are going straight, curved, or zigzag? How many are going fast and forward in a straight line?

- Use a Venn diagram to model these attributes. See the lesson "Get Set" in the following section on algebra for more information on using Venn diagrams to depict sets, union, and intersection.

- Encourage children to use flowcharts or cues to develop a mental image or schema of how to execute movement patterns. For example, forward roll = squat, tuck, bottom up, roll, return to feet. Tennis forehand = ready, turn, racket back, step, swing low to high, home base.

- Use the process of inductive reasoning to help children discover general facts from more simple, specific facts. In a lesson on traveling on the feet, do not tell the children your objectives for the day at the outset. Begin by asking them to walk about the space. Ask them what they are doing with their feet (placing one foot in front of the other, alternating steps). Ask them if they know any other ways to move their feet. They might answer "jump" or "hop." Ask them what they do with their feet when they jump or hop. Define each. Ask them if there are still other ways to use the feet to move about space. Help them discover the remaining types of steplike weight transfer: "So what did we do today? We used our feet to move about space. . . . How many basic types of steplike weight transfer are there? [Five.] When we move about space with our feet, what is that called? [Traveling or locomotion.] How might we define traveling? [Moving from one place to another.] Are there ways to travel other than using our feet only?" [Yes, we can use hands and feet together, rolling, sliding, rocking.]

- Use the process of deductive reasoning to help children discover specific facts based on narrowing ideas from general concepts. For example, have the children throw for distance in any way they choose. You can even have them experiment with throwing while standing facing the target without using their whole arm (ball up to ear, but elbow down by side) and without taking a step. Gradually introduce them to a more efficient throwing pattern by allowing them to step. "Which foot is better to step with? [Opposite.] Can you throw better facing the target or starting with your side to the target and turning? [Side to target.] What about your arm? Is it better to throw with your arm in or your arm cocked with your elbow out away from your ear?" [Elbow up and out.] There are many other skills that you can teach using deductive reasoning to help the children to discover the most mechanically efficient way to perform.

- Early experiences in logic include *if-then* statements. Practice making these types of statements with the children using creative movement. "If the road is bumpy, then the ride will be rough. If the ice is smooth, then skaters will glide across it. If we hurry, then we'll get there faster. If it is really cold outside, then it might snow." We encourage you to develop your own *if-then* statements, as well as to have the students do so, and ask them to put these statements into movement sequences.

▪ Help children to define specific movement skills using *if and only if* statements. For example, "A hop is a hop if and only if the steplike weight transfer is from one foot to the same foot. A skip is a skip if and only if there are steplike weight transfers that alternate between step and hop. A throw is a throw if and only if a held object remains in contact with the body during maximum buildup of momentum (windup) before the object is released."

ALGEBRA

Less Than, More Than, Equal To

Mathematics

Working with math symbols

Physical Education

Selected exercises and manipulative and locomotor activities

Grade Level

1 through 3

As children learn the concepts and symbols of less than, more than, and equals ($<$, $>$, and $=$), there are many concrete applications in physical education. For example, for the equation $5 < 7$, one child or a small group of children could do a locomotor pattern five times, make body shape representing the less than symbol, and finish by doing the same locomotor pattern seven times. Another group could do balances to represent $3 > 1$; a group working with the equation $5 = 5$ could make five throws at a target, a body shape representing an equal sign, then five more throws at the target.

▪ "We are going to play a game of less than, greater than, or equal to. I want you to choose an action or activity (e.g., jumps, ball bounces, bending actions). Perform that action a specific number of times that you choose. Then I will hold up one of the signs, and you must repeat that action, doing it a number of times fewer than, equal to, or greater than the previous time."

▪ Make up a series of task cards and place them at various teaching stations around the gymnasium. Several examples follow. We encourage you to make up your own task cards to fit the ability levels of your students and your teaching situation.

▪ Exercises

1. Perform less than ($<$) 5 push-ups.

2. Perform more than ($>$) 10 sit-ups.

3. Perform <15 toe touches.

4. Perform >5 leg lifts.

    5. Perform a flexed arm hang for greater than or equal to (≥) 10 seconds.

    6. Run in place >30 seconds but <2 minutes.

■ Gymnastics

    1. Do >3 forward rolls.

    2. Do <5 backward rolls.

    3. Do >4 cartwheels.

    4. Do <5 different vaults over the horse.

    5. Try >4 but <10 different ways to cross the balance beam.

■ Ball skills

    1. Bounce the ball <30 times with your right hand.

    2. Bounce the ball >40 times with your left hand.

    3. Throw and catch the ball <25 times against the wall.

    4. Throw and catch the ball with a partner >15 times without dropping the ball.

    5. Shoot the ball at the basket until you make >10 but <20 baskets.

■ Rope jumping

    1. Place the rope on the floor and walk along it >4 different ways.

    2. Place the rope on the floor and jump over it <5 different ways.

    3. Jump a long rope turned by two other people >20 times.

    4. Jump a short rope by yourself <50 times.

    5. Hop a short rope >15 times but <25 times before you change to the other foot.

You're Out in Left Field

Mathematics

Field properties of math: identity and commutative and associative properties

Physical Education

Selected games and dance activities

Grade Level

2 through 4

The identity element for addition is the number zero (0). If we add zero to any number, the sum is still the number. The identity element for multiplication is the number one (1). We have identity elements in all human movements in physical education. For example, we recognize certain mechanics of motion as a skill we term running. A skip is a step-hop, one foot in front of the other, alternating flight phase. What are the identity elements or definitions for a bend, stretch, twist, turn, hop, jump, gallop, slide, throw, strike?

The commutative property of addition states that we may change the order of the addends without changing the sum, that is, 2 + 4 = 4 + 2; or in general, if a and b are any whole numbers, then a + b = b + a. The commutative property of multiplication states that we may change the order of the two factors without changing the product, that is, 5 × 7 = 7 × 5; or in general, if a and b are any whole numbers, then a × b = b × a. In physical education we may help children learn this concept by using several practical examples. While partners are sharing a piece of equipment in physical education, the order in which the partners use the equipment makes no difference, as they will get the same number of tries no matter who goes first. The softball game Run Around the Bases (figure 4.20) is another example of the commutative property. When two children run around the bases, regardless of the order or direction in which they run they will both return to home plate.

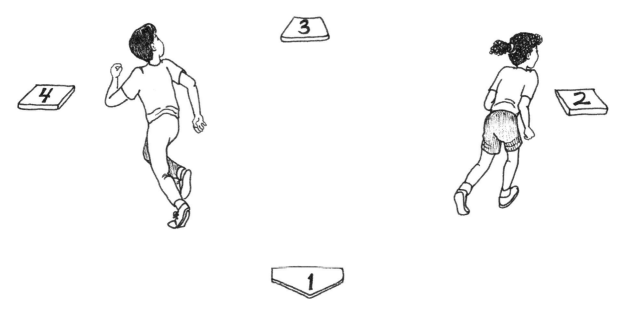

Figure 4.20   Running bases in opposite directions illustrates the commutative and associative properties of mathematics.

The associative property for addition states that when three or more numbers are being added, we may change the grouping of the numbers without changing the sum, that is, (2 + 3) + 5 = 2 + (3 + 5); or in general, if a, b, and c are any whole numbers, then (a + b) + c = a + (b + c). The associative property for multiplication states that when three or more factors are multiplied, we may change the grouping of the factors without changing the product, that is, (2 × 3) × 4 = 2 × (3 × 4); or in general, if a, b, and c are any whole numbers, then (a × b) × c = a × (b × c). In physical education we may help children learn this concept by using several practical examples. When groups of three or four children take turns, changing the order in which the children perform results in the same number of performances. For example, when forming groups of four, have children first pick a partner, then have pairs join with another pair. If partners Arun and Betty join with partners Carlos and Darla, the same group is formed as if partners Arun and Carlos joined with Betty and Darla. When performing a Grand Right and Left in square dance, the four male dancers move counterclockwise and the four female dancers move clockwise, but regardless of the direction in which they move, they finish with their partner and promenade to the home position.

Get Set

Mathematics

Math sentences, sets, Venn diagrams, operations on sets

Physical Education

Selected games and dance and gymnastics activities

Grade Level

3 through 5

Just as children learn to communicate with words and sentences in language arts, they learn to communicate with symbols in mathematics. Here are some common math symbols:

- Capital letters generally denote sets or members of a group.
- Equal signs (=) denote equality between each side of an equation.
- Braces—{ }—denote enclosure for members of a set or group.
- Symbols or names enclosed in braces are understood to refer to members of sets.
- Commas separate the symbols that represent the members of a set when the members are listed between braces.
- Lowercase letters indicate individual members of sets.
- The symbol $\in$ stands for "is a member or element of."
- A vertical or slanted line through a symbol negates that symbol, for example, $\neq$ means "not equal."
- A   B means that A is a subset of B and that B has at least one member that is not a member of A.

Here are some examples of using math symbols to write sets of physical activities:

1. L = {walk, run, hop, skip, . . . , gallop} can indicate "Locomotion is the set of movement patterns that includes walk, run, . . . , gallop."
2. M = {throw, catch, kick, . . . , strike} can be used to indicate "Manipulation is the set of movement patterns that includes throw, catch, kick, . . . , strike."
3. Throw   M can be read as "Throwing is a subset of manipulation."
4. Strike ⊓ L means that striking is not an element of locomotion.
5. Left, right, up, down, forward, backward $\in$ D means that left, right, up, down, forward, and backward are elements of direction.
6. F ⊓ pathway can be read as "Moving forward is not an element of pathway."

Pose movement problems to children, and get them to write their own mathematical sentences to symbolize their solutions. Then have them write a mathematical sentence and perform the solution. Examples are {hop} = transfer of weight from one foot to the same foot; {walk} = transfer of weight from one foot to the other foot; skip = {walk, hop, walk, hop, . . . } (figure 4.21).

Sets represent a collection of objects or a group of ideas. A subset is a part of a set. Union and intersection are set operations. Venn diagrams are often used to symbolize

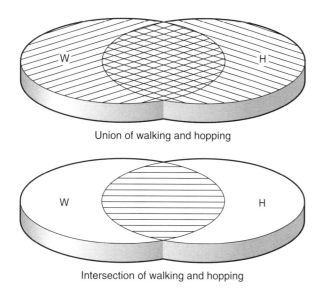

Union of walking and hopping

Intersection of walking and hopping

Figure 4.21   Venn diagrams illustrate the union and intersection of walking and hopping patterns.

operations with sets. In physical education, sets can be used to codify movements of the body. They can also be used in conjunction with mathematical sentences to describe movement sequences.

■ Use sets to group children. Group children by sex, month of birthday, hair color, color of eyes, age (6, 7, 8, . . . , 25). The set of children 25 years old is a null set because there are no children that old.

■ Have the children form a set of body shapes including subsets such as upright, inverted, symmetrical, asymmetrical, low-level, medium-level, and high-level shapes. The concept of shapes during balancing could be thought of as a universal set. Each separate set could be a subset. The union of all possible subsets would include all possible balance positions. An example of the intersection of sets is symmetrical balances at a low level (e.g., front support, back support) as in figure 4.22.

■ Equivalent sets are sets with the same number of elements in them. If you divided a class into groups or subsets of three, you could have each subset perform a separate locomotor skill. The subsets are equivalent because they have the same number of children doing each skill.

■ Have the class begin by performing the set of walking patterns. Practice a variety of ways to walk: fast, slow, long steps, short steps, forward, backward, and so on. Do the same with hopping. Next, do both walking and hopping patterns as a union of sets. Again practice a variety of combinations of walking and hopping. Examples of solutions are walking fast, hopping slow; short walking steps, long hops; walking forward, hopping sideways; and eight walks, four hops. Each could be thought of as a union of different subsets of walking and hopping. Specific subsets you might want the children to try are skipping (step, hop, step, hop, . . .) and schottische dance steps (step, step,

Figure 4.22   Children demonstrate a set of low-level body positions.

step, hop, step, step, step, hop, . . .), which one can think of as the intersection of walking and hopping.

 ▪ Verbally give children directions using mathematical sentences and set terminology. For instance, balance = {high level, symmetrical}. The children should be able to interpret this sentence by practicing many balances at a high level and then many symmetrical balances. Using the intersection of the two subsets, they could practice high-level, symmetrical balances. Other examples are skip = {time, direction} and throw = {distance, force}.

 ▪ Have the children think of their own sets of locomotor or nonlocomotor movements using appropriate terminology, perform the actions, and then write their movement sets using set notation. For instance, one child as a group leader could direct others in his or her group to "run fast while moving in a forward direction." Another might say, "Balance in a twisted shape at a medium level." Descriptions might be written as {moving fast, using a forward direction} $\in$ run or balancing = {twisted shape, medium level}.

Ongoing Strategies for the Physical Education Classroom

 ▪ Organize activity groups by having students count off in twos, threes, or fives. Students can practice multiplication facts and see the math in action.

 ▪ Write numbers on equipment, task cards, stations.

 ▪ Use fractions for describing any skill that involves turning. For example, use fractional terms when describing how to pivot in basketball or during a line dance when students make a quarter turn to the right or left.

 ▪ Ask students to estimate and measure distance, height, or time when you are teaching throwing skills or during running and jumping activities. "Estimate how far you are from your partner while using an overhand throw. . . . How many steps is it from where you are now in the gym to the door?"

 ▪ Keep score during games and practice activities. Students apply addition and subtraction skills frequently when keeping score.

 ▪ While students are listening to directions or forming squads, you can ask the class or groups to sit in a geometric shape (e.g., circle, square, triangle).

Summary

Mathematical concepts taught to children at the elementary level fall into the categories of numbers, measurement, geometry, patterns and functions, probability and statistics, logic, and algebra. We have experimented in our classes with different ways to integrate these concepts in movement settings using different models of interdisciplinary programming. We have always tried to stay true to the principles of maintaining the integrity of each discipline and teaching active lessons. In this chapter we have presented both complete learning experiences and short vignettes of additional learning experiences for you to share with your students.

Try our ideas. Some will work for you. Some may not. Some you may have to modify. Share your ideas with other teachers both in the classroom and in physical education. Try your own new ideas of ways to integrate mathematics with movement concepts. Make mathematics fun and challenging through practical applications in movement.

Integrating Physical Education With Science

During a kindergarten lesson called "Cloud Dance," we lay down and looked up at the sky to notice cloud shapes. We saw alligators, dinosaurs, feathers, trees, and so on. Then we made our bodies into different cloud shapes. We were puffy, fat clouds, long, narrow clouds—all types of clouds. We changed into our cloud shapes slowly and quickly. We traveled across the sky in our cloud shapes to soft, slow, and calm music, then stormy and energetic music. We made up a short sequence in which we started out with one cloud shape, slowly changed into another cloud shape, and quickly changed into a third cloud shape, then traveled across the sky and linked up with another cloud and traveled with it across the sky. At the end of the lesson, the children formed their line at the door by moving in their favorite cloud shape. One child was heard to say "Aww! Do we have to leave now? This is too much fun!"

Bill Nye, the "Science Guy," has a TV program on PBS about science each weekday. He lives by two mottoes. One is, "Science rules!" The other is that science should be fun. One day he might mix some simple chemicals together (water, glue, and Borax) to make "Sticky Icky." You can stretch it, wad it like a ball and bounce it, or use a drinking straw to blow a bubble with a small portion of it to make a balloon to tap into the air. Another day he might get caught in a giant web, like prey caught by a spider. Another TV personality, Slim Goodbody, helps elementary children learn about good nutrition and healthy ways to exercise. Both find very creative ways to capture young children's interest in science, often through active involvement in projects.

Efforts at integrating science with other subject areas, particularly mathematics, are numerous. Research studies as well as practical examples integrating science with other disciplines date back to the 1960s. Werner (1971) conducted a research study integrating selected physical science concepts with physical education in the upper elementary grades. Results indicated a positive learning effect for the experimental group that experienced the integration of science concepts with practical movement experiences. While additional research support concerning the integration of movement with science is scarce, a number of authors (Boorman, 1973; Bucek, 1992; Clements and Osteen, 1995; Gilbert, 1977, 1992; Joyce, 1994; Pica, 1995; Werner and Burton, 1979; Werner, 1996; Cone and Cone, 2005) have continued to pursue efforts at integrating science with physical education and dance in practical settings (figure 5.1). In each instance these attempts at interdisciplinary work with children were pursued because they made the learning environment meaningful and showed positive learning effects in children.

Because of the technological age and culture in which we live, children in the elementary schools must have a variety of meaningful science experiences that lead them to an understanding of the world around them. Leading science educators have constructed a framework for science education (South Carolina Department of Education, 1995) that includes the nature and philosophy, process skills, and knowledge of science. *National Science Education Standards* (National Research Council, 1996) defines what students should know and be able to do at specific grade levels.

Students engaged in the nature and philosophy of science develop attitudes and ways of thinking and looking at the world that reflect an appreciation for what science is. Attributes of science commonly described include intellectual honesty, continuous inquiry, tolerance of ambiguity, openness to new ideas, curiosity, reflection, ability

Figure 5.1   Children learn what happens when they see a little oil in a pond, then create an environmental dance about pollution and environmental balance.

to make informed decisions, communication and sharing, and being empowered to participate. Because of these attributes it is thought that science should be learned in the following ways: (1) becoming actively involved in hands-on experiments; (2) doing problem-solving activities designed to facilitate learning as a result of inquiry; (3) relating instructional experiences to everyday life; (4) engaging in a sequence of activities proceeding from concrete to abstract; (5) making connections to other disciplines and from grade to grade; (6) working with others; (7) making effective use of technology; and (8) talking, writing, and communicating.

While not all scientists approach their subject in the same way, Gega (1994b) and other science educators agree that certain steps or processes are fundamental and are invariably employed by scientists at one time or another: Observing, classifying, measuring, inferring, predicting, communicating, and experimenting are the process skills of science. To help children learn to become scientists and maintain enthusiasm for the scientific process, it is important to engage them in each of these steps through practical, hands-on experiences rather than the learning of science theory in a textbook.

The knowledge of science is divided into content areas. These areas include life or biological sciences, earth and space sciences, and the physical sciences. Topics in each of the sciences are more fully developed in later sections of this chapter.

Scope and Sequence for Science

Science experiences through physical education are numerous. The application of science to physical education is almost unlimited. Classroom teachers and physical education specialists often overlook these possibilities. Most classroom teachers are interested in using physical education in every situation in which it would help to broaden the pupils' experiences in school. This desire has been frustrated, however, owing to difficulty in obtaining the necessary material or the lack of a ready-made source of ideas that integrate science with other disciplines.

If children are to have learning experiences that relate science concepts with physical education, teachers should be aware of problems and everyday occurrences that are of real concern to children in their daily lives. While we were developing materials for this chapter, our main concerns were collecting a variety of ideas for science lessons to include in one source and making these lesson ideas as practical as possible. We reviewed several science textbook series, projects of leading science organizations such as the American Association for the Advancement of Science, and methods textbooks (Gega, 1994a) on teaching elementary school science. We found that science concepts were based on and taught through units in the biological and life sciences, earth and space sciences, and physical sciences (table 5.1).

Table 5.1

Scope and Sequence of Science Concepts Taught in Elementary Schools

CONCEPT	GRADE						
Biological life sciences	K	1	2	3	4	5	6
Your body	✘						
How living things help you	✘						
What plants and animals need		✘					
Your senses		✘					
Growing seeds			✘				
Foods and you			✘				
Your bones and muscles				✘			
The ways of plants and animals				✘			
Your body and nutrition					✘		
The world of animals					✘		
Transport systems of the body						✘	
The plant kingdom						✘	
The world of small living things						✘	
Control systems of the body							✘
Life cycles and new generations							✘

CONCEPT	GRADE						
Earth and space sciences	K	1	2	3	4	5	6
Explaining time	✖						
Our home, the earth		✖					
Investigating air and water		✖	✖				
Weather			✖		✖		
The environment			✖				
Earth, moon, and sky				✖			
The changing earth					✖		
Conserving the earth's resources						✖	
The earth's crust							✖
Space: the new frontier							✖
Exploring climate							✖
Physical sciences							
Observing things	✖						
Changing things	✖						
Where things belong		✖					
Things on the move		✖					
Forces in action			✖				
Measuring all around you			✖				
Exploring matter and changes in matter				✖		✖	
Heating changes				✖		✖	
Electricity and magnetism					✖		
Energy					✖		✖
Force, motion, and machines						✖	
The structure of matter							✖

PRIMARY-GRADE SCIENCE SKILLS AND CONCEPTS

During the primary grades, the major concepts taught within the biological or life sciences include the body, the senses, bones and muscles, how living things help people, what plants and animals need, growing seeds, foods, and the ways of plants and animals. While studying earth and space sciences, children learn about time; the earth; air and water; weather; the environment; and the moon, sky, and celestial bodies. While studying the physical sciences at the primary level, children learn how to observe things, how things change, where things belong, how things move and also about forces in action, measuring, exploring matter and changes in matter, and heating changes.

INTERMEDIATE-GRADE SCIENCE SKILLS AND CONCEPTS

At the intermediate level, the major concepts taught within the biological or life sciences include the body and nutrition, the world of animals, transport systems of the body, the plant kingdom, the world of small living things, control systems of the body, and life cycles and new generations. In the earth and space sciences, children learn about weather, the changing earth, conservation of the earth's resources, the earth's crust, space exploration, and climate. Topics in the physical sciences at this level include matter and changes in matter; heating changes; electricity and magnetism; energy; force, motion, and machines; and the structure of matter.

Learning Experiences

This chapter presents five complete learning experiences (table 5.2). They demonstrate two of the interdisciplinary teaching models presented in chapter 1. The learning experiences have been designed to include skills and concepts from physical education and science. For each learning experience we include a name, suggested grade level, the interdisciplinary teaching model, objectives, equipment, organization, a complete description of the lesson, and assessment suggestions. In addition, we offer tips on what to look for in student responses, suggest how you can change or modify the lesson, and present ideas for teachable moments to provide further insights into each learning experience.

Table 5.2

Science Learning Experiences Index

Skills and concepts	Name	Suggested grade level	Interdisciplinary teaching model
Science: biological sciences—identifying body parts, major muscles, bones Physical education: balancing	The Hip Bone Is Connected to the Thigh Bone	2-3	Shared
Science: physical sciences—simple machines Physical education: lifting, pulling, pushing, rolling, throwing, striking, kicking	The Simple Things in Life	2-3	Shared
Science: flower and plant identification Physical education: body shapes, movement sequences	April Showers Bring May Flowers	3-5	Partnership
Science: biological sciences—transport systems Physical education: fitness—cardiorespiratory running, jumping, skipping	Rainbow Run	3-5	Shared
Science: earth sciences—weather patterns, cloud formations, wind Physical education: body shapes, time, force, and space concepts	Weather or Not	4-5	Partnership

The Hip Bone Is Connected to the Thigh Bone

Suggested Grade Level

Primary (2 and 3)

Interdisciplinary Teaching Model

Shared

The purpose of this lesson is to integrate the children's growing awareness of their body, when learning about the musculoskeletal system in science, with how their body parts function in a movement setting.

Science

Biological sciences—identifying body parts, major muscles, bones

Physical Education

Balancing

Objectives

As a result of participating in this learning experience, children will improve their abilities to

- balance on a variety of large and small body parts using good form;
- create balances on the floor and completely or partially on small apparatus;
- develop a simple balance sequence—balance–weight transfer–balance; and
- name parts of the body on which they balance and the muscle groups, bones, and joints that support them (figure 5.2).

Equipment

Although this lesson could be taught on the floor, it is best to use gymnastics mats, floor exercise mats, or wrestling mats. Pieces of small apparatus such as benches, or cardboard boxes filled with newspaper, should be scattered around with enough space between them to permit freedom of movement. If this lesson is to be taught outside, a large parachute could be spread out on the grass to protect the children's clothing.

Organization

Children work individually in scattered formation or with partners, depending on the number of mats and pieces of apparatus available.

Description

"Good morning. As you come in, have a seat in front of me on the floor. What body parts are touching the floor as you are seated? Tom?" (Seat, bottom, rump.) "Any other body parts? Theresa?" (Hands, feet, thighs, shins.) "Right. I see many of you in different body positions as you are seated. Well, I've been talking to Mr. LeGrand, and I've found out that in science you're learning about your bodies: your muscles and bones. In our gymnastics lesson today we'll try to use that information by giving scientific names to the body parts we balance on as we build a sequence.

"Can anyone remember the name for your seat or bottom? Lauren? [Gluteus maximus.] Well done. And the bones connecting at the hip joint (hip bone) are called the ilium, ischium, pubis, and femur (our long leg bone). We've also said that some of you

Figure 5.2   Children balance on their *(a)* abdominal muscles, *(b)* gluteus maximus, *(c)* femur, and *(d)* metacarpals.

are seated with your hands (carpal, metacarpal, and phalange bones), feet (calcaneus, tarsal, and metatarsal bones), thighs (femur bone and quadriceps muscle), or shins (tibia and fibula bones) touching the floor. When I say 'go,' we are going to get out of our seated position and spread out on the mats. There is enough space, so I don't want any more than two people to a mat. Go. . . . Stop.

"Everyone sit in a long, seated position with an erect posture. Your seat (gluteus), hamstrings, calves (gastrocnemius), and heels (calcaneus) should be in contact with the floor. Point your toes away from you. Bend over and reach with your arms toward your toes. Hold the position for 15 seconds. Sit up straight again. Straddle your legs, reach first toward your left leg and hold it for 15 seconds, then reach toward your right leg and hold it for 15 seconds. Sit back up straight and bring your legs together. Put your palms (metacarpals) on the floor beside your hips and press up into a back support position. Make your body straight as a board and feel the tightness in your tummy (abdominal muscles) and seat (gluteus). Lean onto one hand with weight also on your feet and rotate your other hand over your head until you are in a front support position (push-up position)."

▶ Continue with more stretching exercises until the children are warmed up. During each exercise, mention as many muscles and bones that are being used as you think will be helpful to the children.

"Good warm-up. You sure are learning the names of many of your bones and muscles. We'll continue class now by balancing in different ways. First we'll try many ways to balance right on the floor. Then we'll try some balances on the equipment. Finally, we'll select three balances and develop a short sequence. When you do your sequence, I'll give you a worksheet so that you can name the body parts (bones and muscles) you balance on for each of the three balances. When I say 'go,' show me one way to balance. Perhaps think of balancing on large or small body parts. Go. That's it, Jamaal. You're balancing on a forearm (radius and ulna bones) and your whole thigh (femur and quadriceps). Great, Keshia. You're balancing on four small body parts. Two hands and two feet, abdomen toward the ceiling, in a back-bend position. Way to go, Carol. An elbow and two knees (patella). Ian, that is an interesting way to balance—on your seat (gluteus) in a *V* shape. That makes you use your abdominal muscles. Each time you hear me give a signal (clap or drumbeat), I want you to change your balance into a new position. [Signal . . . signal. . . .] Stop. You are working hard, but I want to point two things out.

"First, I want you to use good principles of balance when you try things. What that means is that all of your support positions should be strong. If you are balancing on your hands, your elbows or shoulders should be directly above. Use good vertical alignment. Same with your legs: hips or knees above your feet. I also want to see firm muscles—no sagging bodies. The second thing that I want to see is a real commitment to a chosen shape. What that means is that if a particular body part is straight or stretched, I want to see extension out through the end. If your intent is to create a rounded surface, I want to see a curved shape. Also think of where your head is and where you are looking to make a complete body shape.

"Let's try some more balances. We'll hold each balance for 5 seconds before you hear the signal to try a new balance. Ready, [signal]. . . . That's it. I see much better quality in your shapes. . . . Stop.

"Next, we'll use the boxes or benches I have placed at each workstation to balance on. I would like to show you two different ways of balancing that I would like you to consider. First, you can balance on the equipment by placing part of your body on the equipment and part on the floor. I'll show you what I mean. I can put my two forearms (radius and ulna) on the floor and my two shinbones (tibia) on the bench or box. [Demonstrate.] Or I could put my two hands (metacarpals) on the floor and my two calf muscles (gastrocnemius) on the box or bench with my body straight and abdomen facing the ceiling. [Demonstrate.]

"The second style of balancing on the equipment that we will work on is to balance with our whole body on the equipment. For example, I can sit in a *V*-seat on my gluteus muscles and lean back on my hands. [Demonstrate.] When I say 'go,' I want you to try several ways to balance with your whole body on the equipment. Remember, I want good strong balances, and I want you to hold each balance for 5 seconds. Go. . . . Stop.

"Next, you can choose either a partial or complete balance on the equipment. I want you to work on your own without a signal and to try at least five different balances. Hold each one for 5 seconds. Make sure that you do each balance well, using the principles we've already talked about. Go. . . . Good work, Ian. I see you balancing completely on the bench in a shoulder stand. You have achieved a good balance by vertically aligning your hips, knees, and ankles over your base. That's it, Suzi. Good partial balance on the box. Your body is straight as a board with your left forearm (radius and ulna) on the box and your left foot (metatarsals) on the floor. Your side is facing the ceiling. . . . Stop.

"Everyone come gather around this mat. For our final activity we are going to develop a short sequence. Your sequence will consist of three balances linked by transition moves such as roll, swivels, steps, or twisting actions. Your sequence may be on the mat only or on the equipment and the mat. As you develop your sequence, I want you to use this special worksheet I have. [Distribute handout; see example in figure 5.3.] I want you to draw a stick figure of each of your three balance positions, label the body parts (bones and muscles) that support your balances, and identify your two transition moves with word cues. Look at my example on the worksheet as I demonstrate, then you can get to work. First, I'm in a *V*-seat on the bench. I'm balancing on my gluteus maximus, leaning back on my hands. Then, I use a swivel move to my second balance, which has my stomach (abdomen) on the bench and my hands (metacarpals) on the floor. Finally, I do a forward-roll transition move to two feet (metatarsals and calcaneus bones) and immediately stand in an erect *Y* position with my arms stretched diagonally toward the ceiling. Does everyone understand how to do the sequence? How many balances are required? [Three.] Do you have to do your sequence on the equipment? [No.] How many transition moves are there? [Two.] What do you have to write on your worksheet? [Draw each of the three balances. Name the body parts, muscles, and bones we balance on for each balance. Describe the transition moves.] You're ready to go, then. Work hard. I'll come around and help or make suggestions. Go. [Allow several minutes for students to work.] Stop. I can see that you're making progress. Make sure your first balance is held with stillness, as if to say, 'Watch me, I'm going to begin.' Then start your sequence using good, smooth, flowing transitions, and end your sequence with another balance with stillness, as if to say, 'I'm finished now.' Also make sure you begin drawing your three balances and write out the names of the body parts you balance on. Get back to work. . . . Stop.

"What I want you to do now is get with a partner who has not seen your sequence. Take turns sharing your sequence and your worksheet. The observing partners watch the sequence and give help when needed on the worksheet to identify body parts, bones, and muscles used as supports in each balance. Use as many scientific names as you can so we can show Mr. LeGrand how smart you are. If you are not sure of the name of a body part, bone, or muscle, ask me or look at this big musculoskeletal chart I have hung here on the wall. We want to make sure we're scientifically accurate. Go. . . . Stop.

"It is time to leave now. Let me collect your worksheets. I want to share them with Mr. LeGrand so he knows we are learning about how our bodies work in physical education. Good-bye for now."

Assessment Suggestion

Give each child a chart of the musculoskeletal system. Have the children identify or label selected bones or muscles. Or, at the end of class, balance in one to three poses, and have the children identify, name, or label the specific body parts, bones, or muscles on which you are balancing.

Look For

- Some children may have trouble deciding on balances to perform. You can provide a series of pictures of possible balances (see Werner, 2004). Other children may want to copy a friend's balances. That is okay at first, but gradually stress and place value on unique balances, using original ideas, and working within one's own abilities.

- Stress quality balances using good principles of support. Children should balance from positions of strength. There should be no weak, sagging bodies.

- During sequence work, watch for three good balances with smooth transition moves.

- Emphasize the quality of written work on the worksheets. Drawing may vary from full-body pictures to stick figures. The key is using accurate names for body parts, bones, and muscles because the focus of the lesson is on integration with life sciences (anatomy).

Name: _____

Example

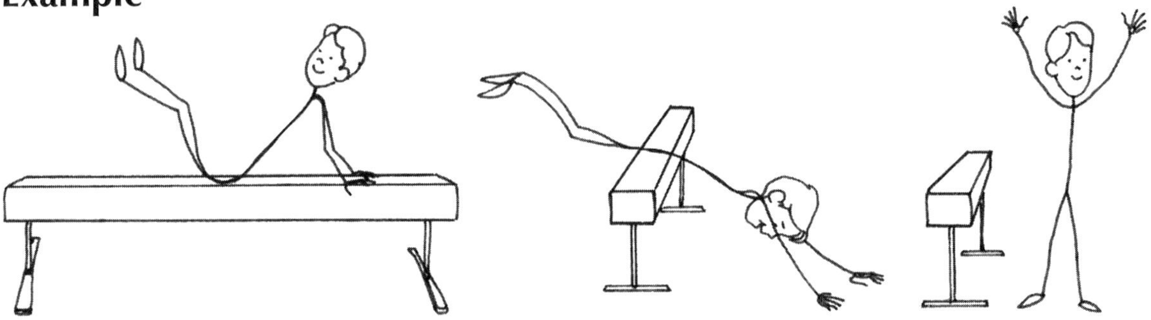

Balance 1: *V*-seat on bench

Transition cues: Gluteus maximus and hands

Balance 2: Log position

Transition cues: Swivel with a 1/2-turn weight transfer onto abdomen abdomen on bench; hands on floor

Balance 3: *Y*-stand

Transition cues: Forward roll chin to chest; grab shins; stand (return to feet) arms symmetrically out and up; stand on metatarsals, calcaneus

Your Sequence

Draw three pictures of your balances on or off equipment. Identify the body parts on which you balance (bones, muscles). Use cue words to describe your transition moves (weight transfer).

Balance 1: _____

Transition cues _____

_____

_____

_____

Balance 2: _____

Transition cues _____

_____

_____

_____

Balance 3: _____

Transition cues _____

_____

_____

_____

Figure 5.3 Balance sequence worksheet.

How Can I Change This?

- Children can develop a partner balance sequence and use the same worksheet to identify the body parts, bones, and muscles used for support.
- Provide a worksheet, and have the children identify muscle groups that are flexed and stretched during warm-up. Have them identify bones and joints that are moved by the muscles during specific exercises such as jumping jacks, bent-knee sit-ups, or push-ups.
- Have the children identify body parts, bones, muscles, and joints used in various sport actions such as throwing, kicking, catching, and striking.
- Develop a short aerobics routine or a set of light weightlifting exercises that work selected muscle groups. Do the routine or exercises with the children, and identify the muscles, bones, joints, and body parts involved with each.

Teachable Moments

- Collect action pictures of athletes in various sport, game, dance, and gymnastics settings. Have the children analyze selected pictures and attempt to identify the body parts, bones, muscles, and joints used in a given skill.
- Collect action pictures of people at work in everyday life (e.g., truck drivers, computer operators, assembly-line workers, firefighters). Have children analyze selected pictures and attempt to identify the body parts, bones, muscles, and joints used in a given work task.
- Have children analyze pictures of buildings, bridges, and other structures for strong foundations and principles of balance. Compare the concepts of strong foundations and principles of balance used in construction with those used in building efficient body balances.

The Simple Things in Life

Suggested Grade Level

Primary (2 and 3)

Interdisciplinary Teaching Model

Shared

As children learn about simple machines in science, you and the classroom teacher can coordinate efforts to help children understand how machines assist people to do work and understand that the human body uses primarily third-class leverage systems to perform most manipulative tasks. Third-class levers offer increased speed and range of motion but require a lot of force production to do work.

Science

Physical sciences—simple machines

Physical Education

Lifting, pulling, pushing, rolling, throwing, striking, kicking

Objectives

As a result of participating in this learning experience, children will improve their ability to

- lift, push, and pull objects while using the body in an efficient manner;
- throw, strike, kick, and perform other manipulative actions while using the body in an efficient manner;
- use simple machines such as an inclined plane, lever, wedge, screw, and pulley to do work;
- understand the differences among first-class, second-class, and third-class levers; and
- learn that the human body uses mainly third-class levers to perform manipulative actions.

Equipment

A seesaw or teeter-totter (2-inch × 100-inch × 12-foot [5-centimeter × 2.5-meter × 3.5-meter] board and cement block); a slide; a horizontal bar with a single or double pulley system attached; a wheelbarrow or dolly; can openers (electric and church key); a scale; a nutcracker; scissors; a wedge mat (inclined plane); and five balls each for kicking, throwing, and striking

Organization

This lesson is designed to be conducted at several different stations outside, on or near the playground. Children work together in small groups and rotate to each station.

Description

"Hello. Today we are going to talk about and do some experiments with machines. We'll also talk about how our body is a machine and performs work. See what I've got here? Yes, it's a can opener. Before we had electric can openers like this one, we opened all of our can lids and even soft drink cans with hand-operated, or manual, can openers. Does anyone know what kind of machine this manual can opener might be? Any guesses? It is a lever. A lever has a resistance arm, a force arm, and a fulcrum. In fact, this is a first-class lever. The resistance is the top of the can. The fulcrum is the edge of the can where the opener hooks around the edge. The force comes from our hand out at the end of the opener (first class = resistance, fulcrum, force). [Demonstrate opening a can with the manual opener.] Did you know that when we cut paper with scissors, we are also using a first-class lever? [Demonstrate cutting paper with scissors, and point out the resistance, fulcrum, and force.]

"Do you know what this is? [It's a nutcracker.] Good, Sara. Watch. I have some nuts here. No matter how hard I squeeze with my hand, I cannot open the shell. And yet if I put a shell in the nutcracker, the force of my hand can easily open the nut. That is another example of a simple machine at work. A nutcracker is an example of another type of lever. It is called a second-class lever. The fulcrum is at the closed end of the cracker. The nut (resistance) is in the middle, and the hand (force) is out at the end of the handle (second class = fulcrum, resistance, force).

"I know you have been studying about machines in science. Can anyone tell me the names of some other simple machines besides a lever? [Wedge.] You're right, Billie. Can anyone think of an example of when a wedge is used? [A knife cutting butter, an ax splitting wood.] What about other machines? [Pulley, screw, inclined plane.] Can anyone think of where pulleys are used? [Sailboat, elevator, auto shop to lift an engine out of a car.] Examples of where screws are used? [Meat grinder, cement mixer.] Inclined planes? [Escalator, ramp in a parking garage, slide on a playground.]

"You already know a lot about machines. Today in physical education we are going to do some experiments about how we use simple machines to do work and how our own bodies work as machines when we do sport activities. What we are going to do is divide our class into five cooperative groups and then rotate to each of five stations that I have set up. While at each station you will perform each of the tasks and answer the questions on the worksheets provided. At the end of class we will all get back together to talk about what we have learned about machines."

▷ Escort the children to each station, and briefly explain the activity at each station. Then divide the children into five groups by name—for instance, pulley, lever, wedge, and so on—and at a signal have them begin. After 5 to 7 minutes at each station, rotate groups until all the children have visited each station.

Station 1

Equipment: a dolly or wheelbarrow, two or three cases of paper or food from the cafeteria

Activity: Have the children try to lift the heavy boxes in pairs. (Teach them how to lift properly using straight backs and the large muscles of the legs.) Then have them put two or three boxes on the dolly or wheelbarrow and not only lift the boxes but also move them a distance and back as an example of transporting a load (figure 5.4).

Worksheet questions:

▪ What type of machine is being used? (Lever, second class.)
▪ Where is the fulcrum? (Axis of the wheel.)
▪ Where is the resistance? (Boxes on the dolly.)
▪ Where is the force? (Lifting out at the end of the handles of the dolly.)
▪ Is it easier or harder to carry these boxes using the machine?
▪ Diagram the lever in the space provided.
▪ Where have you seen this type of machine being used? (Grocery carryout, bellhop in hotel, porter at airport, bricklayer carrying bricks or mortar.)

Figure 5.4 Wheelbarrows or dollies help transport heavy loads.

Station 2

Equipment: a seesaw or board-and-block teeter-totter, two or three cases of food or paper

Activity: Have the children put the heavy load on one end of the seesaw with the fulcrum exactly in the middle. Have them try to lift the load. Because the distance of the resistance to the fulcrum *(RA)* equals that of the force *(FA)*, their lifting force *(F)* equals the weight of the boxes *(R)*: $F \times FA = R \times RA$. Next, have them shift the fulcrum so that it is only 1 or 2 feet (0.3-0.6 meters) from the load. Then have one child show how the heavy load can be lifted by just one person (figure 5.5).

Worksheet questions:

▪ What type of machine is being used? (Lever, first class.)
▪ Where is the fulcrum? (Cement block.)
▪ Where is the resistance? (Cases of food.)
▪ Where is the force? (Child lifting at the end of the board.)

Figure 5.5   The farther away from the fulcrum a force is applied, the easier it is to lift the box.

- Diagram the lever in the space provided.
- How can you make it possible for just one person to lift a very heavy load? (Shift the location of the fulcrum so that you have a short resistance arm and a long force arm.)
- Where have you seen this type of machine being used? (Crowbar, scissors, can opener, tire iron to put tires on rims of wheels, lifting with a shovel.)

Station 3

Equipment: A slide and a gymnastics wedge mat, a case of food or paper, a piece of rope 20 feet (6 meters) long, and a spring scale. If you don't have a wedge mat, a hill or mound on the school playground or an inclined plane made from gymnastics benches would work great.

Activity: Weigh the case of food or paper. Then attach a rope to the box, attach the spring scale to the rope, and place the box at the bottom of the slide. Pull the box up the slide and see how many pounds of force are needed to make the box move. Have the children slide down the slide or roll down the mat or hill (using a forward, backward, or log roll), then do a roll on level ground.

Worksheet questions:

- How heavy was the box? _____ pounds.
- How much force did it take to make the box move up the inclined plane? _____ pounds.
- Is that force more or less than the weight of the box?
- In which roll that you did, down an inclined plane and then on level ground, did you move faster or more easily? (Inclined plane.)
- Why? (An inclined plane helps to work with gravity to overcome friction and resistance.)
- Inclined planes help do work

  a. only going uphill (box up slide).

  b. only going downhill (down the slide or hill).

  c. both up and down.
- Name some inclined planes in everyday life. (Escalator, stairs, trough on cement truck, parking ramp, grain elevator.)

Station 4

Equipment: horizontal ladder or chin-up bar, a case of food or paper, a piece of rope 20 feet (6 meters) long, one or two pulleys, and a spring scale

Activity: Weigh the case of canned goods from the cafeteria. Attach a rope to the box through the pulley system. Attach the spring scale to the rope. Pull down on the rope to lift the box. Using the scale, see how many pounds of force are needed to lift the box with a one-pulley system and a two-pulley system.

Worksheet questions:

- How heavy was the box? _____ pounds.
- How much force did it take to lift the box with one pulley? _____ pounds. Two pulleys? _____ pounds.
- As you add more pulleys, does it take more or less force to lift an object?
- Name some examples of pulleys that are used in everyday life. (Elevator, block and tackle to lift a car engine, boom vang and mainsheet on a sailboat, building crane.)

Station 5

Equipment: balls; bats; batting tees; open area to throw, strike, and kick; tape measure

Activity: Throw five times, and measure the farthest throw. Punt or kick a ball off the ground into the air as far as you can five times. Measure the farthest kick. Bat five balls off a tee, and hit them as far as you can. Measure the farthest batting attempt.

Worksheet questions:

- What kind of machine is your body when you do these sport skills? (Lever.)
- What class of lever is your body under these conditions? (Third class: fulcrum, force, resistance.)

- Where is the fulcrum? (Body joint—shoulder, hip.)
- Where is the force? (Muscles.)
- Where is the resistance? (Ball out at the end.)
- Diagram the lever in the space provided.
- Rank your skills in order of distance. Shortest _____ , middle _____ , farthest _____
- Why do you suppose you can kick and bat farther than you can throw? (Longer force arm, mechanical advantage, bigger and stronger muscles used.)

"Okay, stop. Everyone come over here by the board and sit down. Who can tell me the names of the machines we used in class today? Yes, Keshia. [Lever, pulley, inclined plane.] Great. Can anyone remember how many classes of levers there are? [Three.] What is a first-class lever like? Ronald. Yes—the fulcrum is in the middle. How does it help you? [You can lift something really heavy if you have a long force arm, like a crowbar.] When do we use our bodies as third-class levers? [When we throw, kick, and strike balls.] I can see you are learning a lot about machines, and as time goes on we'll see more and more examples of how we use our bodies as machines. Bye for now."

Assessment Suggestion

The worksheets used at the stations provide adequate assessment of the children's knowledge of simple machines and the application of that knowledge in movement settings.

Look For

- Children should be taught to lift heavy objects properly. Rather than bending over and lifting with the arms, children should bend at the knees, keeping the back vertically aligned and the center of mass of the object close to their own center of gravity. They should lift with the strong muscles of the legs.
- Children should stay on task, work together, and all contribute answers on the worksheets. In a cooperative learning experience, no one child should dominate.
- Monitor answers on the worksheets. Make sure that children understand the problems being solved and that they can transfer knowledge to examples of machines in everyday life.

How Can I Change This?

- For a simpler lesson, require children to identify only the major category of machine being used at each station. Have them work individually and write their answers on a note card.
- If you don't have all the equipment (scales, dollies, inclined mats, etc.), focus the lesson on levers used in the human body. Emphasize that the body uses mainly a third-class leverage system (figure 5.6) to manipulate objects. Third-class levers offer speed and range of motion (mechanical advantage), but the body has to use a lot of energy to produce force, so it is not a very efficient machine.
- At a higher level, help the children calculate the mechanical advantage gained as a lever arm (hand, paddle, racket, baseball bat) is extended from 1 to 2 to 3 feet (0.3 to 0.6 to 0.9 meters).
- Use the formula $R \times RA = F \times FA$ to calculate answers to problems on leverage. Use the known weights of the boxes and the approximate lengths of the resistance or force arms.

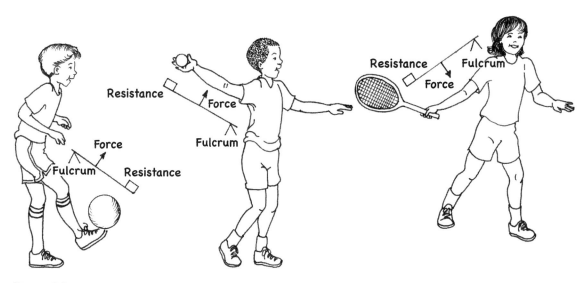

Figure 5.6 The body uses mainly a third-class leverage system in throwing and striking objects.

Teachable Moments

■ Bring in pictures from magazines to show different types of machines being used. Have the children bring in their own pictures of different types of machines, and make a collage on the bulletin board.

■ Encourage children to find pictures of people doing physical work (chopping wood, using a wheelbarrow, turning a screwdriver, pouring cement, throwing a ball, batting a ball, etc.), and create a small booklet that categorizes work by type of machine: class of lever, pulley, inclined plane, wedge, or screw.

April Showers Bring May Flowers

Suggested Grade Level

Intermediate (3 through 5)

Interdisciplinary Teaching Model

Partnership

Students learning about the identification of different types of flowers and plants can use this learning experience to develop creative movement sequences based on body shape and time–force concepts.

Science

Biological sciences—flower and plant identification

Physical Education, Dance

Developing a movement sequence based on body shape and moving to a selected piece of music that features short pauses and time and force fluctuations—AB pattern

Objectives

As a result of participating in this learning experience, children will improve their ability to

- identify, name, and state different qualities of a minimum of five flowers;
- demonstrate a variety of body poses that contrast in shape and size in relation to flower shapes and sizes; and
- cooperatively work with a partner or small group to choreograph a movement sequence that includes held poses during moments of silence and appropriate loco-motor movements to an ABA theme.

Equipment

A fresh bouquet of flowers or pictures of different flowers are needed to show students that flowers come in different shapes, sizes, colors, and so on. In addition, a CD player and *Music for Creative Dance: Contrast and Continuum,* Volume II, Track 3, Checkerboard by Eric Chapelle will be needed to complete this dance experience.

Organization

Students will work alone to create individual shapes and do initial work with the ABA theme music. Then, they will work with a partner or small group to create a short movement sequence combining held poses in different shapes and contrasting locomotor actions based on the time, flow, and energy of the music. As you are teaching this experience, feel free to break it into two to four lessons depending on how far you get in any one lesson. Just remember to have children warm up and rehearse the previous lesson before moving on to new material.

Description

"Good morning, everyone. I have been talking to Ms. Jones about what you are learning in science class. She tells me that you are learning about flowers as you study biology. Can anyone tell me what our state flower is? Yes, Susan, it is the yellow jasmine for South Carolina. I used to live in the state of Wisconsin, and the violet is the state flower there. As you can tell, I am very interested in flowers as well, so Ms. Jones and I have decided to work together on our unit of study. In the classroom you will learn about how to identify and classify flowers, what makes flowers and plants grow, and what the technical parts of a flower are.

"In physical education–dance we are going to focus on the shapes of flowers and use that information to create a movement sequence. I have brought to class today a nice bouquet of cut flowers. As you look at the bouquet, what do you notice? Yes, Joseph. The flowers are different colors. Why, yes, Veronica, they also come in different sizes! Look closely at the petals. The petals have different shapes. Well, we too can create different poses with our bodies by varying our shape and size. That is where we will start our lesson today as we warm up. First, spread out and find a nice personal space. Think of one of the flowers you just saw. Does it have rounded petals or pointed ones? Show me a rounded shape with your body. Show me a pointed shape with your body. Change your level and create a rounded shape. A pointed shape.

"Gather in quickly. Now I am going to play some music. Before the music starts I want you to choose a shape and hold it still. When the music begins to play I want you to move to the texture of the music. Let's listen first. What are you hearing? Is the music fast or slow? How about loud or soft? What about smooth and flowing or percussive and jerky? Show me by moving your hands in self-space. Yes, I agree with you. I see your hands moving slowly, softly, smoothly.

"Let's spread out now. Show me your first flower shape pose. Hold it. When the music starts, move about the floor slowly, softly, smoothly. Begin. . . . Stop. That is a good start to our sequence, but we can make it better. The reason I say that is that you were all moving mostly forward in a straight line and you weren't using your whole body to respond to the music (mostly walking with the legs). Let's see if you can slide, pirouette, and use curved pathways. Use your arms and hands to change levels. Bend and extend at the knees and waist to change levels. As you move through space, keep the same emphasis on slow, soft, and smooth. Get into your flower shape to show me you are ready. When you hear the music, begin moving through space again. Yes! Wow! What improvement!

"Come in again and let's look more closely at the flowers. Does anyone know the name of this one? Yes, it is a rose. More specifically it is a Jefferson Rose. Oh-oh! Watch out! Its stem has thorns. Yikes! What about this flower? It is called a chrysanthemum. Some people call it a mum for short. This one is a daisy. Here is a daylily, and here's a daffodil. This is a tulip. Take a close look at the petals of all of them. Some are rounded. Some are pointed. Some flowers are small and dainty like this baby's breath. Others are bigger and more bold like this magnolia blossom. They are all so different.

"When I say 'go,' we are going back to work on our flower sequence. But we are going to add on now. You will pick a first flower shape. Then, you will move slowly, softly, smoothly to the music. When you hear the music stop, I want you to stop in a second flower shape. What I am going to look for, though, is for you to change your flower shape. Make it very different from your first shape. I want to see contrast. If you are small, delicate, and round in your first shape, then perhaps be big, bold, and pointed in your second shape. Let's see how many different flower shapes I can see in your bodies. Get up. Spread out. First flower shape. Hold it still. [Begin music.] Stop. Practice just this much of the sequence two or three times through. Self-shape, A, different self-shape. Stop. Gather in here close to the music again. Now I want you to listen to part B of the music."

▶ Play the CD.

"What do you notice about the music? Raise your hand. Yes, Michelle. It is faster, more energetic. We might think about this as the flower growing and getting nutrients from the soil. [If the classroom teacher is talking about plant parts and about nutrient exchange, you can liken this to xylem and phloem traveling up and down the plant stems. [Emphasize to the children that you expect their whole body to show the energy flow.] The flower is also getting energy from the sun and rain. It is getting larger and ready to blossom. Let's try to move to part B of the music. I expect to see more energy—some jumping, hopping, skipping. Use your arms and whole body to project this new energy. You are alive! Get up. Spread out. Show me that you are ready by getting into your second (different) flower pose."

▶ Play part B several times, allowing the students to experiment with their locomotor movement actions.

"Stop right where you are. Now, this is where it is going to get a little tricky. When I say 'go,' I want you to find a partner and want the partners to sit back to back. When everyone has a partner and is sitting, I will know that you are ready to listen. Go. You have 15 seconds . . . 5, 4, 3, 2, 1. Good, you did that quickly. We are going to continue building our sequence now. So far you have been working by yourself. But now you have a partner. Look where you and your partner are in the room. This is your partner space. First, we will practice making partner flower shapes. I want them to contrast with, yet complement, each other. Let me demonstrate with Shonda. I'm going to choose a twisted leg and trunk shape with my arms and elbows extended away from my body and rounded so that my hands and fingertips are close together. Shonda now has some choices as I want her shape to be different from mine but yet complement mine. We are the beginning of a bouquet of flowers. She could be beside, in front of, or in back of me. Her arms could be above or below me. She could be larger or smaller than me.

Her shape could be pointed, symmetrical, or asymmetrical. Shonda, choose a shape. Very nice. I think we have the beginnings of a great bouquet.

"Now I want everyone to try several partner flower shapes. Go. Pick the one you like best and remember it. Show it to me. . . . Stop. Sit down. Think of where you and your partner are right now. When I say 'go,' you are going to split away from your partner into self-space. I will play part B of the music, and you will move about with good energy. As part B is playing, each of you will gradually move back to your partner space and create your partner flower shape. It doesn't make any difference who gets to your partner place first; but when you arrive, stop and make your flower shape. When your partner arrives, he or she will get into the complementary shape. You know how long part B takes, so don't arrive too early and become still while the music still has a long time to play. Timing and arrival will be important to show good flow or continuity to our sequence. Okay. Let's practice. Stand and move away from your partner. Show me an individual flower shape to show me you are ready."

> ▶ Play part B only. Music stops; students are into their partner flower shapes. Take time to have students practice several times to allow each set of partners to get their arrival time down and their partner flower shapes memorized. (For the end of the sequence, they will also need to remember where in the room this partner flower shape occurs. Giving the children a piece of paper to draw their positions on may be a good idea: individual shape, lively part B music shape, partner flower shape.) "Good. Excellent work. Stop. Come gather around the music again.

"We will now add the next part to our sequence. I want you to listen to the music first. It has an ABA theme. So far we have heard and performed part A, then part B. After each part there is silence for several seconds when we make our still flower shapes. When the music returns, you will again hear part A. Let's listen. ABA. The second time through, the music is slow, soft, and smooth again. However, you are with a partner now. So this is what we are going to do. You will travel through space using slow, soft, smooth movements with your partner. One will lead and the other will follow. You choose who will lead and who will follow. Let's practice this much. I'll play part A of the music, and you work at leading and following."

> ▶ Practice several times and give each person a chance to lead and follow. Stop several times and point out examples of children working well together—showing slow, soft, smooth movement; staying together and making their movements the same so you almost can't tell who is leading or following.

"Stop. Good work. Now, this is how we are going to end our sequence. Find another set of partners so that you have a group of four. Sit down next to the other set of part-ners. (Each group of four should be spread out so that the groups are spaced equally throughout the room.) We now have four flowers, so we will make a bouquet. Each flower will be a different shape, yet you will be close to each other to make a bouquet. One shape might be higher or lower, round or pointed, larger or smaller, or sym-metrical or asymmetrical. Use your close space well. Perhaps you will be somewhat intertwined. Let's try several possibilities. Experiment with a bouquet flower shape. Practice time. . . . Stop.

"Remember that part A of the music will be playing and you will be traveling in a leader–follower relationship prior to making your bouquet. The trick is going to be having awareness of where your second set of partners is so that you can arrive together just when the music comes to a stop (bouquet pose). So now I want your group of four, the two sets of partners, to go back to your partner flower pose place. Get into your partner flower pose. When part A of the music starts, do your slow, soft, smooth leading and following movements. Be aware of where your second set of partners is located and move ever closer to them. Approach them. Gather together, but not too soon. You want to arrive just in time for when the music stops and you show your bouquet pose. It doesn't matter which set of partners arrives first. Just stop at your bouquet pose place and wait for your partners to arrive. Practice this several times. Partner flower pose, part A (lead–follow), bouquet pose. Stop. Everyone gather in here close to the music.

"Finally, we will put our whole sequence together. Who thinks they know the parts to the whole sequence? Raise your hand. Yes, Josey, what do you think? Self-shape, A, different self-shape, B, partner flower pose, A (lead and follow), bouquet pose. Great! You have a good memory. Let's get to work. Practice the whole sequence several times. Work on still flower poses. Stress variety on the flower poses. Work on contrast in parts A and B of the music. Work on good transitions between moving and being still. Work at partnerships and groups of four arriving in a timely manner. Stop. As a conclusion to our flower dance sequence, I have asked Ms. Jones and Dr. DeTuelo to come into our class. I want to show them how well you can perform your sequences and also to tell them some of the things we have learned about flowers and plants during our unit of study."

Assessment Suggestions

■ Use the rubric in figure 5.7 to assess the children's work. Use the rubric for each child, for each set of partners, or for the groups of four. Assess the children yourself, or allow the groups of children to assess each other. You could also train a parent volunteer to assess the movement sequences.

■ Videotape the performances for later analysis and evaluation.

Look For

■ After they have studied flowers, have the children make body shapes that clearly define some of the qualities of flower petals. Some are frilly, lacy, and delicate. Some are furry and soft. Others are bristly and prickly.

■ The children need to create smooth transitions between moments of stillness in their self-shapes and partner and group shapes and their movement to the ABA theme. They need to count out how long each section takes and arrive and depart in time to the music.

■ Cooperative work is essential to the success of this experience. Watch to see that each person gets a chance to voice ideas and contribute to the choice of shapes in their dance—who leads and who follows and so on.

How Can I Change This?

■ Develop the same unit of work based on trees and the use of leaves to identify trees. The leaves of trees are all different. Some are smaller, some larger. Some have pointed ends (red oak). Some have rounded lobes (white oak). Some are symmetrical (tulip tree). Some are asymmetrical or polymorphous (sassafras).

■ All snowflakes are different. Study some under a microscope. Then have the children cut snowflake designs out of paper and develop a lesson or unit of work based on the shape of snowflakes and the grouping of snowflakes to make a snowball or a snowman or snowwoman.

Teachable Moments

■ Compare flowers and plants to humans. Talk about annuals and perennial plants and how they propagate. What are some ways plants and flowers reproduce?—seeds blow in the wind, animals eat seeds and deposit fecal matter, bulbs spread and multiply.

April Showers Bring May Flowers

Name(s) of children _____

Variety of flower shapes—big/small, same/different, curved/pointed   Yes   No

Evidence of responding properly to music

    Part A—slow, soft, smooth   Yes   No

    Part B—vibrant, vigorous, percussive   Yes   No

Held poses; showed stillness   Yes   No

Clear beginning and end   Yes   No

Good transitions from one part of the sequence to the next   Yes   No

Worked responsibly by self, with partner, and with small group   Yes   No

Individual Worksheet—Flower Facts

Name the state flower. _____

Name three other flowers. _____

State three other facts you have learned about flowers: species/families, growth cycle, ways flowers propagate, where flowers get nutrients from, how flowers are living/ organic things. _____

_____

_____

_____

Figure 5.7   April Showers Bring May Flowers rubric.

- Discuss transport systems in the human body and in plants. Humans have a cardio-respiratory system. How do plants and flowers live and breathe? Humans have a digestive system. How do plants and flowers get nutrients to grow and stay alive?

- Plant flower seeds in different pots and conduct an experiment. Give selected plants a good growing environment—water, sunlight, food, good soil conditions—and other plants less desirable growing conditions. Analyze what happens. Discuss the results and compare the needs of plants to the needs of humans for love, nurturing and care, good food, adequate fluids, a home, someone to take care of them, and so on.

Rainbow Run

Suggested Grade Level

Intermediate (3 through 5)

Interdisciplinary Teaching Model

Shared

Students learning about the body's transport systems in science can use this learning experience to gain practical lessons in how the systems are affected by exercise.

Science

Biological sciences—transport systems

Physical Education

Fitness—cardiorespiratory activities (running, jumping, skipping)

Objectives

As a result of participating in this learning experience, children will improve their

- physical fitness,
- ability to measure heart rate, and
- understanding of how the body's transport systems are affected by exercise.

Equipment

Color-coded cones or posters and magic markers, a "rainbow" card for each student, rubber bands, and jump ropes. The rainbow card is a white index card showing a rainbow in colors matching the colors of the cones. (Each index card should have a different rainbow on each side of the card because the children will do this rainbow sequence two times.) It is important that cards have different rainbow color sequences, or students will all be going to the same cone at the same time.

Organization

Students work alone and with a partner in a large indoor or outdoor space.

Description

▶ Before students arrive, prepare the work area for activity. Rainbow cards with rubber bands should be spread out for easy access. Cones or posters for the rainbow run should also be set up at appropriate distances. (The distance of the run is determined by the distance from the starting area to each of the cones.) Jump ropes should be spread so that they do not tangle when students need them.

"Everyone come in and have a seat by a card and rubber band. Hello, everyone! I am very excited because today we are going to explore how the transport systems of the body are affected by exercise. The transport systems are the circulatory system, the respiratory system, and the excretory system. The circulatory system is made up of the heart, blood, and blood vessels. The system that takes air into the body is the respiratory system. It consists of the lungs and the passages through which air travels, such as the nose, throat, larynx, and bronchial tubes. The third transport system is the excretory system. This is the system that takes away waste products from the body and includes the kidneys, the skin, and the lungs.

"We are going to choose only one part of each of the transport systems for our class today. Let's focus on the heart (circulatory), the lungs (respiratory), and the skin (excretory). What happens in one system affects the other. For example, think of a time when something really scared you. Maybe you were separated from an adult in a big store. You were worried, and you were having trouble finding the adult. How did your body react? Your heart, lungs, and skin? Your heart probably began to beat a little faster, you started to breathe deeper and faster, and sweat began to bead up on your face.

"Just for a minute, let's think about how your heart is beating right now. You might know that your pulse is the beating in the arteries with each heartbeat. You can find your pulse by holding your index and middle fingers against your wrist at the base of your thumb. This is where your radial artery is. Go ahead and try to feel your pulse. Let me know if you can't find yours, and I or some other student will help you. You can also feel your pulse at the carotid artery in your neck or at the temporal artery in front of the ear. Let's take our heart rates for 15 seconds. We will all start together when I say 'go.' Count one for each time you feel your pulse beat. Ready, go.

"Now, as you sit relaxed, I want you also to think about your rate of breathing. Are you breathing hard? Are you taking deep or shallow breaths? How about the surface of your skin? Are you sweating? Or is your skin rather dry?

"We are going to exercise now, and after each activity we will examine our selected parts of the transport system: our heart, lungs, and skin.

"Let's look at our activity for the day. We are going to exercise by doing a rainbow run [or walk]. The rainbow run is set up like this [figure 5.8]."

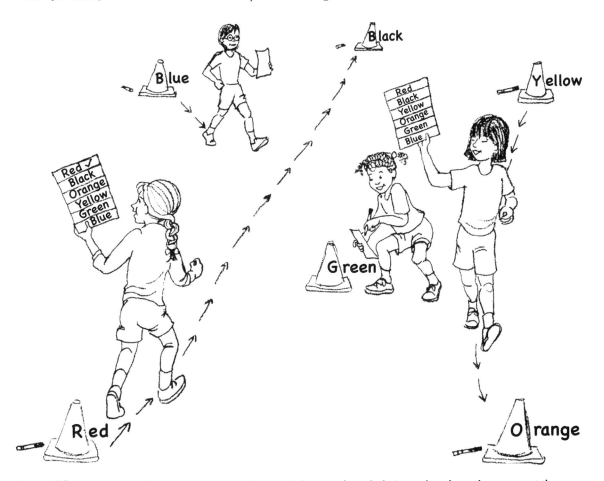

Figure 5.8   Students follow the sequence of their rainbow and mark their card to show they were at the correct station.

"On the field you see a number of different-colored cones [or posters] with magic markers beside them. You will go to the different-colored cones and use the magic marker beside the cone to make a checkmark on your card, which you have in front of you. Your card looks like this [hold up]. It shows the colors of the cones in a certain order. You must move to the cones in the order of the colors of your rainbow. For example, if the first color in my rainbow is red, then I must go to the red cone first, make a mark with the red marker next to the word "red" on my rainbow, and continue to my next color until I finish the last color on my rainbow. Who can explain this again to the class? Good, Joseph, tell the class what we are going to do. . . . Thanks, Joseph. Everyone, remember that you have your own rainbow sequence. Everyone will be traveling a different sequence.

"Okay, go ahead and secure your rainbow card around your wrist with your rubber band. Start off by just walking fast to complete your rainbow. This is not a race to see who finishes first. So as you finish, please walk back over to the starting area and continue to walk fast until everyone is finished. Are we all ready? Go.

"Since everyone is back, let's take our pulse again for 15 seconds. We are taking our pulse for 15 seconds because it is a short time span and easy to count. If we multiply that number by four we can get our heart rate for 1 minute. A 1-minute heart rate tells us how hard our heart is working [figure 5.9]. If your heart is beating 75 to 80 beats or fewer in a minute, your body is working easily or is at rest. If it is beating 90 to 120 beats, you are doing moderate exercise like walking. If it is beating 130 to 180 beats, you are exercising vigorously. To get your body fit, you should be able to exercise with your heart beating in the 120 to 160 range for 5 to 20 minutes without stopping. As your body gets in better cardiorespiratory shape, you can keep exercising for longer periods without stopping. How do your resting heart rate and your walking heart rate differ [figure 5.9]? Can someone tell us what his or her resting and walking heart rates were? Why do you think they are different? What about your lungs? How were your lungs affected by walking? Who would like to share what happened to his or her breathing? Susan. Yes, as you started to exercise, your breathing got deeper. In fact, as you begin to exercise, your heart rate increases and you use more oxygen, which makes you breathe deeper [figure 5.10].

"Let's try the rainbow activity again, but this time let's jog or run instead of walking. Turn your rainbow card over, and you will see a new rainbow for you to use. When I say 'go,' we will start. Same as last time, come back over here and continue to jog or run until everyone is finished. Ready, go.

"Let's take the pulse again for 15 seconds. Wow, your pulse was really easy to find that time, wasn't it? Did everyone have a higher rate that time? What has happened to your skin? Have you started to sweat? Does anyone know why the skin for most of you was dry when we first came into class and now it is moist? Jason? Right, as we continue to exercise, our body temperature rises, and we begin to sweat. Sweating provides water to the surface area of the skin, where it evaporates into the air. This causes the skin to cool. So here is another question. Do you think that you should wipe sweat off your body while you exercise? In other words, should we all run around with towels in our hands to get rid of our sweat? No. The sweat helps keep us cool.

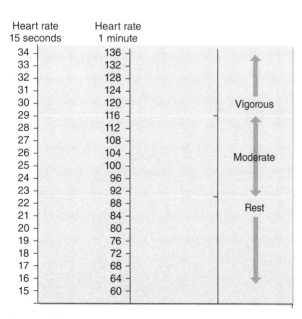

Figure 5.9 Different types of exercise make the heart beat at different rates.

Figure 5.10   Exercise affects the transport system of the body.

"Now let's try a new activity. We are going to jump rope. When I say 'go,' I want you to go over and get a rope and then come back and find a personal space. Let's see if we can increase the pace of our jumping. First, we will all jump at an easy pace for a few minutes, then I want you to jump faster for a few minutes. Last, for 1 minute you will jump as fast as you can—what we call *hot pepper*. Doesn't this sound like fun? Remember, go at your own pace. You know how fast you can go, so pace yourself. Ready, go.

"Let's take your heart rate for 15 seconds. You should be able to find your pulse easily now. Ready, go. . . . Wow, that extra-fast jumping really did something, didn't it? What happened to your transport systems? When I say 'go,' quickly get a partner, and discuss what happened to your heart, lungs, and skin. Go.

"Which partners would like to tell us what happened? Stewart and Jack. Good answer, you could say that as you begin to exercise, your heart rate increases and you also use more oxygen, which makes you breathe deeper. As you continue to exercise, your body temperature rises and you begin to sweat. Sweating provides water to the surface area of the skin, where it evaporates into the air and causes the skin to cool.

"Now that we have rested for a few minutes, let's take one last look at our transport systems. What happened to your heart, lungs, and skin? This is a good time for us to finish our lesson for the day. Let's review just a little. Can someone tell us what the body's transport systems are? Right, Sharon, the circulatory system, the respiratory system, and the excretory system. What parts of these three systems did we examine? Shane. Okay, the heart, lungs, and skin. You will continue to study the body's transport systems in your science class. I have a list of questions for you to complete in the classroom."

Assessment Suggestion

Ask children the following types of questions, to be answered orally or on a worksheet:

- Is your heart rate different when you walk and when you run? When is it faster? Why?
- What do you think would happen if you carried two or three books while you exercised?
- What happens to your pulse rate 30 seconds after you stop exercising?
- Why do you think that we took heart rates for only 15 seconds?
- Why do you breathe more deeply when you exercise?
- Why do you breathe faster when you exercise?
- If sweating causes the skin to cool, do you think that you should try to towel off your sweat as much as possible?

Look For

- Make sure children are taking their pulses correctly at their radial or carotid arteries. Ask children their 15-second counts. If they are in a reasonable range for the type of exercise (resting, moderate, or vigorous using the chart), they are probably counting correctly. A child off the chart probably is making up a number and needs help.
- Make sure children are following the colors on their rainbow and not just following a friend.
- Encourage children to move continuously. This is not a race; it is more about pace. It is not important to be the fastest in class. It is important to maintain exercise over time. Children should learn to monitor their own progress and get in better personal shape over time. They can set their own goals and see improvement over time.

How Can I Change This?

- Change the course to a rainbow obstacle course, where the children have to go over, under, around, and through objects.
- Use a similar rainbow run, but one in which children must dribble a ball, jump rope, twirl a hula hoop, and so on at each cone.
- Perform the rainbow run on the playground. Children can go up and down the slide, swing for a certain time, go across the horizontal ladder or monkey bars, and so on.
- Give children a map and compass, and make the rainbow run an orienteering course.

Teachable Moments

- Encourage the children to be active at other times during the day. If there is a fitness course set up at school, talk to the children about walking or running around the course before school, during recess, or at lunch. Make doing the course a social experience. Encourage them to do it with a friend. It should be fun.
- Active lifestyles should be shared with others. Encourage the children to be active with their parents or friends at home. They can share the knowledge they are learning about fitness, body transport systems, and cardiorespiratory fitness with these people. Prepare handouts for them to take home.

Weather or Not

Suggested Grade Level

Intermediate (4 and 5)

Interdisciplinary Teaching Model

Partnership

Studying about weather patterns, clouds, and storms is common in science in the upper elementary grades. You and the science teacher can work together on this theme. Children learn about weather and cloud formations and use that information to develop a movement sequence.

Science

Earth sciences—weather patterns, cloud formations, wind

Physical Education

Body shapes; time, force, and space concepts

Objectives

As a result of participating in this learning experience, children will improve their abilities to

- use their bodies to create shapes inspired by moving clouds;
- demonstrate the contrast of slow, light, indirect movements with fast, strong, direct movements; and
- identify various cloud formations and weather patterns.

Equipment

Pictures of clouds and other weather information provided by the National Weather Service or local TV stations or newspapers (or specimens of various flowers, leaves from trees, and information about the plants and trees); a tape or record player and music for accompaniment

Organization

Students begin the lesson dancing individually, then finish the dance in a group shape.

Description

"Good morning. Can you believe this day? What great [lousy] weather we are having! I've been talking to [classroom teacher], and I understand you are studying about weather patterns in science. Well, today we are going to create a dance about weather. Our dance will be about the shapes of clouds, the levels at which they occur, wind and its patterns, and the mood of weather. When the sky is almost completely blue on a calm day, did you ever look up in the sky and see white, wispy clouds just floating about? Those clouds are called cirrus, or sometimes mares' tails or mackerel scales. They are at a high level and are rather friendly clouds. When I say 'go,' I'm going to play some cloud music [e.g., "Enter Sunlight," Palmer, 1973; "Windsails," Kupka, 1982]. What I want you to do is listen to the music and move about the general space within the boundaries of the cones. Make sure your movements correspond to the mood and qualities of the music. Stop occasionally to stretch this way and that, expanding and retracting (getting bigger and smaller), and then move on. Be that cumulus cloud floating across the sky. Go. Yes, Amy, Brett! I see you are really paying attention to the music. Nice slow, calm, indirect, floating movements. Super, Glen. You are showing me soft, gentle movements with moments of swaying and stretching while you are in one spot. Stop. Everyone freeze right where you are. Let's watch Amy, Brett, and Glen as they interpret this cloud music with their movement. Watch their gentle, light, or soft movement. Watch how they move indirectly: stopping, starting, changing directions and pathways, using both floor and air space. Notice how they match the slowness of their movements with the pace of the music. See how they stop to gently stretch up, out, in front, behind, and then move on. Stop. Thanks. As you continue to warm up, pay attention to these details (slow, soft or light, indirect). I shouldn't be seeing any running or any direct, powerful, explosive movements. Start when you hear the music. Much better now. I can just imagine I am floating among those cumulus clouds on a calm day. Stop. Everyone come in and sit down.

"Now that you are warmed up, we are ready to put together our cloud dance sequence [figure 5.11]. First, we'll talk about clouds some more. Have you ever noticed that the white clouds are at different levels? They are also all different shapes and sizes. Some are puffy and big, others long and narrow. Do you know what they are called? They are called cumulus clouds. They are rather friendly clouds. For the first part of our dance I want you to choose three cloud shapes. I will play our cloud music again. I want you to float through the sky, using the same type of movements you did during our warm-up. At three different times I want you to stop and hold a cloud shape for 5 seconds. Make each position different: long or round, wide or narrow, big or small. You may change your levels as well. Then move on. I want you to decide when to float across the sky and when to hold a cloud shape. The critical factors are floating softly and gently and stopping to make—how many cloud shapes? Right, three. How long will you hold each shape? Right again. Five seconds. Ready, go. . . . Stop.

Figure 5.11   Students create a movement sequence based on weather patterns— layered, stratus clouds.

"I really like what you are doing, but the music in some ways is hindering what we can do with this dance. So we will continue without music. This time I want us to repeat what we just did, but I want to add the factor of wind. Sometimes the wind is calm and gentle, and other times it is blowing and gusting hard. I still want you to stop and do three cloud shapes, but I want your movements in between to show me calm and gentle versus windy and gusty. You choose the order. Stop and hold your third cloud shape. When everyone is holding his or her last cloud shape, I'll know you are finished. Start by showing me stillness using your first cloud shape. Go. . . . Stop. I can see you are trying, but you can improve in two ways. First, create more contrast between your calm, gentle wind movements and your windy, gusty movements. Windy movements are more strong, powerful, sudden. Gusty means to blow hard, perhaps swirl, then ease up. Gentle winds are more consistently calm, reserved. Second, really exaggerate your held cloud shapes and make sure you hold them for 5 full seconds. Let's try again. First shape. Ready, go. . . . Okay, better. One more time. First shape, go. . . . Stop.

"Now we will build the second part of our dance. Did you ever notice the sky when a rainstorm is approaching? What does it look like? Yes, gray, billowing, threatening clouds. These clouds are low, heavy, full of rain. They are often gathered in a definitive line. These clouds are called nimbus or rain clouds or sometimes cumulonimbus or stratonimbus, depending on whether they are puffy, billowing rain clouds or layered, gray clouds. But, the key name is nimbus or rain. This is what we are going to do. After the first part of our dance when we do three cloud shapes and move using two wind conditions, I want you to gather like a rainstorm and create a line here across the floor. The whole class will create a cloud line as each of you, individually, makes the most threatening cloud shape you can think of. If you can, as you come into the cloud line and assume your cloud shape, link your shape to your neighbors. That would be great. Think of a unified cloud line: a nimbus, angry storm line. Hold that shape. Let's try it. Go back to your third cloud shape. Hold it for 5 seconds. Now we are like the calm before the storm, gathering along this line. Come in slowly, one at a time, gradually gathering mass. Once you come in, link your shape to someone else on either side of you. Touch with different body parts at different levels. Look threatening, menacing. Hold it. Good. Let's try it again. From the beginning this time. Cirrus or cumulus cloud, gentle breeze or gusting wind, another cloud shape, contrasting wind movement, another cloud shape, calm before the storm, nimbus cloud line. Good work. Let's do it again. Start. . . . Stop.

"Now we are ready for the climax. Guess what? Yes, thunder! Powerful, explosive moves. Driving rain. Lots of energy. Sudden movement. The rain and driving wind are moving in one direction across the floor. Show me your energy from the thunder. Explosive runs, jumps, tearing actions. Ready, go. . . . Stop. Let's try that again from the third cloud shape. Ready, cloud shape, gather in a line (calm before the storm), threatening cloud line, hold your shapes (don't worry if you're not always next to the same person). Thunder [drum], explosive movement, driving rain across the floor. Good work. Stop. Come, gather in here for a moment.

"Have you ever seen the destruction after a powerful storm? Do you remember the powerful tornado in Lexington, or hurricane Hugo in Charleston, or the El Niño storms and floods in Malibu? What destruction did you see? [Trees uprooted, houses destroyed, bridges out.] To end our dance, I want you to make groups of three on this side of the floor and create a group shape that resembles the destructive force of nature. First, find two others with whom you can work responsibly. Let's pretend that the thunder and raging rainstorm turn into a gentle sprinkle. This will allow you to slow your energy and calmly find everyone in your group, then create your final destructive shape. Hold that shape to show me you are finished. Let's try that part several times. Slowly move to find your group of three. Create your shape. Hold it. [Practice this part several times.]

"For our conclusion, we will put our weather dance completely together. It is in three parts. First are the cumulus clouds with varying winds, then the cloud line and thunder with driving rain, and finally a calming of the weather and of the group destructive shape. What do you think of practicing it twice through and performing it for [next teacher] when he [she] comes to pick you up at the end of class? [Practice and performance follow.]

"Before you go, I would like to ask you a few questions about clouds and the weather. What are puffy, white clouds called? [Cumulus.] Gray clouds? [Nimbus.] Layered, gray clouds? [Stratus.] Puffy, threatening, gray clouds? [Cumulonimbus.] I'm impressed. You are really starting to know a lot about the weather. And you have learned to communicate your knowledge and feelings about weather through movement. Before we leave, has anyone ever heard a saying about weather? For example, there's 'Pink in the morning, sailor's warning. Pink at night, sailor's delight.' What does that mean? Any others? Yes. 'When the wind is from the west, fishing is best.' When you go home tonight, ask your family if they know any weather sayings or fables. Come back and tell me next class. That's it for now. As you move over to the door to line up, go calmly and gently as a summer breeze."

Assessment Suggestion

Develop a worksheet with pictures of several different types of clouds. Have the children label each picture.

Look For

- The focus of this lesson is on body shapes and an awareness of time, force, and space. As children make their cloud shapes, look for variety through changes in level, dimension, symmetry, direction, and base of support. As children add traveling actions to their sequence, look for contrasts between soft, calm, gentle, indirect movements and powerful, sudden, swirling, sometimes direct movements.
- The emphasis is on expression using a theme from nature. Look for that expression in the soft shapes, the raging storm, and the destructive shapes at the end.
- Focus on the relationships among science, nature, and body movement terminology. Point out the common ground using shapes, time, force, space, and so on.

How Can I Change This?

- This lesson could be adapted to use other themes from nature or the environment. For example, in winter use the shapes of snowflakes as the theme; in spring or fall use the shapes of flowers and tree leaves.
- Use children's literature about clouds (e.g., Shaw, 1947; DePaola, 1975; Locker, 2000) as a stimulus for this lesson, thereby focusing on the integration of language and movement.
- There are many ways to change the content or sequence of this learning experience. For example, children could link cloud shapes together and move across the sky. Children could use traveling actions to represent the change from a soft, gentle, sprinkling shower to a driving rainstorm. They could also create a bouquet of flowers, pile of leaves, and so on as they work on group shapes.

Teachable Moment

Stress the interrelationships among disciplines. Name the clouds; identify high and low weather fronts and clockwise and counterclockwise flow patterns; describe wind forces (breeze, gust, gale, etc.). How fast are hurricane winds? Why does a hurricane occur? Interpret all these phenomena through a focus on movement factors. Use the interrelationships to enhance and enrich language, science, and dance.

Additional Ideas for Developing Learning Experiences

This section offers additional learning experiences to reinforce the science concepts identified in table 5.1: biological and life sciences, earth and space sciences, and physical sciences. Curricular areas, suggested grade level, and a brief description are provided for each activity. These activities are intended to inspire additional ideas for interdisciplinary work between classroom and physical education teachers. We encourage you to develop these ideas more completely. Sometimes the connected model will be most appropriate, while other times the shared or partnership model may be used. Your main concern should be to meet the developmental levels and needs of your students; you can adapt activities to accommodate your teaching schedule, equipment, and available space.

BIOLOGICAL AND LIFE SCIENCES

Body ID

Science

Anatomy—body-part identification

Physical Education

Selected locomotor, manipulative, and nonlocomotor actions

Grade Level

K through 2

 ▪ Have children name and touch different body parts. They touch their pointer finger to their nose, fist to elbow, foot to knee, elbow to knee, elbow to tummy, ear to shoulder, chin to knee, and so on. Have them get a partner and perform the same activities, but touch the called-out body part to their partner's body.

 ▪ Children tap a balloon into the air with different body parts. They use their pointer finger, ring finger, thumb, fist, elbow, shoulder, head, nose, wrist, knee, and so on. They count how many times they can keep the balloon up with each body part, changing and using a different body part each time. They can use a beach ball in place of a balloon.

 ▪ With music (with clear, identifiable 4/4 tempo) playing in the background, have children choose different body parts they can move backward and forward to the rhythm of the music. "Start by using the macro beat, the first beat of each measure (front, 2, 3, 4, back, 2, 3, 4). Choose your arm, leg, elbow, hand, foot, head. What body parts can you move side to side? What body parts can you bend, then stretch, move up, then down, twist, swing, and so on?" Have students do each of these activities with a variety of selected body parts using a macro beat, then switch to a micro beat—move to every count of the measure (bend, stretch, bend, stretch).

▪ Children travel across the room on different body parts. "When you hear the drumbeat, try a different way: two feet, one foot, hands and knees, two feet and a hand, slide on tummy and pull with hands, slide on back and push with feet. What other ways can you think of?"

▪ Children balance on different body parts in a gymnastics lesson and name the parts. "Balance on two knees and an elbow, seat and two hands, forearm and thigh, two shins, shoulders and elbows. What else can you think of?" (See figure 5.12.)

▪ Have the children balance any way they choose but make their feet the highest body part. "Control the balance for 3 seconds. Try making your elbow the highest body part. Now try your tummy, knees, seat. Can you balance with your head, hands, tummy, knees, ankles, shoulders at a medium level? A low level?"

Figure 5.12 Children balance on different body parts and name them.

Oh Deer

Science

What plants and animals need

Physical Education

Locomotor tag game

Grade Level

2 through 4

Oh Deer! (author unknown) is a game of tag that emphasizes the balance of nature. Students are divided into four equal groups: deer, food, shelter, and water. Deer stand on one side of the gym. The habitat components stand on the other side with their backs turned. Establish three signals used by both deer and habitat components: hands over stomach = food; hands over mouth = water; hands over head = shelter. On the signal to go, the deer choose what habitat component they will search for and put their hands in the appropriate place. They may not change components. In the meantime, the habitat components turn around and show what component they are by placing their hands appropriately. They may not change. Deer run across and join hands with a player representing the habitat component they are in search of. They must match. Together they run, hop, jump, skip, leap, or lope back to the starting line. The habitat components then become deer on the next turn representing one successful year of reproduction and finding a satisfactory habitat in which to live. Because the class was initially divided into four groups: 1/4 deer, 1/4 food, 1/4 water, and 1/4 shelter and some of the habitat components are now deer (1/2 the group because of the reproductive cycle), there are fewer habitat components. After the second or third reproductive cycle, part of the now highly populated group of deer will not find what they need to survive. Deer who can't find what they need (food, water or shelter) will symbolically die and go to the habitat component line and make a choice of what they want to be (food, water, or shelter). The game ends when the teacher calls a halt and talks with the students about the science concepts involved.

Sensitivity Training

Science

The five senses

Physical Education

Selected locomotor, manipulative, and nonlocomotor actions

Grade Level

1 through 3

■ Different sounds are produced by different kinds of vibrations. Objects that are dense and vibrate at a high speed produce a high-pitched sound. Objects that are not dense and vibrate at a slow speed produce a low-pitched sound. Make sounds on several types of homemade and commercial band instruments, such as a glass of water, gourd, steel drum, triangle, maraca, drum, guitar, and tambourine. Experiment with the type of sound each instrument makes. Have the children respond appropriately by moving at high and low levels according to the pitch of the sound. Have them move according to whether the sound is vibratory (shake, quiver), flowing (smooth, curving), percussive (pounding, jerky), and so on. Make a short sequence of sounds, then develop a movement sequence to go with the sounds.

■ By listening carefully, a person can tell if a rhythm is even or uneven. An even rhythm or tempo (4/4 time) is one that has the same emphasis on each beat of each measure. For example, one can clap, snap, tap the thighs, step, hop, or jump to each beat of music in 4/4 time. An uneven rhythm or tempo (2/4 or 3/4 rhythm) has an unequal emphasis on each beat of music. An uneven rhythm has, for example, a long/short or long/short/short emphasis. A 2/4 rhythm is appropriate for locomotor actions such as skipping, galloping, and sliding. A 3/4 rhythm is more appropriate for a waltz. Play different rhythms on a drum, or use an appropriate record with different types of rhythms. Have children listen to the beat, clap to the beat, snap their fingers to the beat, move other body parts to the beat, perform locomotor actions to the beat.

▪ The children listen to a rhythmical sequence you create and then make an appropriate movement response. For example, make two loud powerful beats on a drum followed by a long, smooth rubbing on the drum surface. The children should respond by making two quick, powerful body actions followed by one sustained, smooth, flowing action. Make a pattern of long and short squeaking noises using the mouth of a blown-up but unsealed balloon. The children listen and then respond to the sounds that they hear.

▪ To help with auditory sequential memory, tell the children to do a sequence of two, three, or four things, for example, do five sit-ups, then get a ball, and bounce it 10 times; or throw the ball up and catch it seven times, dribble it on the floor 15 times, and kick it against the wall five times. Observe who listens well and performs the sequence correctly.

▪ Turn out the lights in the gym, and have the children follow a flashlight beam with their eyes. Then play a game of Flashlight Tag.

▪ To develop visual sequential memory, have the children watch you do a movement sequence, then copy your sequence. For example, do a forward roll, come out of your roll into a balance on a knee and two hands, go into a sideways egg roll by tucking up into a ball and rolling sideways, and finish in a V-seat resting back on your hands.

▪ Conduct some taste experiments. Bring in foods to taste that are sweet, sour, bitter, salty, and spicy. After tasting the food, the children show their reactions to it through movement. How do the children's movements change according to the type of food they have tasted?

▪ Bring in scented items of different types, such as perfume, ammonia, pepper, sassafras, peppermint, rose petals, and charred wood, in unmarked bottles. Have the children open up one of the bottles carefully and smell the substance inside, then show their reactions to what they smell with different body movements. Have them put their reactions to several different smells into a short movement sequence.

What Goes Around Comes Around

Science
Cycle of life—growing seeds

Physical Education
Selected locomotor and nonlocomotor actions

Grade Level
2 and 3
Develop a movement sequence that shows the cycle of life (figure 5.13): "One plants small seeds in the spring. Showers, gentle rains, and proper soil bring growth. Fields of grain sway in the wind. Fruit matures on trees. Harvest comes in the fall. Fruit is picked. Grain is cut, taken to the mill, and ground into flour. Products are eaten to provide energy to continue the cycle of life."

Figure 5.13   Creating a dance that expresses the cycle of life—a plant sprouting from a seed.

Ecosystems

Science

Metamorphosis

Physical Education

Selected locomotor and nonlocomotor actions

Grade Level

K through 2
Use *The Very Hungry Caterpillar* by Eric Carle or *Charlie the Caterpillar* by Dom DeLuise and talk about metamorphosis. Have the children start out as a caterpillar. They can do moving and eating actions. Then, they can wind into a cocoon (still shape). Finally, they can fly away as a butterfly flitting from here to there and lighting on flowers to rest and feed.

Water Creatures

Science

Metamorphosis

Physical Education

Selected locomotor and nonlocomotor actions

Grade Level

3 through 5

While they are studying the environment, take students to a pond or river and take water samples. Use a small dip net and vials to collect the creatures that live in the water. The students will learn about the fascinating lives of aquatic insects and their life cycles. Essentially there are three main classes of creatures that go through complete or incomplete metamorphosis: the mayfly, the stone fly, and the caddis fly. Mayflies and stone flies go through incomplete metamorphosis in that they progress through an underwater nymph stage and emerge into their aerial adult stage. Dragonflies and damselflies are examples. Caddis flies are examples of complete metamorphosis in that they go from a larval stage into a pupa stage in a cocoon and finally transform themselves as they emerge as an adult winged caddis.

Bring a fly fisherman or fisherwoman into class to talk about the behavior of these creatures and about how he or she uses dry and wet flies to catch trout that may be lurking in the water.

After they have studied the ecosystem of the pond or the river, have the children develop a movement sequence that depicts the metamorphic cycle of crawling on the bottom or the river suspension of nymphs swirling in the water, and the emergence of larvae in the water. Encourage them to change their shape as they transform into the pupal stage in a cocoon and finally emerge into their adult stage and fly away. Also have them depict the movement of the trout swimming in the water from calm pools to rushing ripples in the stream. They can show the fish feeding on the underwater nymphs or breaking the water at the surface to catch a newly hatched caddis fly or mayfly. Perhaps have them include in the movement sequences the act of a fisherman casting a fly, letting it float in the pond or stream, hooking a trout, and playing it in to the catch only to release it back into the environment. (You may want to invite a member of Trout Unlimited to your class to give a talk.)

Dembones

Science

Anatomy—bones and muscles

Physical Education

Selected locomotor, manipulative, and nonlocomotor actions

Grade Level

3 and 4

▪ With a piece of slow, calming music playing in the background (see Brazelton, 1977), have the children place a wadded piece of newspaper in a bent joint for eight counts (two measures), then relax and make that muscle loose (shake it out, make it limp) for eight counts. For example, they can put the wad in the elbow and flex the biceps muscle, in a fist and contract the forearm muscles, behind a knee and flex the hamstring muscle, between two knees and contract the adductors, between two elbows and contract the pectoralis muscles, or under the chin and contract the sternocleido-mastoid muscles. Have them repeat the experience several times on the left and right sides of the body. Talk about what it feels like to have muscles tense and relaxed.

▪ Develop a lesson that emphasizes the use of major muscle groups of the body. After a good cardiorespiratory warm-up that elevates the heart rate, have the children perform selected strength exercises and point out the specific muscles used (e.g., triceps in push-ups, abdominal muscles in sit-ups, quadriceps in squats, biceps in chin-ups, gastrocnemius in toe raises). Stretching exercises can identify other muscles (hamstrings in bending at the waist with right leg over left, trapezius when hugging yourself). Then, depending on the lesson (kicking, throwing, striking, etc.), identify the major muscle groups used and what they do. For example, kicking involves mainly hip flexors (quadriceps) and knee extensors (sartorius). Throwing uses mainly the deltoids, biceps, pectoralis, triceps, and forearm muscles.

▪ Teach children the major bones and joints of the body. As you go over each area, talk about how each part moves. "What can the spine do?" (Arch, bend, twist, turn.) "The hip and shoulder are ball-and-socket joints. How many ways can you make the arms and legs move?" (Bend, swivel, stretch, reach, swing.) Continue exploring other bones and joints by examining what each can do. Develop a creative movement sequence by combining the elements of shape and time, for example, bend at one joint slowly, then stretch another quickly, and so on.

Flora and Fauna

Science

The ways of plants and animals

Physical Education

Locomotor and nonlocomotor movement sequences

Grade Level

3 and 4

■ Bring several leaves from different trees and flowers, as well as blades of different grasses. Ask the children to closely observe the different shapes and arrangements. Some leaves are pointed, others are rounded. Some flowers form in clusters, others are single. Some flowers are large and colorful, others are smaller and perhaps blander. Some blades of grass are narrow, others are broad. After noticing the similarities and differences among the plants, have the children create a movement sequence about changing shapes. Have them choose three different shapes, starting in one shape, changing rapidly to another shape, then changing slowly to the third shape. Shapes should show changes in size, level, formation, and so on.

■ Carefully observe one or several different types of animals. For example, you might choose horses. "What kinds of horses are there? How do different horses move? What about a thoroughbred racehorse? [Fast, straight ahead.] A quarter horse? [Meant for cattle ranching, quick starts and stops, zigzag changes of direction.] A draft or plow horse? [Power, pulling heavy loads.] A Tennessee walker? [Elegant, prancing, pulling a fancy cart.] Are there any other horses you can think of? What other animals can you think of that move in interesting ways? Do not try to be the animal, but try to capture the movement qualities of the animal. What about an ostrich, kangaroo, hippopotamus, elephant? Create a movement sequence that illustrates the types of animal qualities you wish to portray" (See figure 5.14).

Figure 5.14 Creating a movement sequence showing how animals protect themselves: *(a)* bull with horns, *(b)* birds in flight, *(c)* poisonous snake.

Feel That Rhythm

Science

Transport systems of the body

Physical Education

Rhythmical experiences using the heart and lungs as a movement focus

Grade Level

4 and 5

- "While resting, feel your heart beat. Silently tap against your chest to the rhythm of your heart. Snap, clap, or tap that steady rhythm. Hop, jump, or step to that steady rhythm." To get all the children moving together, play a musical march with a steady, even rhythm. Choose an action with the hands, arms, elbows, knees, hips, or feet to keep the beat. To music in 4/4 time with four beats per measure, slow the children's pace to a movement only to the first beat of the measure (move, rest, rest, rest). Double the time with a movement on beats 1 and 3 of the measure (move, rest, move, rest). Then have them move on every beat of every measure (move, move, move, move). "What else do you know that has a steady beat or rhythm? [Robots, machines, dripping water, music, sunrise or sunset.] Create a movement sequence using one of these ideas. Make sure to have a definite beginning and ending."

- "Think about how you breathe. How does your body move?" (Answers will vary from up and down to in and out.) "Take that breathing movement into your arms, head, chest, legs. Show how each body part can move up and down or in and out. . . . Bring in the element of time. Take a long breath and several short, panting breaths with a selected body part. Use your whole body to rise with a long, inhaling breath, then collapse quickly using a quick, direct exhale. Create a sequence by combining these ideas."

EARTH AND SPACE SCIENCES

Time Out

Science

Explaining time

Physical Education

Moving fast and slow; ordering segments of a movement sequence

Grade Level

K and 1

- Create a time line that represents past, present, and future. Order some significant events (cave dwellers—discovery of fire, wheel; medieval times-feudal system; Europeans' discovery of America; industrial revolution; humanity's first flight; computers; space travel; first space colony; who knows?). Develop a movement sequence that illustrates movement during each of these times.

■ "How many movements can you make in 10 seconds? Can you make one movement last 10 seconds?"

■ "Create a movement sequence. Which movement in the sequence comes first, second, third? Can you perform the movement sequence in reverse—third, second, first?"

Where Are You, Carmen San Diego?

Science
Map and compass skills

Physical Education
Orienteering

Grade Level
4 and 5

Teach children some orienteering skills. Use a compass to teach north, south, east, and west. Relate these directions to 90, 180, 270, and 360 degrees of a circle. Play a points-of-the-compass drill called the "Silver Dollar Game" (United States Army Infantry School, 1971). Have the children choose the degree bearing of 120 and walk an equal number of steps (or yards) in this bearing three times in a row. Children should return to their point of origin, having walked the path of an equilateral triangle. Use colored cards or poker chips to mark spots. Develop a simple orienteering course with several coded checkpoints around the school. Students should work with partners in a collaborative fashion to correlate their progress.

Water: The Cycle Goes On

Science
The hydrologic cycle

Physical Education
Locomotor and nonlocomotor movement sequences

Grade Level
3 through 6

The earth's water is always in movement. It is in movement on, above, or under the earth's surface. Because it is a cycle, there is truly no beginning or end. The three main parts of the cycle are precipitation, evaporation, and condensation. Water can change states among liquid, vapor, and solid. Water in a solid storage stage appears in the form of snow and ice. In its liquid state, water is stored in the ground and as freshwater or saltwater. As precipitation it is in the form of snow, sleet, or rain. As runoff it moves into streams, rivers, lakes, and ponds. It gradually flows to the oceans. The sun and the heat process cause evaporation into the sky where condensation causes clouds to form.

Have the students create movement sequences based on the water cycle. Held shapes can be ice crystals, snowflakes, or droplets of water. Water in its various stages can be depicted as still, as moving slowly and calmly, or as an active, raging storm or river rapids. Choose several action words or phrases (five to eight) and have children explore their movement potential. Then select a few (three to five) and have the children put them into a sequence with a beginning, middle, and end. Choose words or phrases that show contrast or are unique or most interesting to the students. The children practice the sequences and show them to others in the class.

Weather Channel

Science
Air and water

Physical Education
Locomotor and nonlocomotor movement sequences

Grade Level
1 through 3

- Have the children describe the types of things they might do when the air is still and calm. "What would you do in a soft, gentle breeze? . . . What about a gusting, swirling wind? . . . What about a powerful, ripping tornado?" Have the students create a movement sequence that shows how they would move differently in each of these air conditions. They should show changes of level, energy, speed, pathway, and so on.

- Have children talk about the types of things they do with or in water: wash dishes, take a bath, swim different strokes, catch the largest fish ever, raft down a torrent of whitewater, splash in puddles after a rainstorm, and so on. Enhance the experience by asking them to use movements that create a mood or feeling about the water: disgust when they have to wash dirty pots and pans, the pleasure of a warm bath, the confidence that comes from learning a new stroke when swimming, the excitement of catching a record-size fish, the fear of falling out of a raft in raging rapids, and the glee in getting someone else wet!

Bad Hair Day

Science

Weather

Physical Education

Selected locomotor and nonlocomotor movement sequences

Grade Level

1 through 4

"Weather affects our mood or the way we feel. Show through your movement how you feel on a rainy day; a cold, snowy day; a hot, muggy day; and a damp, foggy day. How and where would you move if a tornado or a hurricane was approaching the area in which you live? Use different directions, pathways, levels, and speeds as you move."

Desert Storm

Science

The environment

Physical Education

Action-word movement sequences

Grade Level

2 and 3

Have the students create a movement sequence based on action words chosen from an environmental theme. For example, a forest fire, volcano, mountain stream, rain forest, or desert sandstorm could be used as a theme. Themes can be broken down into subthemes according to what happens in each environmental situation. In the case of the forest fire, for example, the concepts of smoke, sparks, flames, destruction, and so on can bring out words such as *whirling, swirling, lingering, surrounding, flying, bounding, hurrying, fading, settling, falling, crashing, extinguishing.* After exploring each word, the children should develop a movement sequence that depicts the environmental situation. They can also use creative writing to write short paragraphs or poetry about the environment.

In the Zone

Science

Climate

Physical Education

Action-word movement sequences

Grade Level

4 and 5

- Ask children to explore activities they would do in different climates, regions, or areas of the United States or the world. They can develop short movement sequences that typify the life of people or animals in a desert climate, a frigid zone, a tropical rain forest, a mountainous region, a flatlands area, and so on.

- Have students create a movement sequence that shows what they do during different seasons of the year. Spring signifies planting, growth, longer days, the return of warmer weather, showers, joy, hope, and so on. Summer means vacations, playing, swimming, fishing, going on a trip, baseball, Fourth of July, thunderstorms, and so on. Fall means things like the return of school, harvest, cooler weather, leaves falling, and hurricanes. Winter is typified by cold, snow falling, and activities like ice skating, sledding, and sliding.

Spaced Out

Science

Space: the new frontier

Physical Education

Inventing a game, designing a movement experience

Grade Level

3 through 5

- Students create a movement sequence by going on an exploratory space mission, beginning with a rocket takeoff. They can include a tethered space walk, landing on the moon, performing a work experiment, a computer glitch and technical engineering resolution, return flight, and landing back on the earth.

- Ask children to invent a new game, one that has never been played before. They then play the game as if they were in weightless conditions. Have them write out the rules for the game. Then they can describe the game to some aliens that they meet in outer space and play the game with the aliens.

PHYSICAL SCIENCES

Did You See That?

Science

Observing things

Physical Education

Fundamental movement patterns, mirroring actions, individual movement sequences in dance or gymnastics

Grade Level

1 through 4

■ Have children observe a partner's performance of a sport or gymnastics skill and check for appropriate cues. For example, the observer can check his or her partner's throwing using a checklist of cues such as "side to target, opposite foot forward, trunk rotation, long lever arm, and follow-through" that you provide.

■ Perform a short movement sequence, for example, clap three times, snap your fingers twice, turn once fully around, and sit down cross-legged on the ground. Challenge the children to observe exactly what you do, then ask them to repeat your sequence.

■ While they are working in pairs, have the children mirror each other's movements. The leader can create different kinds of symmetrical and asymmetrical shapes at selected levels. The follower must be acutely aware of any changes of movement by the leading partner and follow so closely that it is almost impossible to tell who is leading and who is following.

■ After developing individual sequences or routines in gymnastics or dance, have the children judge each other's performances. Provide the children with a checklist of items to look for. For example, children can perform a short gymnastics sequence on the floor consisting of three balances with connecting weight transfers. The checklist includes questions such as "Was stillness achieved (for at least 3 seconds) on each of the balances? Were there good lines, extensions, pointed toes and fingers? Was there variety in the choice of balances: upright and inverted, symmetrical and asymmetrical, change of levels, and so on? Were there smooth transitions: no extra or out-of-place movements, no extra steps or adjustments?" Use a rating scale like one used in the Olympics to help the children become critical observers. Have them tell the performer what they liked about the performance. Have them tell the performer how he or she might have improved the performance.

Playground Physics

Science

Motion-related phenomena

Physical Education

Body awareness, energy, strength, safety

Grade Level

2 through 6

Have the children explore different ways to move on playground equipment such as a slide, swings, or climbing bars. For the slide, they can test the speed in relation to the texture of the material. Again for the slide, they can use different body shapes to see if they make a difference in the speed attained. For the swings, they can compare the number of swings they can do in 1 minute or how high they can go while pumping their legs and when they don't pump their legs. For the climbing bars, what is the fastest way to travel across the bars?

Creating Change

Science

Changing things

Physical Education

Creating designs and shapes, then changing them

Grade Level

2 and 3

▪ The children create a dance showing the molecular movement of water in solid, liquid, and gas forms (figure 5.15). The solid form is ice, where molecules are very close together and moving very slowly in a single direction—back and forth. Little space is used. The liquid form is water, in which molecules are farther apart, moving faster, and slipping and sliding past each other. More space is used. The gas is water vapor, with hydrogen and oxygen atoms in water molecules separating and reforming into new molecules of the compounds hydrogen gas and oxygen gas. Molecules are far apart and moving fast in all directions.

▪ Have children work in pairs. One partner is a statue or mannequin in a store front, and the other is the designer. The statue assumes a shape; then the designer changes the shape. Work with stretched, curled, and twisted shapes. Have the designer change the statue from one stretched shape to another stretched shape by changing levels, and change the statue from a stretched shape to a twisted shape. Have partners take turns being the statue and the designer.

Clustered   **Spread out**

Figure 5.15   Children can demonstrate molecular movement in solid, liquid, and gas forms.

Balancing Act

Science

Forces in action—principles of stability

Physical Education

Static and dynamic balancing

Grade Level

1 through 3

▪ Conduct some simple experiments regarding stability and balance. "Static balance is when you are still. Can you balance on one, two, or three body parts and hold each for 3 seconds? Can you balance at low, medium, and high levels and hold each for 3 seconds?"

▪ "Our body is best balanced when our center of gravity is over our base of support [figure 5.16]. Use different body parts as bases: feet, hands and feet, knees, seat, forearms, and hips. Find where your center of gravity is. Use your belly button as a point of reference. When your center of gravity is over your base, you are balanced."

▪ "In general, a wide base is more stable than a narrow base, and a low base is more stable than a high base. Work with a partner. One partner should assume a balance position (e.g., on a scale, standing on two feet; three-point football stance, kneeling on hands and knees). The second partner should gently push the balanced person from different directions. Working together under control, push until the balanced person is about to topple. Which balances are most stable? Why?"

Figure 5.16 Our body is best balanced when the center of gravity is over the base of support.

▪ "Sensory organs of the body help a person remain balanced. Stand on one leg. Balance in this position with eyes open, then with eyes closed. Which is easier? Why? [Vision helps orient our body's position in space.] Balance on a knee and hand on the same side of the body, then on opposite sides. Try each with your eyes open, then closed. . . . Try other positions with your eyes open, then closed. Notice that it is much easier to balance with your eyes open. . . . Now try some balances with your arms in close to your side, then spread your arms out. Which position makes it easier to balance? Why?"

▪ "To move, people must temporarily, but under control, place their center of gravity outside their base. Stand up straight. Lean in a chosen direction: forward, backward, sideways. Lean until you feel yourself start to topple. Take a step in that direction to regain your balance. . . . Can you hop forward five times in a row without losing balance? . . . Make one big, long jump and land by bending at the hips, knees, and ankles. Lean forward as you land, and don't let your hands touch the floor. Squat down and place your hands on the floor. Tuck your chin and knees to your chest, bottom up, and over you go. Return to your feet under control."

▪ Have students carry a heavy object, such as a briefcase or a box, as they move across the floor, a raised surface, a bench, or a balance beam. "Try holding the object out away from you in front or to the side as you move, then in close. . . . Which way is easier? Why? In general, for best results, you should lean in the direction opposite the object and hold the object in close to your body."

▪ "Jump in the air and turn a quarter, half, or full rotation. When rotating, pull your arms in for a quick spin. When landing, stretch your arms out to the sides and place your feet wide apart for control. Also bend (give) at the hips, knees, and ankles to absorb your motion. Run, jump, spin and land, or jump from an elevated height to the floor. Each time use good principles of landing to absorb your linear or rotary motion under control—no crashing or falling to the floor."

Do You Measure Up?

Science

Measuring

Physical Education

Selected manipulative and locomotor skills

Grade Level

2 through 4

■ Have children use a book, string, or newspaper to measure how far they can jump, hop, or step. Have them put two actions together, such as two jumps or a jump and a hop, and measure the distance of the combined effort.

■ "Jump as high as you can and place a mark on a wall with a piece of chalk. Measure the height of your vertical jump."

■ "Throw or kick a ball for distance, and use a tape measure to discover the distance the ball traveled in feet, yards, or meters."

■ Use a stopwatch and see how fast the children can run 50 meters, 100 meters, 400 meters.

■ Have children count their resting heart rate using the carotid artery. Then ask them to perform a number of different exercises, such as jump rope, step aerobics, and jumping jacks, for 30 seconds or 1 minute. They count their heart rate again and calculate the difference.

Move Like a Machine

Science

Things on the move

Physical Education

Creative movement sequence

Grade Level

1 through 3

The lever, inclined plane, screw, pulley, wedge, and wheel are types of simple machines. Discuss with the children how different types of simple machines are used in everyday life. Examples include hammers, screwdrivers, bicycles, wheelbarrows, axes, wagons, cranes, and cars. As machines help people work, the machines perform tasks such as pulling, pushing, bending, stretching, twisting, and carrying. Create a lesson in which children explore the various movements that machines perform. Use recorded sound effects or electronic music to allow the students to explore the movements of familiar machines and of machines they create in their imagination. For example, the children could move to the percussive sounds of a hammer; the twisting and rotating of a screwdriver; the creaking of an old door slamming shut; and the rolling of a wagon, bicycle, or steamroller.

Understanding Motion

Science

Newton's laws of motion

Physical Education

Selected locomotor and manipulative skills, creative movement sequence

Grade Level

4 and 5

▪ Newton's first law of motion is about inertia and momentum. It states that a force is required to start an object in motion, stop it, or change its direction. To help children gain an understanding of this law, conduct a number of experiments in your physical education class (figure 5.17). Some balls, bowling pins, and a box or bench to jump from are needed. (1) An object such as a ball will remain at rest unless acted on by an outside force. When we throw, kick, or strike a ball our body provides the outside force. (2) A push or pull must be exerted for an object to be set in motion. When we roll a ball at a bowling pin, the pin will remain stationary until it is hit by the ball. When the ball hits the pin, the pin moves in the direction of the applied force. "In what direction will the pin move if it is hit straight on, from the right side, or from the left side?" (3) Have students run and then try to come to a sudden stop. From a moving start, they jump onto and then off of the box or bench and try to "stick" the landing. "Often you have to take extra steps to come to a stop, or you may even lose control and crash to the floor. The reason is that you have acquired momentum that is difficult to control."

▪ Newton's second law of motion is about acceleration and deceleration. Momentum is directly proportional to the mass of the object and the speed at which the object is moving. Try an experiment with some scooter boards or roller or in-line skates. Push people of different masses or have them build up to different selected speeds on skates when they reach a specific line on the floor of the gym or playground. Then they stop and let momentum take over. Help children observe and record the results of the distances rolled before coming to a stop. After analyzing the results, help children discover that if objects have equal mass, a greater speed will yield greater momentum. If bodies are moving at equal speed, a greater mass will yield greater momentum.

▪ Take several balls of different sizes and masses, such as basketballs, tennis balls, shot puts, medicine balls, and cage balls, out to the playground. First have children toss a ball easily onto the field. Then have them throw the same ball at the same angle but as hard as they can. Observe and record the place where each of the balls lands and the distance each ball rolled. Why did the second throw go farther in the air and on the roll? (More force was applied; it was traveling faster; it had more velocity; it had more momentum.) Next have the children throw balls that differ in weight or mass. They will discover that it takes more force to throw a heavy object a given distance. For example, a child could throw a softball 10 feet (3 meters) with much less force than he or she would need to throw a medicine ball or shot put 10 feet.

Figure 5.17 **Momentum causes a skater to remain in motion after effort is stopped.**

■ Newton's third law of motion is about action and reaction. For every action, there is an equal and opposite reaction. "While sitting or kneeling on a scooter board, if you push backward, in which direction will you travel? [Forward.] While swimming, if you push the water backward, in which direction will you travel? [Forward.] When jumping, if you push down hard against the floor, in which direction will you travel? [Up.] Think of as many other examples of applying Newton's third law of motion as you can."

Push-Pull

Science

Force and motion—work, energy, resistance, friction, linear and rotary motion, centrifugal force

Physical Education

Experiments in human movement

Grade Level

4 and 5

■ A force is a push or a pull exerted against an object to start, stop, accelerate, decelerate, maintain, or change its motion (figure 5.18). To make this point, conduct several demonstrations in your class using large pieces of equipment, for example, a piano, a balance beam on a transport dolly, a horse or parallel bars on a transport dolly, or a portable chalkboard. Have the children work in pairs to put the equipment in place before class or put it away after class. Teach them how to lift or push heavy objects

Figure 5.18 Force should be applied in the direction of the intended movement.

safely (straight backs, lift or push with the legs). Try to get them to figure out where force needs to be applied to push the object in a straight line or to make it turn around. In general, to push in a straight line, the force should be applied near the center of gravity. To achieve rotary motion, the push needs to come from the end of the object. After the equipment is put in place, conduct a regular gymnastics class using the equipment.

■ Work is a force acting on mass through a distance. In simpler terms, work means the ability to push or pull an object over a distance. Point out to the children that whenever they move their bodies or manipulate an object in physical education or at play, they are performing work. Running, jumping, hopping, skipping, throwing, striking, and so on all are examples of moving mass over a distance.

■ Energy is required to produce force and move objects from one place to another. The human body applies force in the form of muscular energy, which is derived from burning calories from eating the proper foods. Kinetic energy is the energy of motion. When we lift, push, pull, carry, throw, or strike something we are using kinetic energy. The body applies force to objects indirectly through the use of potential energy. A drawn bow, a stretched slingshot, and a taut spring are examples of potential energy that becomes kinetic energy on release.

■ In order for a body or an object to move, the forces acting on it must be unbalanced. "Stand in a balanced position. Lean forward, backward, or sideways. Feel the instant that you begin to lose your balance. This is the moment that your center of gravity moves outside your base. Take a step to regain your balance. . . . Squat down and place your hands on the floor. Tuck your head and knees to your chest. Raise your bottom and look under your legs. Once again feel the instant you lose your balance and roll over in a forward roll. This is the moment your center of gravity moves outside your base."

■ Resistance is an opposing force that makes it difficult to move a body or an object. Friction is a type of resistance between the surfaces of two objects. Friction is necessary to start and stop motion. To gain efficient movement, it is desirable to create enough friction or resistance for movement to take place but not so much or so little that inefficiency of execution results. Conduct some experiments in the gym by having races under different conditions. Have the children try racing with socks on, in bare feet, and in gym shoes and consider which ways make it easiest to get a good start and a quick stop. Have the children observe the results of their attempts. Record the results. Point out that athletes use various athletic shoes with special designs, such as football cleats, baseball spikes, and basketball sneakers, to gain traction on the surfaces on which they move. Sometimes it is desirable to reduce the amount of friction between surfaces to enable more efficient movement, for example with use of ice skates, in-line skates, and skateboards.

■ There are three circumstances in which friction affects motion: starting friction, sliding friction, and rolling friction. Starting friction exists when a person begins to move him- or herself or an object. Starting friction causes the greatest resistance to movement and is the hardest to overcome. Sliding friction exists when an individual attempts to drag or slide one object over another. Rolling friction exists when a person rolls one object over another. Conduct some simple experiments in the gymnasium. Have the children work in pairs. Have one partner try to pull the other a short distance with a jump rope. The resisting partner should be wearing gym shoes and standing with his or her feet wide apart in the direction of movement. The children will find out that starting friction is great under these circumstances. Next, have the resisting child stand, kneel, or sit on a carpet square with the carpet side down. Once again, the pulling partner should try to pull the resisting partner a short distance. Make observations, calculate the force, and record the results. Finally, the resisting partner should sit or kneel on a scooter board. The pulling partner should try to pull the resisting partner a short distance. Make observations, calculate the force, and record the results. The children should discover that it takes much less force to overcome rolling friction than it does to overcome sliding or starting friction.

▪ Linear motion is motion in a straight line or a direct pathway. Develop with the children a dance sequence that compares moving in straight lines or direct pathways with moving in curved lines or indirect pathways. Both air and floor pathways should be considered.

▪ Rotary motion is movement of a body around an axis. This type of motion may occur in any or all of the three body planes: around the vertical, horizontal, and transverse axes. Conduct a lesson that helps children learn about the principles of rotation around an axis. In general, shortening the radius of rotation causes a faster rate of rotation. Lengthening the radius causes a slower rate of rotation (figure 5.19). Tucking up tight into a ball in a gymnastics roll causes a fast rotation. Opening up at the end of a roll causes a slower rotation. During *V*-seat spins in gymnastics (Werner, 2004), tucking up tight causes a fast spin, and opening up makes the spin come to a stop. Dancers, roller skaters, and ice skaters all use these same principles to control their spins on a vertical axis. To spin fast, performers tuck their arms in tight. When stopping their spins, performers thrust their arms out to the sides. To help children gain an understanding of these concepts, have them jump into the air from the floor or from an elevated surface such as a box or bench. Have them make quarter, half, or full turns while in the air. To assist in the takeoff and spin, children need to throw their arms in the direction of the spin and then tuck their arms in quickly. To stop the spin and control the landing, they need to spread their arms and legs out to the sides and flex to absorb the landing. To make this a safe experience, insist that the children always land in control on their feet. Falling and crashing to the floor out of control is not acceptable.

▪ Radius of rotation around an axis is also a factor in learning how to pump while swinging. In principle one must lengthen the radius of rotation while working with gravity. When moving against gravity in an upward direction, one must shorten the radius of rotation. One can achieve a long radius by establishing a low center of gravity on the down phase of the swing. One can achieve a short radius by establishing a high center of gravity on the up phase. While this concept may be difficult to explain in detail to children, you can teach them to bend and stretch their legs at the appropriate times to achieve a successful pumping action. For example, when swinging from a sitting position, they should learn to straighten their knees on the down phase and bend their knees on the up phase.

▪ Centripetal and centrifugal forces also affect the motion of a person or an object moving in a circular pathway. Centripetal force is the name given to any force directed inward toward the center of a circular path of motion. Centrifugal force is the inertial tendency of a body or object in motion to move out or away from the center of the circular path. Centrifugal force causes a person or an object to travel in a straight line if released in some way from the axis of rotation. Once again,

Figure 5.19 Using the arms to help stop rotary motion.

several practical examples can be used to help children understand these concepts. When a person throws a ball overhand or pitches it underhand, a windmill-like windup establishes a rotary motion while the ball is held. The muscles of the arm and hand serve as the centripetal force by pulling the ball inward and keeping the ball in contact with the hand as it travels in a circular pathway before release. On release, centrifugal force causes the ball to move away from the body in a straight line tangential to the circle at the point of release. You can present similar examples by having children pivot around a vertical axis using a discus-like hurling action to aim a hula hoop at a traffic cone target or throwing a Frisbee for distance.

Forces in Action

Science

Force to produce movement, summation of forces, absorbing forces, angle of release, angle of deflection

Physical Education

Using muscles to produce and reduce force (strength), experiments to understand angles of force and deflection

Grade Level

4 and 5

▪ The amount of force needed for a particular task depends on the purpose of the movement. Since muscles supply force for each movement that a body makes, people should be aware of certain facts about muscles and how they work so that they can use their muscles efficiently. For example, the large, strong muscles of the body are able to exert more force than the smaller, weaker muscles. In general, the muscles of the legs, hips, and thighs are larger and stronger than those in the arms and lower back. Have the children help you when you place large pieces of apparatus (boxes or bags of balls, gymnastics boxes or benches, etc.) as you begin a class. Teach them how to lift heavy objects by keeping a straight back and lifting with the larger muscles of the legs (figure 5.20).

▪ In addition to lifting, teach children how to carry heavy objects. In general, they should hold the object in close to their center of gravity. They should lean away from the resistance (heavy object) in proportion to the weight of the object in an effort to keep their center of mass over their base of support. Have the children experiment by carrying a heavy briefcase, a pail of water, or a heavy box across a balance beam or across the floor.

▪ Even small-muscle coordination tasks such as cutting, pasting, and writing require each muscle to be as strong as possible to work efficiently. To develop strength, dexterity, and coordination of the smaller muscles of the hands and forearms, provide situations for children to squeeze tennis balls, wad up pieces of paper with their hands, put nuts and bolts together, play with construction toys, and use small muscles in other ways. Excellent recorded resources for these

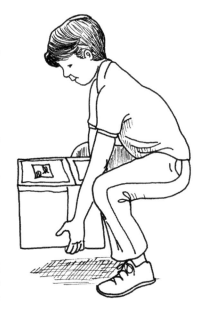

Figure 5.20 Teaching children how to lift and carry heavy objects.

small-muscle development activities are "Squeeze and Relax" and "Finger Thumping" (Brazelton, 1977).

▪ Muscles are able to exert more force when they are placed in a stretched position before they contract. This principle serves as the basis for the windup or ready position of nearly every sport action. Discuss this principle with your students, and then have the children practice their windup before throwing a ball, backswing before stroking a tennis ball, and so on.

▪ When teaching a lesson about throwing, describe to students the principle of summation of forces. The most efficient and effective total force is developed when the force from each contributing part of the body is applied in a single direction in a sequential order over as long a period of time as possible. Try an experiment. Have the children face a target a good distance away. Have them throw toward the target with their arms only—no stepping action, no trunk rotation. Mark and record the distance of the throw. Next, have them throw with a stepping action of the same foot as the throwing arm. Again mark and record the distance of the throw. Finally, with their side to the target, have them step with the opposite foot, turn their trunk appropriately, and release the ball with a cracking action of the arm, wrist, and fingers. Mark and record the distance. The children should discover that the last type of throw produces the best results when throwing for distance. The summation of forces from each contributing body part enables a greater number of muscles to apply the force over a longer distance and a greater period of time until momentum reaches its maximum at the point of release. The sequential contribution of various body parts to the force of the throw also allows for greater leverage, which will increase the force and efficiency of the throw. The same rules apply during kicking and striking various balls in different sport activities.

▪ When one is absorbing the force from a fall or landing from a jump, there should be a gradual reduction of force. Have the children jump from a height such as a box or bench and land on the floor. At first allow them to land rather stiffly on their flat feet. Point out how loud they land as their feet hit the floor. Next, use the cues "bend" or "give." By creating some tension in their leg and feet muscles (preparation) and coiling like a spring as they bend at the hips, knees, and ankles during landing, they will land softly and make much less noise.

▪ Teach the children a safety roll to help them learn about how to absorb their body weight over time and surface area. When falling or performing a forward or safety shoulder roll, a person who tries to land and roll by using a large portion of the body and by absorbing the force over as long a distance as possible lands more softly and efficiently.

▪ Teach the children the principle of absorption of force during a lesson on catching. At first allow them to catch a ball, or preferably a beanbag, with their hands held rather stiffly out in front or to trap the ball against their chest. Point out that their catches make a lot of noise. Then teach them to reach early to make contact with the ball or beanbag and "give" with the force by bending at the elbows and pulling the object in to their trunks. Have a contest to see who can catch without making any noise.

▪ The angle at which an object is struck or released will affect the distance it travels (figure 5.21). Have the children conduct a throwing-for-distance experiment. Each child should throw one or more balls as hard as possible with a rather high trajectory (pop fly). Measure and record their distance. Next, have them throw one or more balls at a rather low trajectory (line drive). Measure and record their distance. Finally, have them throw one or more balls at an approximately 45-degree angle. Measure and record their distance. The children should learn that to project a ball or object into the air over the greatest distance possible, the angle of release should be 45 degrees.

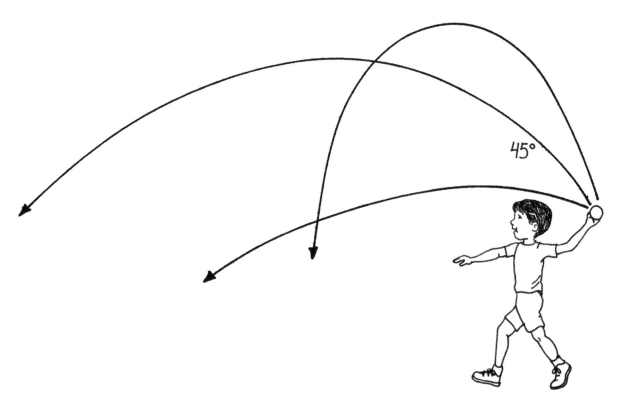

Figure 5.21 **Throwing a ball at 45 degrees for the greatest distance.**

▪ The angle of deflection equals the angle of approach. In the game of billiards, this concept is very important for sinking balls after the cue ball rebounds off a side cushion, but the same concept applies to bouncing a ball off the backboard and into the goal in basketball. Stations can be set up to teach about this concept using these or other activities, such as bounce passes in basketball, striking a ball against a wall at an angle and observing the resulting angle of the returning ball, and a chest pass against the wall to a partner 5 feet (1.5 meters) away.

Magnetic Field

Science

Electricity and magnetism

Physical Education

Creative movement sequences with a focus on attracting and repelling; appliances that are run by electricity

Grade Level

3 and 4

▪ Create a short dance sequence by having the children move about the room as if they were all magnets with only a north pole. What would happen? They would repel each other; and as a result, the magnetic force would become so great as children approached one another that they could get only so close before they would move off in different directions. The children's movement selections should show choices in moving on different levels, in different directions, and at different speeds. They can also experiment with bringing specific body parts close together, showing greater tension as parts come closer together, and moving quickly away in different directions.

■ Pretend that the whole class is working in a magnetic field (figure 5.22). Have each child choose whether he or she wants to be a north or south pole. Use a signal or code for identifying poles, for example, red band or pinny or thumbs up for north, green band or pinny or thumbs down for south. Children should move around the room in different ways such as hopping, skipping, sliding, and crawling. As they approach another person, they will come closer and attach to each other by holding hands if they are opposite poles. They will repel and move away from each other if they are like poles. Once two poles attach they must move around together while linked. Eventually everyone in the class will end up attached.

■ "What appliances in your home are run by electricity?" While the children work in small groups, have them choose a specific appliance and develop a short movement sequence that shows how the appliance works. As groups take turns, have the observing groups guess what appliance is being demonstrated.

Figure 5.22   Opposite magnetic poles attract.

Ongoing Strategies for the Physical Education Classroom

■ Use science terminology when providing technique instruction: terms such as momentum, velocity, inertia, fulcrum.
■ Acknowledge the day's weather conditions. Discuss how and why weather influences the use of facilities, types of activities, safety issues, and participants' attitudes.
■ Use activities that employ different weights and sizes. Ask the students about the impact of weight change or object size on the activity.
■ Connect the daily activity with body functions and systems. Talk about the benefits and reasons for keeping fit.

- Emphasize safety and good body mechanics during lifting, carrying, pushing or pulling equipment, or the performance of skills.
- Discuss advances in technology design and how they have changed the equipment and activities in the physical education classroom.

Summary

The scope and sequence chart in table 5.1 shows that there are many science concepts taught to children in elementary school. Concepts taught in science include those within the biological and life sciences, the earth and space sciences, and physical sciences. We have experimented in our classes with different ways to integrate these concepts in movement settings using different models of interdisciplinary programming. We have always tried to stay true to the principles of maintaining the integrity of each discipline and teaching active lessons. Here we have presented both complete learning experiences and brief descriptions of additional learning experiences for you to try with your students.

Try our ideas. Some will work for you. Some will not. Some you may have to modify. Share your ideas with other teachers both in the classroom and in physical education and dance. Try your own new ideas of ways to integrate science with movement concepts. Make science come alive through practical applications in movement.

Integrating Physical Education With Social Studies

A class of fourth graders went by bus to a nearby living history farm representative of life in the 1800s. The children got to experience milking a cow, shearing a sheep, and gathering eggs from the chicken house. They saw a man plowing a field with a horse-drawn plow. They saw sorghum being ground up and made into syrup. They saw a woman dyeing wool blue (using indigo), yellow (using onion skins), and brown (using bark from a walnut tree). They saw a spinner combine wool and angora (from a rabbit) to make yarn. They saw a woman making lye soap in a cauldron over a wood-burning fire. They saw a blacksmith making tools and a cooper making barrels. They got to ask questions and interact with each of the craftspersons. They wrote in their journals about their experience. Recurring themes of their writing were an awareness of how labor intensive life was during that time period and an appreciation of how many advantages they have in today's society. After all, when they need things, all they have to do is go to a store.

Unlike other curricular areas addressed in this book, the social studies comprise a number of different disciplines. According to Banks (1985), social studies in the elementary curriculum has the primary responsibility to "prepare citizens who can make reflective decisions and participate successfully in civic life of their communities, nation and the world" (p. 7). A review of social studies texts (Harcourt, 2005; Houghton Mifflin, 2005; Scott Foresman, 2005) revealed that at least eight disciplines make up the content foundation of elementary social studies programs. They are history, geography, civics, economics, sociology, anthropology, political science, and philosophy.

Each of the disciplines in social studies may be thought of as addressing product skills. In addition to teaching these skills, social studies provide an environment in which children can learn skills that pertain to building human relations. For example, contemporary curricula at the elementary level often include character education (Lickona, 2004). Students learn about virtues, morals and character issues such as accepting, cooperating, courage, empathy, feeling, fortitude, friendship, gratitude, hard work, honesty, humility, integrity, justice, kindness, love, motivation, peer pressure, persistence, positive attitude, respect, responsibility, self-control, and self-esteem. Schools that adopt a character education program often stress a virtue a week or a virtue a month. There are many ways in which physical education lessons can contribute toward helping students learn and understand each of these virtues.

Students can profit greatly from the integration of social studies experiences with physical education experiences. This integration makes learning experiences more meaningful in both disciplines. Relationships within families, school and community, citizenship, character education, history, mapping and globe skills, national identity and culture, and geography can be studied and enriched through participation in physical education activities.

Both contemporary elementary social studies and physical education curricula also emphasize critical thinking and collaborative learning. The Houghton Mifflin social studies curriculum (*Social Studies,* 2005) stresses critical thinking as a goal in teaching social studies so that students become citizens who make informed and reasonable decisions. The texts note that teachers can help students become better critical thinkers when they help students in

- seeking a clear statement of the question,
- using and mentioning credible sources,

- seeking reasons,
- looking for alternatives and alternative viewpoints,
- being open-minded, and
- changing their position when the evidence warrants.

No doubt integrating movement and social studies contributes to the actualization of these characteristics of critical thinking.

Scope and Sequence for Social Studies

The scope of elementary social studies usually includes specific topics by grade levels. Because social studies is made up of so many disciplines, the scope and sequence are quite elaborate. It should be helpful to examine the content of elementary social studies by grade level (table 6.1).

Table 6.1

Scope and Sequence of Social Studies Concepts Taught in Elementary Schools

CONCEPT	GRADE						
	K	1	2	3	4	5	6
Family	✕	✕					
Home		✕					
Neighborhoods	✕	✕	✕				
Communities	✕	✕	✕	✕			
School	✕	✕					
Travel	✕						
Necessity of rules	✕						
Urban, suburban, and rural life		✕					
Family life, past and present		✕					
Citizenship		✕	✕	✕	✕		✕
United States				✕	✕	✕	
Famous people			✕				
How people live and work				✕	✕		
First Americans					✕		
Settling the land					✕		
Our own state					✕		
How people change				✕			

(continued)

Table 6.1 *(continued)*

CONCEPT	GRADE						
	K	**1**	**2**	**3**	**4**	**5**	**6**
Geography of the United States						✖	
History of the United States						✖	
Economics of the United States						✖	
Political system of the United States						✖	
History of western hemisphere						✖	
Geography of western hemisphere							✖
The world, past and present							✖
The world, regions							✖

PRIMARY-GRADE SOCIAL STUDIES SKILLS AND CONCEPTS

The focus in kindergarten is on awareness of self in a social setting. Kindergartners begin to connect their home life with group life at school. They also study neighborhoods, communities, occupations, ways to travel, and the need for rules in social settings. First graders learn about themselves in primary social groups, including family (past and present), school, neighborhood, and community. Within communities, first graders study citizenship and the differences between urban, suburban, and rural life. Second graders study about neighborhoods, communities, famous people, citizenship, and how people live and work. Third grade social studies focuses on communities and emphasizes sharing earth and space with others who are working and changing. Third graders are introduced to their own country and continue to study citizenship. Other primary-grade topics that are taught include mapping skills; expressions of culture; character education; community celebrations; heroes; caring for resources; and buying, selling, and trading with others.

INTERMEDIATE-GRADE SOCIAL STUDIES SKILLS AND CONCEPTS

The major emphasis in fourth grade is on the students' home state, including study of geography, state government, history, citizenship, and economics. The fifth grade program highlights the United States and focuses on geography, history, economics, and the national political system. The subject of study in sixth grade is usually the people, cultures, and geography in the western hemisphere and the world. Additional intermediate-grade topics that permeate the curriculum entail map and globe skills including knowledge of latitude and longitude, archaeology and early civilizations, character education, and old ways and new—change over time.

Learning Experiences

This chapter presents six complete learning experiences (table 6.2). They demonstrate two of the interdisciplinary teaching models discussed in chapter 1. The learning experiences have been designed to include skills and concepts from physical education and social studies. For each learning experience we include a name, suggested grade level, interdisciplinary teaching model, objectives, equipment, organization, complete description of the lesson, and assessment suggestions. In addition, tips on what to look for in student responses, suggestions for how you can change or modify the lesson, and ideas for teachable moments are offered to provide further insights into each learning experience.

Table 6.2

Social Studies Learning Experience Index

Skills and concepts	Name	Suggested grade level	Interdisciplinary teaching model
Social studies: modes of transportation, with a focus on the development of the bicycle Physical education: locomotor patterns	Moving Through the Years	K-3	Shared
Social studies: studying occupations, vocations, and the life process and how products were manufactured in the 18th and 19th centuries Art: art of the masters and contemporary artists that exhibits everyday life experiences and vocations. Students can draw pictures or sculpt models of people involved in their occupation. Physical education: creating poses and action sequences that depict a selected vocation	The Good Old Days	2-3	Shared
Social studies: customs and cultures—greetings from around the world Physical education: locomotor patterns and axial, gesture-like patterns	Have a Good Day	K-2	Partnership
Social studies: customs and cultures—games children from various countries play Physical education: locomotion, balance, and coordination	Games From Other Countries	4-6	Shared
Social studies: Olympic history Physical education: throwing using force	Heave, Hurl, Fling	4-5	Partnership
Social studies: learning about the history of Scotland, John Knox and the Reformation, and Hogmanay as a New Year celebration Visual arts: drawing and sculpting pieces of art to represent a ritual Music: appreciating and singing music associated with a ritual Physical education: creating a dance emphasizing activities that occur during a ritual	Hogmanay	3-5	Partnership

Moving Through the Years

Suggested Grade Level

Primary (K through 3)

Interdisciplinary Teaching Model

Shared

Studying transportation is common in elementary social studies. Students can use what they learn in this lesson to better understand the historical development of transportation and to improve expressive movement skills.

Social Studies

Modes of transportation, with a focus on the development of the bicycle

Physical Education

Various locomotor patterns to express the movement in types of transportation

Objectives

As a result of participating in this learning experience, children will improve their ability to

- move like different types of vehicles,
- develop and perform a movement routine that focuses on the evolution of the bicycle,
- move in ways that reflect an understanding of the concepts of fast and slow movement,
- move in ways that reflect an understanding of the concepts of bound and free-flow movement, and
- identify the different types of bicycles in the evolution of the bicycle.

Equipment

A picture file of the evolution of bicycles will be needed for this lesson. Some social studies textbooks include such pictures.

Organization

The students will work individually in mass or scattered formation. They will also work with partners in scattered formation.

Description

"Hello! Today we are going to take a look at transportation, which is how we travel. Every day our lives are affected by different types of transportation. Can you think of ways transportation has affected your life since you woke up this morning? Some of you were transported to school in cars, buses, trucks, trains, or subways or on bicycles or skates. Maybe you even transported yourself here by using your own two feet. Another way in which transportation has affected you has to do with the food you eat in the cafeteria. The food was transported here in some way. The bananas that are served might have come by boat, freight train, or truck. We can think of many ways in which transportation has touched our lives in the hours that we have been awake this morning.

"Let's get moving. I want you to pick some type of transportation. You might choose a car, boat, helicopter, skateboard, or something else. When I say 'go,' move like your method of travel. For now you are not, for example, riding *in* the car or the boat; you are moving *like* the car or boat. You don't need to sound like your type of transportation. Let's move quietly. Who would like to show us what we are looking for? Erin. Everyone, let's see if we can figure out Erin's means of transportation. Thanks, Erin. What were you moving like? Okay. You were a jet. You had a takeoff that started off slowly but very quickly increased speed until you were moving very fast. Once you reached your traveling speed, you stayed at that speed for a while. Now everyone, go. . . . Freeze.

"Think about the speed of your movement. Were you going fast or slowly? Did your speed truly represent the speed of your mode of transportation? This time I want you to think about the way your mode of transportation changes speeds. Think of your type of transportation, for example a huge flatbed truck, moving from still (or parked) up to full speed and gradually back to parked. Really think about your mode of transportation. Usually the larger modes of transportation take longer to arrive at top speed and also take longer to slow back down. Ready, go. . . . Freeze.

"When I say 'go,' make a bridge with a partner by the time I count to five. Ready, go. Show your partner your change-of-speed sequence. See whether your partner can tell what you are moving like. Then switch and have your partner take a turn. When you have finished, stand beside your partner so that I'll know you have completed the task. Now ask your partner what you can do to make your sequence look more like your type of transportation, from parked, to full speed, to parked. When I say 'go,' each of you work to improve your routine. Ready, go. . . . Freeze.

"We have so many ways to travel. Let's get to know a little more about transportation. There are three types of areas in which we can travel: on land, over water, and in the air.

"Let's focus on land travel. This is very interesting! The invention of the wheel started real land transportation. Guess how long humans have had the wheel? About five thousand years. Once people understood the wheel, they could transport themselves and their belongings more easily. What would be some of the first kinds of transportation that used wheels? Oxcarts, chariots, covered wagons, buggies. Later came the bicycle and 'horseless carriage,' or automobile. *Automobile* means 'a machine that moves by itself.'

"The bicycle was popular well before the car was invented. Bicycles were the most popular way to travel in cities. The first bicycles had no pedals; the riders sat on a seat and moved by walking [show picture]. These cycles were called *hobbyhorses* [figure 6.1]. The next cycles, which were invented in the 1860s, were *velocipedes,* and they looked like this. [Show a picture of a velocipede.] As you can see, the velocipedes had a big front wheel and two very small rear wheels. The larger the front wheel, the faster the cycle could go. Gradually the front wheel became smaller, and the bicycle came to look more like the bicycles that we ride today. The bicycles of today are really awesome. With the technology that we have, some bicycles are designed to go very fast. Have any of you seen bicycle racing? Those athletes are really moving, aren't they?

Figure 6.1　A picture of a "hobbyhorse."

"Let's move like different types of cycles. First, take a look at the velocipedes again. [Show picture.] How do you think those velocipedes moved? I'll tell you that riders had to be careful not to run over rocks or holes because they could crash very easily. Now when I say 'go,' I want you to begin to move like a velocipede over a city street. Ready, go. . . . Freeze. I notice that many of you are going slowly and are moving in what we call a bound flow. You want to stay in control, avoiding other cycles, bumps, and rocks. Let's move again like those early cycles. Ready, go. . . . Freeze. Molly, please show us the way you were moving. She is doing a nice job of moving like a velocipede in a slow, bound flow. Thank you, Molly. Everyone, let's give that movement another try. Ready, go. . . . Freeze.

"Different cycles emerged over the years. The *ordinary* could go much faster than the velocipede. [Show picture.] Next came the *safety* [show picture], which looks much like the bicycles that we ride today.

"Let's move like the ordinary and the safety. The ordinary we can see still had a large front tire and smaller back tires [figure 6.2]. Riders sat over the front wheel about 5 feet [1.5 meters] off the ground. When a rider fell off, it was difficult to get back on. Sometimes a rider would have to push the ordinary a good distance before he or she found something to stand on to mount the bike. The wheels were rubber and had wire spokes with steel rims. How do you think movement on the ordinary was? Probably more like movement on the velocipede than on the bicycles we ride today. More bound than free flow. Bound flow is really controllable, like the jump you would make from one slippery rock to another in a creek. Free flow is almost unstoppable, as when a child runs down a hill.

"The safety [figure 6.3] looks similar to the bicycles that you might have at home. Of course, the safety did not have all the modern features that we have today. What do you think movement of the safety over a city street was like? More bound or free? Yes, more free flow.

"When I say 'go,' I want you to move like an ordinary until you hear the drumbeat. Then begin to move as a safety would move. Who can tell us what we are going to do? Jeff? Right, move like an ordinary until the drumbeat, then like a safety. Ready, go.

Figure 6.2   A picture of an "ordinary."   Figure 6.3   A picture of a "safety."

"Freeze. I want you to keep the same idea, but now begin with an interesting starting position, move like an ordinary bicycle, and then on your own change into a safety bicycle. Gradually increase speed, then slow down and stop in a finish position. Who can quickly tell us what we are going to do? Phillip? Okay, good answer. Everybody ready. Go.

"Freeze. You all are moving very well. Let's add another part to your sequence. Again you will begin with an interesting starting position, but then move like a velocipede (with caution, you need to avoid those potholes, rocks, and debris); gradually transition into an ordinary cycle (you are still somewhat cautious); then into a safety, increasing speed and then gradually slowing to an interesting finish. So the sequence is like this: starting position, velocipede, ordinary, safety, ending position. Ready, go.

"Freeze. Adam and Lauren have agreed to show us the sequence that they have come up with. . . . Thanks, you two. Now I want you to continue to work on this sequence. Focus on making the first part of your sequence slow with bound flow, which is cautious and restrained, just as Adam and Lauren did. This is sort of like learning to ride a unicycle, a cycle that has only one wheel. Have you ever seen someone ride a unicycle? Have you ever tried to ride a unicycle yourself? Think about the way you would ride if you were trying to balance on a unicycle, which would be much like trying to ride a velocipede. Ready, go.

"Freeze. You are working hard. Let's add a final part to your sequence. Remember that at the start of the lesson we talked about modern bicycle racing. Racers go very fast. Most of you have probably ridden your bicycle very fast down a hill. Well, that is what I want you to add to the last part of your sequence. So let's say that your safety bicycle turns into a current-day racing bicycle [show picture]. You are going to be moving very fast, as if you are traveling down a big hill. This is called free flow. For the ending, you must slow down and finish in an interesting way. So, Sarah, tell us what we are going to do for our whole routine. Good. Ready, go.

"Freeze. Students, you are going to continue to work on your routines. I want to emphasize starting your routine with a slow, bound movement and gradually changing into a free-flow, fast movement. Ready, go.

"Freeze. Let's show our routines. We will have six or seven of you go at a time. The others of you can just have a seat on the floor until you are asked to show your sequence. . . . I enjoyed seeing your sequences, but I would like you to refine your routines a little more. When I say 'go,' I want you to get with a partner to work on your routines. Ready, go. Now I want you to show your routine to your partner and ask for help in making it look better. Then switch and have your partner show you his or her routine. Remember, we are telling a story here. What is our story? It is the development of the bicycle, which is a form of land travel. . . . Freeze. Let's show our routines again.

"You are going to find this next task very interesting. How many of you have heard of a bicycle built for two? These are also called tandem bicycles. They have two seats, two sets of handlebars, two wheels, and two sets of pedals. The tandem bicycle was popular during the late 1800s and early 1900s. Many couples dated, or courted, on tandem bicycles. With the same partner you had before, you are going to come up with a 'tandem routine.' Choose one of your routines and perform it as if you are on a tandem bicycle. Remember, this is leading and following. The person on the front of the bicycle is the leader. Ready, go.

"Freeze. Students, let's show what we have so far. We will have four sets of partners go at one time.

"You did very well at working with your partner on your tandem routines. That is about all the time we have today. Let's review. What was the first bicycle called? The next one? And the next? On what type of movement did our routines focus?

"Let's end with a funny story. At first, automobiles were unpopular with farmers. Drivers who were not careful ran over dogs, cats, and chickens. Cars also scared horses that were pulling wagons or buggies. I think this next part is funny. When farmers saw a car that was broken down, they would often yell, 'Get a horse!'

"Okay, thanks for the hard work on your routines. See you tomorrow."

Assessment Suggestion

After the sequence is completed, ask students to write down their sequences. Have an observer check that his or her partner followed the written sequence and that all parts are included. Encourage the observer to provide feedback about the inclusion of all parts and about the expressiveness of the sequence.

Look For

- Emphasize that all routines (or movements that are connected) should be repeatable, should have a starting and an ending position, and should use smooth transitions from one movement to the next.

- A focus of this lesson is on moving fast and slowly. As children move like their chosen modes of transportation, look for gradual changes in speed. Also look for speeds that are really representative of the type of transportation. For example, a huge ocean liner never would move as fast as a small speedboat.

- A focus of this lesson in on bound and free-flow movement. Look for students to make their bound flow really bound. A good example of bound flow is jumping on slippery, wet rocks in a creek. Also look for free movement to be almost unstoppable, as when a child runs down a hill. Point out the contrast in bound and free movements as the children move.

- When students work on leading and following, look for accurate matching of movements.

How Can I Change This?

- The lesson could focus on the evolution of other types of transportation, for example, the evolution of the automobile.

- Students could be asked to mirror, instead of match, movements in the partner sequence.

- Students could develop a sequence that focuses on different types of transportation during a certain time period, for example the early 1900s. The sequence could include moving like trains, airplanes, bicycles, and automobiles of that era.

Teachable Moments

- Stress the relationship between the disciplines of physical education and social studies. Emphasize how types of transportation move and how our bodies move through space.

- Be sure that students can identify the specific types of bicycles. Ask which bicycles would emphasize different types of movements: slow, fast, bound, free.

The Good Old Days

Suggested Grade Level

Primary (2 and 3)

Interdisciplinary Teaching Model

Shared

Students use knowledge about occupations gained in an integrated social studies and art unit to create shapes and movement sequences that represent the actions of different occupations.

Social Studies

Studying occupations and vocations is common in elementary social studies. Students can use what they learn in this lesson to better understand the life process and how products were manufactured in the 18th and 19th centuries.

Art

Art of the masters and of contemporary artists often exhibits everyday life experiences and vocations of people. Students can learn about these art pieces as well as draw pictures or sculpt models of people involved in their occupation.

Physical Education

Creating shapes and action sequences that depict a selected vocation

Objectives

As a result of participating in this learning experience, children will improve their ability to

- combine locomotor and axial movements in a repeatable sequence of three or more movements;
- create a sequence with a beginning, middle, and end while working by themselves or with a partner;
- create a dance that communicates and interprets a selected life process or vocation;
- create a movement problem, demonstrate multiple solutions, choose the most interesting solution, and discuss the reasons for that choice; and
- interpret through dance an idea taken from another medium.

Equipment

A series of pictures that illustrate the work of everyday life or vocations (such as van Gogh's *Peasant-Woman Tying Sheaves, The Reaper,* and *The Thresher,* 1889, van Gogh Museum, Amsterdam; Brueghel the Elder's *The Harvesters, Harvesters,* and *Rabbit Hunt,* 1565, Flemish Museum; and Green's *Homage to Sheets, Two Baskets,* and *Fishing from Shore,* 1989-2000, *Gullah Images, The Art of Jonathan Green,* University of South Carolina Press, Columbia, SC, 1996) will be needed for this lesson.

Organization

The students will work individually or with a partner in scattered formation.

Description

"Good morning. As you know when you come into class, I always take roll. As I look at some of your surnames or last names, I can tell what some of your forefathers did for a living. For example, we have Taylor, Miller, Sawyer, Cooper, Tanner, Schumann, Collier, Mandrel, and Smith families here in school. Does anyone know the origin of these names? Well, a tailor was a seamstress or a person who sewed clothes. A miller was one who processed grain (wheat, oats, etc.) at a grist mill. A sawyer was a lumberjack, a person who cut down trees or worked in a sawmill. A cooper was a barrel maker. A tanner was someone who tanned hides of animals to make leather products such as coats, hats, and gloves. A *schumann* (German) was a cobbler, who made shoes. A collier was a coal miner. A mandrel is a miner's pick, and most likely a person with that name mined for coal or gold. 'Smith' is short for 'blacksmith' or 'tinsmith,' so a person with that name did that as a trade. Do you know the origin of your family name? Ask your parents and come back and report to me.

"I have been talking to your classroom and art teachers, and we have decided to work together for our next unit of study. Together we are going to learn about our history from the 1800s and early 1900s. In social studies you will learn about the lifestyle of people working during that time period. You will learn about the tools and machines used to perform labor tasks. People did not always have it as easy as they do now with modern technology. We have collected some of those types of tools so you can see how they worked. You will also be asked to do some of your own research in books and on the Internet to find examples of people doing work during that time period. You will write a story about what you learn on a chosen topic such as farming, cooking, baking, tree cutting, blacksmithing, weaving, or washing clothes.

"In your art class you will discover some of the famous paintings of artists showing the lifestyle of people during that time period. For example, Vincent van Gogh is well known for his paintings—*Peasant-Woman Tying Sheaves, The Reaper,* and *The Thresher.* Let's look at those paintings. Boy, that looks like hard work. I'm glad that I am living in these modern times. You will also draw pictures or sculpt pieces that depict different trades or vocations.

"At the same time you are working in the classroom and in art on this topic, you will be working on a dance project. We will start working by ourselves and then select a partner to work with to create a movement sequence that will combine four or five action words using a chosen theme. For example, if you choose farming, you might use words such as *tilling, planting, cutting, bundling,* and *threshing.* Each of these words is an action word or verb. Let's get started by getting up and spreading out. We will explore each of these words as we warm up. Does anyone know what the word *tilling* means? Yes, Patty, *tilling* means preparing the soil for planting. Some ways to do that would be to dig the dirt with a shovel, plow the land with a horse and plow, or even hoe the dirt. Let's do some of those actions. We'll start with the word *plow.* I want to show you these pictures. Here's one of a horse farmer. See the horse pulling and the farmer walking behind the plow. Here is another with a person pushing a hand plow. Boy, that was hard work! One movement is pulling and the other is pushing, but they both involve direct, powerful, sustained movement. How can we do these actions? I want to see the strain and tension in your muscles. That's it—long, slow, direct, and powerful actions. I want to see that in your arms, legs, and back. Push, then pull. Go forward, backward, maybe sideways. Stop.

"I see some people trying to look exactly like the action in using the tool or machine in the picture. What I am looking for is a liberal or creative interpretation of these actions. Can you do a plowing action with different body parts in self-space? Can you do plowing actions while moving about on the floor? Let's get back to work. That is much better. I see powerful pushing actions with the arms. Some people are bent over at a medium level, pulling backward as they move across the floor straining with their legs. Sally is pushing sideways to the left with both arms and a step of the left foot, then to the right with two arms and a step of the right foot. How else can you do a plowing action? Next, try digging the soil. Remember to interpret the words creatively. I am looking for powerful, direct, sudden actions this time. Punch down into the earth, out into space. Use your arms, your legs. Then, hoe the soil."

▶ For the remainder of this lesson, explore other words related to farming. Show the children tools that would have been used in the planting, cutting, bundling, and threshing processes. For example, perhaps you have an old corn-planting tool. Perhaps you can find a sickle or scythe that was used to cut grain by hand in the fields. Creatively interpret each of the words you use by getting at the essence of these words. How much force or power do the movements require? Do they use space directly or indirectly? Are they sustained or sudden actions?

▶ For the remainder of the unit (two to four lessons), explore other early labor processes. Baking or cooking, blacksmithing, soap making, lumberjacking, washing clothes, making candles, shearing sheep, dying wool, weaving, milking cows, basket making, carpentry, and wood carving are good choices. The following list gives suggestions for action words that are appropriate to explore through movement. We encourage you to add your own words and think of other jobs to add to the list.

▪ **Baking, cooking, canning:** *break* eggs, *sift* flour, *mix* ingredients, *knead* dough, *rise* (bread or cake), *cut, serve*

▪ **Blacksmithing:** bellows, heat and fire, *pound, bend* and *shape, cool*

▪ **Lumberjack:** *chop, saw, haul, split*

▪ **Washing clothes:** *agitate, wring, hang* on a line, *dry* in a breeze

▶ In cooperation with the classroom teacher and art teacher, find pictures of people doing each of these activities. Or one of the children may have a parent who is proficient in one or more of these vocations as a hobby whom you could invite to class. You might even live near a living history farm, a museum, or a place where people engage in reenactments of Revolutionary or Civil War battles.

▶ If possible, take the children on a field trip to learn about life in the 1760 to 1840 time period.

▶ In dance or physical education class the children will be allowed to work on their own or with a partner. They will choose a theme or vocation and select four to six action words to describe the movements relevant to that theme. They will then develop a movement sequence to interpret their chosen action words. As the children develop their sequence, they must start and end in a shape that creates an image typical of the work they are doing. Children should be encouraged to use their own words based on reading or research they have done on their theme. As a teacher you should encourage children to be analytical as well as to interpret their words liberally. They should not restrict their movements to make them look exactly like the action in using the tool or completing the process. For example, if a child or set of partners chose kneading dough, you might expect to see actions that are powerful, sustained, and indirect. These movements might be done with different body parts in self-space or as students move about on the floor. The actions are not about standing still and using only the hands and arms to mix dough.

▶ In the last lesson of the unit when all of the sequences are well rehearsed and memorized, each of the students or sets of partners will perform their work for the rest of the class. They may read the story they have written about what they have learned about their chosen vocation or job. They may also show the artwork that they drew or made in conjunction with this unit of study.

▶ At the end of the unit, you and the other teachers should discuss the topic of vocations and occupations with the children, focusing on comparisons from one time period to another.

Assessment Suggestion

Figure 6.4 shows a suggested rubric for evaluating the children's movement sequences based on their chosen vocation or job.

Good Old Days Movement Rubric

Sample Theme—Farming

Clear beginning individual/partner shape: pulling/pushing a heavy plow

WORD	BSER COMPONENTS			DANCE/MOVEMENT
	Space	Weight	Time	Interprets Component
	Dir/Flx	Frm/Lgt	Sud/Sus	Yes/No
Till	✖	✖	✖	
Plant	✖	✖	✖	
Grow	✖	✖	✖	
Cut	✖	✖	✖	
Bundle	✖	✖	✖	

Clear ending individual/partner shape—bundle, pile of straw, vegetables

Figure 6.4   The Good Old Days movement rubric.

Your Theme _____

Person(s) in group _____

Clear beginning individual/partner shape—draw picture here:

WORD	BSER COMPONENTS			DANCE/MOVEMENT
	Space	Weight	Time	Interprets Component
	Dir/Flx	Frm/Lgt	Sud/Sus	Yes/No

_____
_____
_____
_____
_____

Clear ending individual/partner shape—draw picture here:

Figure 6.4 *(continued)*

(continued)

Good Old Days Movement Rubric *(continued)*

Scoring for rubric

3—Clear beginning and ending shape with all selected movements interpreted correctly and consistently using BSER components

2—Clear beginning and ending shape with most (three or four) selected movements interpreted correctly and consistently using BSER components

1—Beginning or ending shape (or both) not clear; one or two selected movements interpreted correctly or consistently using BSER components

Figure 6.4

Look For

▪ Emphasize clear beginning and ending shapes that represent the occupation or vocation chosen. If the children are working as partners, stress that each person should relate to the other as if they were working together.

▪ Stress a liberal or creative interpretation of the selected action words and not a literal translation of the true action. How much power or force is used—heavy, light? What is the use of space—direct, indirect? What is the relationship to time—sudden, sustained?

▪ Do the students use contrasting movements to make the sequence interesting to watch? For example, are some movements strong and powerful while others are soft and light? Are some sudden and quick while others are slow and sustained?

▪ Are there transitions from one action word to the next in an attempt to show a smooth flow through the sequence?

▪ Have the students chosen words that effectively represent their occupation or vocation? Have they practiced several possibilities of performing each word? Have they eliminated some words or actions that didn't work well in their sequence? Have they added others? Have they ordered the words in a logical sequence? Have they practiced the sequence often so that they can repeat it the same way each time?

How Can I Change This?

▪ Students could be encouraged to combine different words that represent "a day in the life." Examples are *cooking, washing, weaving* and *sewing, chopping* (wood), and *hunting.*

▪ The lesson or unit could focus on modern-day occupations and vocations. For example, students could research the life of a coal miner, a shrimp boater or fisherman, an astronaut, a automotive mechanic, or an industrial engineer.

▪ Use folk dances as a venue to teach children about occupations and vocations. For example, Jolly Is the Miller is a folk dance about how a grain mill works; Tanko Bushi is a folk dance about coal mining; Chimes of Dunkirk is about clocks; Gathering Peascods is about farming and harvesting; The Little Shoemaker is about how shoes are made; The Fireman's Dance is about the job of a firefighter.

Teachable Moments

- Invite parents and community members to class to share their occupations. Have the children ask them questions relating to the actions involved in their everyday work.
- Have a discussion with the children about how various jobs were done in earlier periods as compared to how they are done today.
- Visit a living history farm to witness how activities took place on a daily basis before the Industrial Revolution. Children could play games with toys from that time period, milk a cow, shear a sheep, plow a field, make a candle, watch a blacksmith in action, and so on.

Have a Good Day

Suggested Grade Level

Primary (K through 2)

Interdisciplinary Teaching Model

Partnership

We strongly urge you to make this lesson part of a collaborative effort by several teachers. Themes of study including important life milestones (births, religious rites of passage such as baptisms or bar mitzvahs, weddings, funerals), seasons of the year (new year, planting, harvest), and holidays are clearly interdisciplinary. As children explore customs and cultures of different people around the world through a theme approach, they can celebrate similarities and differences among groups of people.

Social Studies

Customs and cultures: greetings from around the world

Physical Education

Locomotor patterns of walking and skipping and axial, gesture-like patterns involved in greetings

Objectives

As a result of participating in this learning experience, children will improve their ability to

- perform simple locomotor and gesture patterns to the rhythm of music,
- move using the specific rhythms designated in each part of a dance,
- perform selected folk dances that reflect greeting customs from other cultures, and
- recognize a variety of ways that people from different cultures and vocations greet each other.

Equipment

A record, CD, or cassette player and music for the French folk dance "Bridge of Avignon" (Michael Herman's Orchestra, 1958) or the Danish folk dance "Dance of Greeting" (Michael Herman's Orchestra, 1958) or the African folk dance "Jambo" (Weikart, 1989, record 7).

Organization

To learn the specific steps of the dance and the greeting customs, the children will work individually in mass or scattered formation. Then the children will form a single, large circle with an assigned partner and corner to perform the selected folk dance.

Description

"*Buenos dias. Bon jour. Jambo. Guten tag [guten morgen].* Do you know what any of those phrases mean? Ashley? [Good day or hello.] Right. *Buenos dias* is a greeting in Spanish. Good day. The other three are the same greeting in French *(bon jour),* Swahili *(jambo),* and German *(guten tag).* What do we say to each other in the United States when we greet each other? [Hi; Hello; How ya doin'; What's up; What do you say, man.] You're right. Those are all verbal ways people greet each other.

"In our school we are studying the theme of customs and cultures of different people around the world. This will help us come to understand that while we all may do things differently, we are alike or similar in many ways. For example, as you have learned in your class with Ms. Crosse, most cultures celebrate or honor specific important life milestones, such as births, namings, graduations, weddings, and funerals. Most cultures also celebrate the beginning of new seasons of the year, such as the new year, planting, blessing of the fleet, and harvest. Most countries also celebrate special holidays. Can you name any we celebrate here in the United States? [Martin Luther King Day, Valentine's Day, St. Patrick's Day, Memorial Day, Mother's Day, Father's Day, Fourth of July, Columbus Day, Washington's and Lincoln's Birthdays, All Saints Day or Halloween, Hanukkah, Kwanza, and Christmas.] Why do we celebrate them? Yes, some are religious holidays, others celebrate our war dead, our independence, national heroes, and so on.

"The reason I greeted you in different ways today is that we are going to learn to physically greet each other in different ways and put those greetings into a dance. What is one way we often greet someone we know using our bodies? Kelly. [Wave hello.] A wave is one way, any others? [Hug, high five, give skin.] We'll use those ways of greeting each other, plus some other ways of greeting people from different historical time periods, different vocations, and different cultures as we develop our dance.

"Let's begin by spreading out into general space. The music I have selected ["Bridge of Avignon"] has two parts, A and B. In part A, or the chorus, there are eight measures or 32 counts. During that time we will skip 16 times. To make it easier to remember we will count eight skips two times. Let's put the music on and do just part A. Then we'll stop and listen to part B. Ready [music on], skip, 2, 3, 4, 5, 6, 7, 8, skip, 2, 3, 4, 5, 6, 7, 8. Listen (da, da, da, da, da-da), Skip. . . . Stop. Remember, this is not a race. Try this again, and skip to the music. . . . Stop.

"Now we are ready to do part B. You have already heard the special music signals (da, da, da, da, da-da) for part B. That is the time we will greet each other. Because this is a French dance, we'll start with some French greetings. This dance originated in Avignon during the 14th to 16th centuries. The royalty used to dress very formally in fancy costumes. [Bring in pictures of Louis XIV or other pictures showing period dress.] They would greet each other by bowing or curtsying [figure 6.5]. [Demonstrate.] As the music indicates, we will offer a greeting to someone nearby two times: boys bow, girls curtsy. Let's practice this much: part A and B one time. Ready [music on], skip, 2, 3, 4, 5, 6, 7, 8, skip, 2, 3, 4, 5, 6, 7, 8, greet, greet, stop.

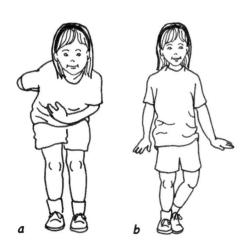

Figure 6.5 Greetings: *(a)* bowing and *(b)* curtsying.

"Very good. You're getting it, but as you can tell, there is more music and there are more ways to greet each other. This time try a different way of skipping—forward, backward, while turning, and so on—each time the chorus plays. And each time part B comes on, we'll do a new greeting. The first time we'll be French mademoiselles and monsieurs and curtsy or bow. The second time we hear part B, we'll salute like the gendarmes (French military soldiers or police). The third time we'll do a prayerful, holy greeting (hands folded) like the Catholic priests, monsignors, or nuns. The fourth time we'll pretend we are greeting our good friend with a big wave. Remember to skip about in general space during the chorus each time and to greet two different people near you (look them in the eye) on part B. I'll help you with my cues. Ready, [music on], skip, skip, bow/curtsy, bow/curtsy, skip, skip, salute, salute, skip, skip, prayerful, prayerful, skip, skip, wave, wave, stop. Very good so far.

"Now I want you to get a partner and stand next to your partner as we form a single, large circle. Stand, face your partner, and shake his or her hand. Say hello. Stand with your back to your partner. The person you are now looking at is your corner. Take a step toward your corner, shake hands, and say hello. I want us to do the greeting dance, as we now know it, from this formation. For the first eight skips in part A, we'll join hands and skip clockwise in a large circle. Then we'll do eight skips counterclockwise. On part B we'll greet our partner, then turn and greet our corner. Who can tell us the order or sequence of the greetings? Jennifer. Bow or curtsy, salute, prayerful, wave. Can everyone remember that? I'll give you word cues to help you remember. Ready. . . . Stop.

"There are still three more times for part A and two more times for part B before we get to the end of the record. We'll keep part A always the same, but I'm going to give you and your partner 1 minute to agree on two new ways to greet each other. Think about how people from other time periods, cultures, and so on might greet each other—for example, a Native American greeting, a high five, "Give me some skin," a hug, and a cool wave. Go. . . . Stop. Now turn and talk to your corner for 1 minute and agree on two more ways you'll greet each other.

"Okay. Let's try the whole dance. Remember, skip clockwise, skip counterclockwise, greet, greet. I'll cue the type of greeting each time. There will be one extra part A or set of skipping steps after our last greeting sequence. Ready, [music on], skip, skip, bow/curtsy, bow/curtsy, . . . stop. Good hard work, children. You performed the sequence quite well. I saw only a few mistakes that we can polish up, but for now we'll stop. Bring your partner over here and gather around me in front of the board.

"You now know how to say hello or greet each other in at least six different ways. Who can tell me one way and who might greet that way? Heather? [A soldier salutes.] Mike? [A religious person bows in a prayerful way.] John? [A French person might say *bon jour.*] Ira? [A person from the Middle East might hug and bring cheeks close together on both sides.] Simon? [A Native American might raise his arm in a peaceful way.] Maria? [A Spanish person might say *buenos dias.*] Judi? [An American youth might give a high five or some skin, that is, pound fists together.] Very good, everyone. What I'm hoping you are learning from your study about cultures and customs is that while people have some differences in the way they do things, we all have a lot in common that makes us alike. We all celebrate similar occasions and have the same needs and interests as humans. Good-bye for now. *Au revoir. Abientot. Adios, hasta la vista. Sayonara.*"

Assessment Suggestions

- Videotape small groups of learners and ask students to complete a self-evaluation of the dance.
- You can also complete an analysis of the video.

Look For

- Watch to see if children have beat awareness and skip to the music. If some students are having trouble, reduce the skill to walking to the music or take some time to clap to the music.

- Make sure children understand that their greetings are to occur for the whole duration of part B. Racing through just to get done and then waiting for part A to start again is not proper.

- After having done the dance sequence individually, the children might show some confusion in getting a partner, forming a circle, and learning about a corner. Be an especially good manager during this transition.

How Can I Change This?

- Teach a different international dance of greeting, such as the Danish "Dance of Greeting" (Michael Herman's Orchestra, 1958) or the African "Jambo" (Weikart, 1989, record 7).

- Develop a creative dance about a birthday party (Cone and Cone, 2005), or to celebrate planting or harvest season, or victory or independence, or other special event.

- While teaching about the culture or customs of another country, teach a game or sport from that country (Kirchner, 1991).

Teachable Moments

- Invite others from the community with different cultural heritages to share their language, costumes, food, life in their culture, cities in their place of origin, special festivals, and national heroes and heroines.

- Use a globe or map to point out where the countries are located. What other countries are near? What are the major bodies of water and other major geographical features of a country? What are each country's main industries?

Games From Other Countries

Suggested Grade Level

Intermediate (4 through 6)

Interdisciplinary Teaching Model

Shared

Studying characteristics of different countries is common in upper elementary social studies. Students can learn children's games from various countries to enhance their understanding of the cultures of the countries.

Social Studies

Customs and cultures: games from various countries

Physical Education

Locomotion, balance, and coordination

48617446R00021